MW00440603

"John Johnson's lucid reading instead, it's breathtakingly beaut intellectualism wherein the Bible has been treated as a dusty textbook or antiquated legal treatise, *Under an Open Heaven* actually seeks to accomplish for its reader what the Bible seeks to accomplish with its reader: namely, to draw us all into the wild, powerful, graceful arms of Jesus. I can't recommend this book enough. Words simply fail me."

—A. J. SWOBODA, pastor, professor, and author of
The Dusty Ones and *Messy*

"This is a delicious exposition of John's gospel! Dr. Johnson makes the writings of John contemporary with his alert references to modern life throughout the commentary—a fresh incarnation of The Incarnation."

—F. DALE BRUNER, author of *The Gospel of John: A Commentary*

"John Johnson's insights are always intelligent and often paradigm-shifting for the reader. His unique take on the book of John opens up new and unexpected gospel treasures. Dr. Johnson brings compassion, a careful reading of Scripture, and a pastor's heart to this book. Highly recommended."

—MATT MIKALATOS, author of *Into the Fray*
and *My Imaginary Jesus*

"John Johnson's writing is that of a well-read, urbane pastor-scholar with poetic sensibilities. His text is sprinkled with neatly turned phrases, and he employs illustrations and select quotations with the touch of an experienced preacher. In a word: his prose is engaging. But above this, Johnson is a penetrating expositor and theologian. . . . One is reminded of some of the writings of Frederick Buechner. A beautiful book and a fresh entrance into John's gospel."

—R. KENT HUGHES, senior pastor emeritus, College Church,
and author of numerous books

"John combines the seasoning of decades of pastoral leadership with the honing of seminary classrooms worldwide to his explorations of the profound depths of John's gospel. The combination of the messiness of life and the depths of the academy gives place for wrestling with the ironies of John. For those who want to know Jesus in real life, *Under an Open Heaven* is a delight."
—Dr. Gerry Breshears, professor of theology, Western Seminary, and coauthor of *Vintage Church*

"In this excellent work, Dr. John Johnson presents traditional insights from the gospel of John in fresh new ways. The author persuasively directs our attention to the authentic Jesus rather than the Jesus of our preconceived notions. He escorts us into the conversations of the persons who stand alongside the Son of God in the fourth gospel. By reading this book, we are not afforded the luxury of neutrality or avoidance; we are challenged to measure our relationship to the real Jesus by examining the characters in John's gospel, who serve us as mirrors for identity. This work is not for those who think they have mastered the Master in John's gospel; instead it is for believers who are willing to discover themselves through the Jesus who is Wholly Other. I highly recommend this work for those who are willing to read it at the risk of not only being informed but also transformed."
—Dr. Robert Smith Jr., professor of preaching, Beeson Divinity School, and author of *Doctrine That Dances*

"You will hear Christ in this book. He will call you, encourage you, and challenge you to follow Him. And along the way, you will learn a lot about John's gospel."
—Dr. David Hansen, author of *The Art of Pastoring*

UNDER
AN OPEN
HEAVEN

A NEW WAY *of*
LIFE REVEALED
in JOHN'S GOSPEL

JOHN E. JOHNSON

Kregel
Publications

Lindsay.

*For those
who have urged me
to press on*

John 10:10

CONTENTS

FOREWORD

THE GREAT FAILURE MOST OF US FACE AS BELIEVERS ISN'T SHAKING our fists in open rebellion against God; that's far more likely the sin of those who don't believe. Our ruin is far more likely to be minimizing the impact of Jesus by treating Him as the supreme historical figure who left us a challenging example and some inspiring words.

In other words, we live with an open book but a closed heaven. The phrase "What would Jesus do," though well-intentioned, is radically, even dangerously, misguided. It's not what would Jesus do, but rather what *is* Jesus doing?

In *Under an Open Heaven*, Dr. John E. Johnson says that we must live with an open book *and* an open heaven. Jesus didn't just die, and He didn't just rise. He ascended, He rules, and He sent His Spirit, all of which have wide-reaching implications for day-to-day life.

These are the questions Dr. Johnson wrestles with in *Under an Open Heaven*: Is God real? Does He make a major difference in our lives? Does His presence go beyond inspiration and hope to become one of empowerment and active engagement?

With the knowledge of a professor, the real-life understanding of a pastor, and a somewhat surprising familiarity—at least to me—with popular culture, Dr. Johnson combines three worlds to produce one engaging study. Heaven isn't closed. Jesus came to open it up, and Dr. Johnson invites us to lift up our heads, open our eyes, turn our palms upward, and experience the life-changing presence of God.

Jesus told us that if our eyes see, we will be full of light. Dr. Johnson opens our eyes and thus floods our souls with God's light. We see faith as more than a memory, more than a celebration of a glorious victory. Rather, it is walking with our eyes wide open to all that God is doing today—challenging our presumptions, countering our fears, revealing the foolishness and precariousness of our prejudices, and inviting us to absolutely refuse to settle for anything less than God's light.

Dr. Johnson has a particularly brilliant line in chapter 10 that encapsulates much of his book: "We find that keeping our heart in this journey is the most important mission of our lives—and the hardest." He follows later with this question from Jesus: "Is your trust in Me bigger than your disappointment?" These are clearly the words of a pilgrim who has occasionally ascended the heights of faith while never losing his memory of what it felt like to sometimes travel in the depths.

It is a treat to have our minds informed, our hearts convicted, our eyes opened, and our souls warmed as we engage with people who spoke face-to-face with Jesus. Dr. Johnson helps us see Christ's humanity in a way that opens up His divinity.

If you read *Under an Open Heaven* carefully and thoughtfully, you will realize that as much as you are reading the words of an academic or pastor, you are in the presence of a poet—not in form, but in concept, expression, and thought. Dr. Johnson is in love with God and the world God has made; and his delight and even fascination in the way truth impacts this world, rips open the veil blinding us from heaven, and shines its penetrating and life-giving light into our souls borders on exuberance.

As it should.

Life is different, life is better, life is more meaningful, more intimate, and more divine when we live it under an open heaven.

—GARY THOMAS

ACKNOWLEDGMENTS

ON ANY GIVEN WEEKEND, IT IS DIFFICULT TO PREDICT THE IMMEDI-
ate reaction church attenders might have to a sermon. If you go to
church, there are some Sundays you might rave and others you might
rant. You may find yourself frantically searching for what to say
should you inadvertently run into the pastor after a service. Words
like "That was lovely" might provide quick cover for an awkward
moment. But then you realize these words are a more appropriate
comment pertaining to the flowers gracing the pulpit or the sunlight
filtering through the stained glass.

My guess is that many of us, left to our private thoughts, approach
sermons like movie reviewers with grades and comments: "It started
well, but then I got lost in the middle." Or food critics: "I like the taste,
but the presentation could have been better." Or book critics: "That
style reminds me of Eugene Peterson." Or maybe a sound-system ana-
lyst: "When I sit in the middle section toward the back, I can hear you
better."

Perhaps the most common (and most noncommittal) response
pastors hear is this one: "Thanks for the reminder." But is this true?
Did all of a pastor's sermon-prep hours simply reinforce what one
already knew? Did the sermon have about as much impact as an email
from the dentist's office, reminding one of an upcoming Wednesday
appointment?

I am guessing most pastors rather hope someone will say, "I never
thought about that before," or "I didn't realize that about God." Or
maybe, "I did not realize this about myself." Those comments would

indicate that the preacher reached beyond the obvious, plumbing the depths of both mind and spirit. My hope is that this book is more than a review of a well-known gospel. Many (yes, many) books have been written on the gospel of John. My intent is not to simply add another commentary to the shelves. I want this book about John to go beyond the obvious and touch your soul and expand your life. To achieve that for my readers, I have drawn from thirty-two years in the trenches of pastoral ministry. I have spent a fair amount of time in the basement of a seminary library working through books on John, as well as listening for whatever has been coming my way. Writing a book has been likened to the building of a chicken coop in high wind. You grab anything loose and nail it down fast.[1] More countless hours and much labor have gone into writing and rewriting. And over the course of two summer retreats on the Pend Oreille River, I have sought to hear from God.

I have many to thank for their help, beginning with my family, who allowed me to hibernate at times to complete this project. Thanks Heather, Nate, and Kate. Likewise, I am indebted to my church, Village, for giving me needed off-duty space. I have been honored to be their pastor. I am also grateful for a seminary, Western, that has respected times when my office door is closed to do research.

For the company of twelve who prayed regularly over this project —thank you! Numerous others read various chapters and gave helpful comments. In particular, I am grateful to Nancee Dickson for keeping me on the straight and narrow path that one must walk when constructing sentences and developing ideas, as well as my administrative assistant, Memry Walker, who did much of the compiling. Chris Comp, who helped with the hidden details some writers (like me) would prefer to avoid, and Lehman Pekkola for his creative sketches using ink and gouache for the book's interior illustrations. I am especially grateful for the counsel of David Sanford, who exhorted me to stay with it, and David Van Diest, who was critical to securing a publisher. Finally, thank you to my editors, who include Janyre Tromp and Paul Brinkerhoff, and Kregel Publications for making all of this possible.

BEFORE WE BEGIN . . .

Oh, that you would rip open the heavens and descend,
make the mountains shudder at your presence.

ON JULY 12, 2014, AS REPORTED IN *THE NEW YORK TIMES*, POLICE found the body of George Bell in the living room of his apartment, "crumpled up on the mottled carpet."[1] The stench-thickened air confirmed that he had been dead for some days. Actually, as they began to piece together George's life of seventy-two years, it appears he had been sort of dead most of his life.

The bodies of people like George Bell often end up in "communal oblivion at the potter's field on Hart Island in the Bronx, the graveyard of last resort." In the case of George Bell, the body was kept for months while investigators tried to determine if there were any family or friends to receive what few assets remained.

Wading through the "unedited anarchy" of an apartment trashed with balled-up, decades-old lottery tickets, shopping lists, and holiday cards, they found a few pictures. The snapshots recorded the humdrum of life. There was no evidence of any significant events. George had "lived in the corners, under the pale light of obscurity."

George was an only child, and he lived with his parents until they died. George never married. He eventually got into the moving business, transporting furniture to business offices. George was quite the juicer. After work, he often used his paycheck to drink in "titanic proportions." Other than escapes to the bar, he seldom went out.

Unfortunately, George injured his spine lifting a desk, forcing him to go on disability. His sedentary lifestyle, mixed with his ravenous appetite, pushed George to nearly 350 pounds. Over time, life became emptier and emptier. He would bump into other tenants in north central Queens and share a brief greeting. He sometimes passed the time meandering around in his Toyota, but his car had its own sedentary experience. Over nine years, the odometer never broke three thousand miles. George never really went anywhere. His friendships were few. Once he just hung out for hours with a fishing partner in the parking lot of a Bed Bath & Beyond. But the days just bled into one another, an endless loop of deadening predictability. The very few who knew George saw a man living in a small world "just waiting to die."

Many of us live in our own confined spaces. While few of us live in George's extreme desolation, we are restricted by lots of things— small imaginations and old habits. Fear works to enclose us. There are voices we cannot shake that tell us we will only go so far in life— that it is too late to live a life that matters. But it doesn't have to be this way. As Cornelius Plantinga Jr. challenges, what if there were words to "break open closed systems, to smash fixed conclusions, and summon the brave new world of God"? What if something were "unshackling us from dreary conventions, and opening the way for possibilities no eye has seen, no ear has heard, no imagination has ever conceived"?[2]

What if . . . ? The good news is that all those glorious what-ifs are true. Jesus and His kingdom have broken in. To use the language of the gospel of John, the heavens have opened, and the force of the Trinity "like an ice-axe [has broken] the frozen sea inside of us" (1:51).[3] Two worlds have collided in the coming of Jesus. Divine mystery has clashed with human ignorance; appearance has been shaken by reality.[4] Jesus's birth forever challenged a closed world. He entered into our world and opened up a conversation. The gospel of John carefully records the implications of this new open system using Christ's conversations with ordinary humans.

In this book we will examine thirteen of those conversations and study how an open heaven has opened up unimaginable opportunities. Conversational language and lengthy dialogue are distinctive features of the gospel of John. Each conversation is a literary painting of humanity, teaching us something of ourselves and our own perplexities as we encounter theirs. They move us to live on a different plane. The words appear to be ordinary, spoken to simple people. But things are going on well below the surface. Alice Munro, a Canadian novelist, describes the characters in her book as "deep caves paved with kitchen linoleum."[5] It's an apt description of those Jesus converses with in John.

Some of the conversations are initiated by Jesus; others are prompted by people who come to Him. Each one invites us into the world of the characters. They represent an odd collection of people, ranging from family to followers, from those at the bottom of culture to those at the top. The conversations are quite pedestrian. At times they are messy, full of pauses and interruptions. Ultimately, in each conversation, we see something of our own dilemmas and struggles. What begins as a private conversation enlarges to a sermon for everyone.[6]

My aim is to demonstrate that each dialogue is not random but intentional, moving along and developing the larger plot. Together they fulfill the purpose of the book: that both believer and unbeliever might become convinced that Jesus is the Christ, the Son of God, and that by believing we might have eternal life (John 20:31).

MAPPING OUT OUR JOURNEY

Before we begin this journey, I would like to introduce you to some of the terrain we will encounter. John is filled with irony. Irony has been described as the "mother of confusions,"[7] and it fits. Apparent contradiction lurks everywhere. You will find yourself expecting things to go in opposite directions. God steps into the world He has created, but creation does not even recognize its Maker (John 1:10–11). Jesus, the Son of God, comes to His own people, but they have little interest in receiving Him. They are off on other priorities. Jesus grows up in a family, but His unbelieving brothers seem put off by His existence (John 7:5). Think of the irony—the One who is perfect love is dismissed by His closest family circle!

Even in His approach to ministry, things seem contrary. He initiates the greatest global mission ever, recruiting misfits to carry it out. It has always been the way of God. As Plantinga puts it, "God hits straight shots with crooked sticks."[8] Jesus prepares them to lead the church but then sends them out to a world that soon takes most of them out.

You begin to realize that grasping the ways of Jesus in John is a bit like shoveling smoke. "There's plenty to take hold of if only one could."[9] In one of the greater ironies, "born again" language is only used with the religious (John 3:3). One would think that Jesus would save these words for Pilate. Oddly, those in the gospel who market themselves as the ones in the know, the seers of Israel, are, ironically, more blind than those they pretend to lead (9:39–41). In the garden, the soldiers need lanterns to arrest the one who has come as the Light of the World (18:3–12).

Jesus goes to regions we least expect. He asks for water and then offers water. He calls people to follow Him in His kingdom and then runs when people attempt to make Him their king. He says now is not the time and in the next moment acts as if it's the perfect time. He uses signs as a means of demonstrating His messiahship, but He issues some of His harshest words to those who would ask for a sign. "The mighty are lowered, the humble exalted, and the savior dies on the cross."[10] And so it goes.

Clearly, John is not the simple read we expected. Ironically (there's that word again), John is often the gospel passed out to new believers with the advice to start their spiritual journey here. John is promoted as Christianity 101; it is prolegomena to the rest of the course.

Elementary, rudimentary, straightforward—take your pick. John was the working text my Greek professor used to teach us baby Greek. The vocabulary is simple and the grammar is not so complex. But it's a setup. What appears to be a gentle hiking trail turns out to be a technical climb. Seemingly accessible, yet beyond our grasp. Inviting, yet threatening. As Martin Luther quipped, these "simple words" are at the same time "inexpressible words."[11] Hmm, we must have overlooked the small print on the label that reads "industrial strength." This is high Bible. In structural terms, it is the keystone of the arch. In contrast to the other gospels that are "earth up," John is "heaven down." John is impressionist art; Matthew, Mark, and Luke are portraits. (There's a reason the art found within the book is abstract!) We are in language from another realm. No wonder the apostle John is known as "the Theologian" in Eastern tradition.[12]

The arrangement of the book is also challenging. A contemporary review of John's gospel in a secular publication might read something like this: "Structurally, the book is a bit of a mess. It is more a collection of conversations, lurching from one character to another. Few of the characters generate sympathy. The effect is often disorienting and sometimes off-putting. Better editing would have made for an easier read."[13]

IT'S WORTH THE TREK

Years ago, Edwyn Hoskyns warned any student of John that he "will not be true to the book he is studying if, at the end, the gospel does not remain strange, restless, and unfamiliar."[14] There are times you will need to air your brain out, moments you will wonder, "Is God messing with me?" Short answer: *Yes*.

But even if we find ourselves over our heads, we are gripped by a force, a voice, a Person from another realm calling for us to stay at it. There is a summit to be reached, a message that desperately needs to be heard. There is a life to be discovered. Heaven has invaded earth. We are drawn in, and we find benefits to every step.

As we journey, we also find John to be incredibly relevant. When this gospel was written, the world was in turmoil. Jerusalem was collapsing, the empire was eroding, and the early emerging church was in a fight for its survival. The community was coping with a rigid Jewish institutionalism, a Hellenistic world of pagan idols, and an abusive Roman authority. This triad teamed up to make war on the church. These early believers needed words to get them through the night. They needed to know that everything had changed with Jesus's coming.

We need such words to get us through our dark nights and a world that remains in turmoil.

Navigating through John, we can't help but notice something else—a pastoral texture. The apostle John is a pastor, so we expect language befitting a shepherd. I take it that John, one of Jesus's twelve, writes this book to his congregation, one most likely in Ephesus. At points his language moves from singular to plural, hinting that the message is from a Christ follower to Christ followers (1:51; 3:11). Like any pastor, John wants his congregants to live in light of God's finished, present, and future work. All too many were—and are—living as if the heavens are still closed, oblivious to the fact that the old system of sacrifices and law has been replaced with the new. We will discover that we no longer have to settle for life as it was before Jesus ripped things open. God is up to something profound and unexplainable. Under an open heaven, the church can anticipate becoming a formidable force. Each chapter in this book is a description of life as it is now to be lived.

This book is not intended to be a verse-by-verse commentary on the gospel. It is not a regurgitation of other commentaries with an introduction and conclusion (some pastors call this a sermon). It has aspects of a commentary and some kinship to a sermon. It is a theology of sorts, an overall survey of John, as well as a devotional reading of the text that will lead you to change your approach to God and therefore life. You will find questions at the end to facilitate additional personal study or group discussion. Ultimately, it represents my pilgrimage as a Christ follower, a pastor, and a professor.

The aim is for serious scholarship, respecting those of us in the church who want more than anecdotes and entertainment. I don't want to just get something said—I want it to be heard, pondered, and hopefully enacted. If I am faithful to the task of writing, I am doing what I hope to do in my preaching—splash cold water on any of our complacencies. If I succeed, the reader will be persuaded not only to study these conversations but to enter into each one, listening for what the Spirit may be saying.

1

LIFE IS ABOUT EXPANDING ONE'S VISION

A Conversation with Nathanael

JOHN 1:43–51

> *"You will see greater things than this." Then [Jesus] said, "I assure you: You will see heaven opened and the angels of God ascending and descending on the Son of Man."*
>
> —JOHN 1:50–51

THE GREY IS A CHILLING MOVIE ABOUT A GROUP OF UNRULY OIL-RIG roughnecks who survive a plane crash in Alaska's wilderness. In merciless weather, they must endure injuries and a vicious pack of rogue wolves. As the wolves take out these men, one by one, the question begins to surface: Is God still out there? Even the film's lead character, John Ottway (Liam Neeson), the roughest of the rough, demands to know. At the end, he is the only one left. Desperate, facing imminent death, he pleads to God for help. He screams out, "Do something!" But the only sound he hears is silence. He senses God is nowhere to be found. The heavens appear to be sealed shut and the key thrown away. The scene ends with this desperate yet self-confident line: "F— it, I'll do it myself."

How many times do we feel alone in the midst of circling predators? They may not be literal wolves but threats that feel like death in the midst of life. There are dead lines at work, dead ends in certain relationships, and dead weights that keep us down. There are the ever-present financial worries that attempt to eat us alive. For some of us, there emerges a dull sense that life is not going as we hoped. For others, there is a heightening awareness of "the accumulated crumbling of one's bodily systems while medicine carries out its maintenance measures and patch jobs."[1]

We all know (at least intellectually) that this is our plight in a broken world. We always face struggles, though the forces that beset us change with the years. We take on many of these "wolves" with our prayers, but our words are sometimes met with silence. It's as if we live under some God-imposed dome. Our fear is that if we are able to break out, we might find that heaven's doors are shut and the curtains are pulled tight. We find ourselves echoing the same question raised in *The Grey*: Is God still out there?

Over time, it is easy for a low-grade skepticism to begin to take root, the sort that threatens to overthrow faith. Along with the main character in *The Grey*, we gradually come to a place where we believe that any saving action is up to us.

IT IS NOT UP TO US

The gospel of John is out to challenge this outlook on life. Throughout, John describes life under a wide-open heaven, where everything has changed. Jesus broke through the sealed dome and entered into this self-reliant world to declare it is not up to us. And amazingly, He is still here and He is not silent. He came to confront the wolves that threaten death with His promises of life, even an abundant life (John 10:10). It's not His intention that we live desperate, inconsequential lives sealed into our doomed state nor merely succumb to the passage of time. He has opened the doors, pulled back the curtains, stepped into this world, and opened our eyes to see otherworldly realities. Each conversation in John enlarges our picture of an interactive God, telling us what life under an open heaven is about. He intends to remove our self-imagined restrictions, take us through the barriers, and bring us out to the edges.

To begin, John leaps into an apparent void with his story. It has been nearly four hundred years since God has spoken through a prophet. Miracles have largely ceased after Mount Carmel; visions and dreams have diminished. By the end of the Old Testament, an unresponsive people have seemingly pushed God into early retirement.[2] Meanwhile, empires come and go. Rome is now the dominant force oppressing Israel. And the Jews are desperate for God to unretire, to throw open the doors of heaven and answer their prayers. Though they desperately long for a messiah who will overturn Rome and vindicate Israel, they insist that this messiah must conform to their expectations of what a messiah is like. In the meantime, they have to rely on their own wits, their own strength. They have to defeat the wolves themselves.

And then, an opening. God breaks His silence. How appropriate that He is introduced in John as "the Word"—God is now audible, oh yes, and visible as "the Word became flesh" (1:14). Like someone returning from a long journey, He suddenly emerges and speaks. There is this Godward force changing the landscape. He directs the winds. He creates Burgundy out of H$_2$O. He speaks with the kind of power that can level the old-growth cedars of Lebanon. He rebukes and invites and liberates us from any notion that we are forced to go it alone. Something about the Word, Jesus, causes men to drop everything and follow.

It still happens.

YET WE TRUST OUR TUNNEL VISION

Andrew and other early disciples drop everything to cast their lot with Jesus (1:39). They're convinced they've found the Messiah. But some, like Nathanael, hold back. He looks at Philip and others and wonders if their bull-manure detectors are broken. There have been too many failed promises. Expectations have hit painful dead ends. There have been plenty of bogus messiahs in and around Galilee. The time for messianic dreams to be fulfilled is surely now, but the résumé of this character does not fit. The man is a Nazarene, but they expect the Messiah to come from Bethlehem. Anyone with basic Sunday school training knows this. (Later, in 7:41–42, this will be a huge sticking point for others.)

Furthermore, Nathanael and others like him are incredulous that the one prophesied in the Old Testament—the fulfillment of all the biblical prophets' longings and visions—would come from a place as irrelevant as Nazareth. The anticipated King who conquers the dark oppressor cannot emerge from some backwater town![3] To Nathanael this is insane, floating on ludicrous, lost in a sea of nonsense.

Imagine today anyone suggesting that the Messiah will be born in a homeless shelter, move to a place like Norton, Kansas, work a minimum-wage union job, hang out with riffraff, need to borrow a junker car for a parade in His honor, wash dirt off His workers' feet, get Himself arrested and convicted of a crime, and finally be sentenced to the death penalty. Nathanael depends upon his own sight. He has his expectations. Messiahs do not do this.

The tone of Nathanael's response in John 1:46 is flippant (and maybe a little hostile). Even his own hometown, Cana, is a village larger and more prosperous than Nazareth, that speck on the map nine miles to the south. It's so obscure it is not mentioned in a list of sixty-three Galilean towns in the Talmud. But chances are there's a crosstown rivalry of sorts. These are communities that harbor deep suspicions of one another (just like the rivalry between Scappoose and St. Helens on the north side of Portland, and nearly every other small town adjacent to another).

Nathanael is just being realistic. Like most skeptics, he's sensible enough to question far-fetched claims to fame. The more significant the claim, the more it requires exploring, questioning. If Nathanael is to believe in this emerging new voice, he has to see it. Jesus has to meet *his* expectations and fit into *his* categories. He has to respond at a prayer's notice, especially when wolves circle his path. The Messiah has to come in glorious and grand terms, in ways that make sense. If not, Nathanael will suspend judgment until he has sufficient evidence. Until the real Messiah shows up, Nathanael will deal with unanswered prayers. He will keep relying upon himself.

Skepticism is not necessarily a bad thing. It's a form of protection against believing too much. Suspicion guards us from giving credit card information to Nigerian lawyers or obeisance to weeping icons of Mary. With John Ortberg, each of us declares: "I don't believe in Bigfoot or Stonehenge or the Loch Ness monster. I don't believe Elvis is still alive and working as a short-order cook at Taco Bell. . . . I don't believe extra-terrestrials periodically visit the earth and give rides on their spacecrafts, partly because they never seem to land in Pasadena and give rides to physicists from Cal Tech."[4]

Nathanael just wants reliable proof. He is like some people I know who sit in the pews with their arms folded, wearing an incredulous Missouri spirit that says, "Show me." Maybe Jesus is the Messiah.

Maybe He did walk on water and declare sovereignty over creation. Maybe. But what if an academic like Doron Nof, a professor of oceanography at Florida State University, has it right when he acknowledges that Jesus walked on water, but it was an isolated patch of floating ice due to global cooling?[5] The greatest fear of a skeptic is to be taken in. Nathanael will need to hear more before he makes a decision.

Maybe we need to hear more. Doubts about God also find their way into our lives. How do I reconcile a congregant's tragedy with the words of the sage, "No disaster overcomes the righteous" (Prov. 12:21)? Where is God when the world seems to be oppressing me— when my ongoing prayer requests seem to evaporate into thin air? Why am I not experiencing this peace "which passeth all understanding" (Phil. 4:7 KJV) now that I have cast my worries upon Him? Why didn't He alert me to the symptoms before it was too late? Why am I the subject of an investigation that is fueled by a lawsuit-happy person wanting to make a quick buck? Why doesn't God intervene before some mindless shooter steps into a Charleston African Methodist Episcopal church or walks onto a southern Oregon campus?

Even pastors occasionally "hang on to faith by [their] finger nails"![6] Doubts creep into the pulpit. How can I preach certain parts of Joshua that sound disturbingly like genocide? What about these dietary restrictions? (Does God really have something against lobsters?) We preach revival, but we sometimes wonder if God will ever show back up. In our darker moments, we might wonder if He ever did. Was it just old-time media hype? If God is God, why doesn't He intervene when my sermon seems to lose heat? If the Spirit of God is so mightily present, and the Word is sharper than any two-edged sword, how is it some remain so unaffected?

James 5:16 declares that the intense prayers of the righteous accomplish much, but what have my pastoral prayers really accomplished? Does the prayer of faith really heal the sick? If Jesus is this living water, why am I so dry? Open doubts and honest searching fill in some of our space, encroaching on trust and sensibility, threatening to make a shambles of our faith. We expect God to ride into our lives and conquer the inescapable consequences of being finite creatures in a broken world. When it doesn't happen, we wonder if anything can be done.

Like us, Nathanael has to be careful with his skepticism. If we hold on to doubts too long, they can curdle into unbelief. In *Not Sure: A Pastor's Journey from Faith to Doubt*, John Suk describes how skepticism worked like a slow erosion in his soul. He began asking questions: Is the creation story real? Were the exodus accounts exaggerated? What about Israel's ethnic cleansing? As he puts it, "It was as if different corners of my brain were holding onto contradictory ideas and maps all at the same time."[7] Uncertainty replaces certainty, and unbelief shoves belief aside.

Nathanael is on the brink of missing the true Messiah because he's holding the wrong map.

ENCOUNTERING THE ONE WHO SEES

Jesus may not impress Nathanael with His street address or nonmilitary bearing, but He blows Nathanael away with what He knows and what He can see (John 1:47–48). The Son of God speaks to him as if He has known him his whole life. He comes across as one who has fathomed Nathanael's deepest being. This is because He knows Nathanael better than Nathanael knows himself. God does not perceive us fragmentarily; He knows us and everything exhaustively. He knew Nathanael in eternity past when He conceived him in His mind. He knows all about Nathanael's present moral choices. He sees his whole future. Jesus is fully aware that Nathanael is not a man prone to cunning and treachery; Nathanael is the antithesis of deceit. He is devout. Jesus compliments Nathanael's integrity, all while acknowledging and accepting his open doubts and questions.

When Nathanael asks Jesus how He knows him, Jesus unnerves him with His answer: "Before Philip called you, when you were under the fig tree, *I saw you*." Something supernatural has just happened. In these words, Jesus pierces Nathanael's sense of hiddenness. How does He know? Here is someone who knows his rising and his sitting. Something has opened. There is exposure.

This is someone who knows our movements, *sees our lives*.

Some years ago, when I was in Stavanger, Norway, and wearied with denominational meetings, I decided to escape. I had read about a geographic wonder called Preikestolen, better known as Pulpit Rock. I thought every preacher who comes to Norway should have the experience of climbing it. So I went AWOL, gone missing from the committee on committees (there really are these committees). I took a ferry, then grabbed a bus, and finally hired a taxi to get to the trailhead. It was a spectacular early October day, and there was no one on the trail except for a few mountain goats. After two hours of climbing, I made it up to the top of this massive cliff, 1,982 feet in elevation. In the solitude, looking out over the Norwegian fjords, I was lifted into an unforgettable spiritual experience. And then it came to me—no one on this earth knows where I am at this moment. But sitting in the presence of God, I realized—He does! "You observe my travels and my rest; You are aware of all my ways" (Ps. 139:3). *He knows our itinerary before it is printed.* He knows how the film ends before we've seen it.

Nathanael is suddenly aware of this reality. Jesus shows this skeptic that He knows when he sits down and when he stands up. Jesus is radically and totally *other than*—other than us and other than our reality. Ironically, this is enough for Nathanael. Skeptical as he is, it does not take much to overwhelm him. It turns out his wonder is not so expansive, his expectations not so great, and his skepticism not so deep.

What about our wonder, our expectations?

OPENING OUR EYES

Nathanael needed his vision expanded. With just a few words, he suddenly sees a Messiah who sees what humanity can't see, who defies what humanity expects, who is completely other. Nathanael falls down and worships. As New Testament scholar F. Dale Bruner put it, "guileless, cool, rational, studious, intellectual [and skeptical]

Nathanael now has an emotional, almost a Southern Baptist conversion."[8] In the span of a moment he moves from skeptic to follower. We expect Jesus will be pleased with Nathanael's profession of faith. But as the conversation reveals, Jesus is not so impressed with Nathanael's response, any more than He is with any of us who impulsively respond to the invitation. People see some miracle or hear a testimony that has stirred their emotions, and down the aisle they go. In some cases, it might be fair to ask the same question: "Is this all that it took to convince you?" Jesus is not so moved by spontaneous reactions to make Him King of their lives (John 6:14–15, 26). He will not assume belief just because people declare they do believe (2:23–25; 8:30–32). Too often, it is short-lived.

Jesus has something greater for Nathanael to see. For us to see. Jesus is about to make one of the most profound statements in Scripture. This will be the true test of faith. Nathanael is about to see a supernatural vision that will shatter his mind—shatter our minds. He will see greater realities, the sort of things prophets and righteous men have longed to see (Matt. 13:16–17). But by God's expansive love, we are allowed to glimpse! Jesus says to Nathanael, "You will see greater things than this" (John 1:50).

He then says to him, "I assure you: You will see heaven opened and the angels of God ascending and descending on the Son of Man" (v. 51). Here's where a more careful look at the text is crucial—critical to the argument of this book. The "you" is plural, twice in this verse. We are *all* invited into a vision that will confront every doubt and unnerve every skeptic. Jesus announces a staggering event, the event prophets longed to see. It's an event that is neither past nor future. The tense implies a present event with effects that continue out into the future. The heavens have opened, and they remain open.

EYES TO SEE THE MOST AMAZING SIGHT

Jesus has inaugurated something, but what is it? The words are baffling, even to Johannine scholars.[9] Is this some bizarre vision, a verbal eccentricity on Jesus's part? He gives no explanation, no commentary, and no clues. The conversation with Nathanael abruptly ends.

No, wait! Is that really it? Did everything just stop? Have we stopped? Sometimes we readers can be like motorists driving sixty miles an hour through Yellowstone. We race past John 1:51 without slowing to see the marvel of these words. But what if we slow down, make a U-turn, stop, and get our binoculars in hand? Might we discover that these words have profound implications for how we understand John, and how we live our lives today? What if every conversation in John goes back to this passage? If so, how do we make sense of these opaque words? We will have to get the dust off of these binoculars, as well as prepare to do some digging.

Glimpses in the Past
We will have to go back a few centuries. Scripture tells us there were occasions when the heavens suddenly opened, giving earthbound dwellers a peek beyond the clouds and a way into the glorious world of God. Micaiah, a prophet of God in the days of Ahab, suddenly saw an opening, revealing the Lord sitting on His throne, seeking a messenger to send to earth (1 Kings 22:19–20); the psalmist received occasional glimpses of divine activity in the heavenly sanctuary (Ps. 68:17); Ezekiel recorded the precise moment he saw the heavens open and a vision of God (Ezek. 1:1); in a dream, Daniel saw the coronation of the Son of Man, coming with the clouds of heaven (Dan. 7:13–14); and in the year King Uzziah died, the skies were pulled back and Isaiah gained a glimpse of God upon His throne (Isa. 6:1).

But these were glimpses. As quickly as the skies parted and a vision was captured, the heavens closed.

Nathanael may have recalled these moments, but it is likely Jesus's words took him immediately to a story much further back. In Genesis 28:10–22, Jacob had his own vision of an open heaven. Like Nathanael, Jacob was a man who did his share of sitting under a shelter. He stayed in his "apartment" under the shade of his tent (Gen. 25:27). His was a sedentary, small world of pleasing his mom, seeking the favor of his father, and stiffing his brother. His was a perspective both narrow and asphyxiating. Jacob's imagination was limited to the mundane. Like so many today, he tinkered at the edge of life's structural issues. He was missing God.

In contrast to Nathanael, Jacob was a man with guile (Gen. 27:35). He was never fully grounded; never seemed to have a true north. As Richard Bauckham observes, he "employed deceit to acquire the paternal blessing that should have been given to his brother Esau."[10] Nonetheless, God revealed Himself to Jacob in a way that served as a precursor to what Jesus revealed to Nathanael. While asleep, Jacob saw a ladder between heaven and earth, and angels ascending and descending. Standing by Jacob, God declared: "I am Yahweh . . . I will not leave you until I have done what I have promised you" (Gen. 28:13, 15).

Jacob realized that gates had opened and heaven had intersected with earth. God is always up to something radical, holy, and earth-shaking. In this case, God was not only manifesting His presence in a decisive way; He was designating Jacob as the inheritor of the Abrahamic promises. Jacob awoke to the realization that he had been presented with a different future. Heaven was no longer some remote and irrelevant realm. Jacob suddenly realized he did not travel alone. With God's presence, life can be more expansive. So Jacob created a marker. He named it Bethel, which means "house of God," so he would never forget. He would forever remember that this was the place where the divide between the realm inhabited by God and the world of humanity was breached.

A Glimpse in the Present

Nathanael's experience matches Jacob's, only it comes through a conversation instead of a dream. It comes in the day rather than in the night. Eyes again are opened. Jesus fills in some of the missing pieces: He is the ladder, God's ramp connecting heaven and earth. He is the one through whom the two realms are linked. The angels descend and ascend, pointing to Jesus who has descended from above and will ascend to heaven (John 3:13).

Whether he realizes it or not, Nathanael is suddenly standing on holy ground. "Jesus is the Christian's Bethel."[11] He is the new temple. John 2 will develop this. The glory of God now tabernacles in Jesus. "He, not the Jerusalem temple, is the primary link between heaven and earth. . . . The life of the temple is now found in Christ."[12] At some point, Nathanael will, like Jacob, exclaim, "Surely the LORD is in this place, and I did not know it" (Gen. 28:16).

HOW AN OPEN HEAVEN CHANGES THINGS

Where is all of this going? Is Jesus simply filling in the details of Jacob's dream? Is there any real application? Is this, along with the other astonishing events of the Gospels, some "nostalgic and triumphalist piece of propaganda" for a desperate church?[13] Or does this announcement of an open heaven signal new, permanent realities? And if so, what are they? Here are six.

The Veil of Separation Has Been Forever Torn
It has to be more than mere coincidence that the same term describing the ripping open of the heavens in Mark 1:10 is used by the same writer to describe the ripping open of the temple curtain separating laity from the Holy of Holies (15:38). The world, according to Mark, is a world torn open by God. From beginning to end, "this is a story of God's powerful incursion into the created order."[14]

With the life, death, and resurrection of Jesus, the obstruction created by sin has been shattered. Forgiveness and reconciliation have replaced alienation and estrangement (John 5:14; 8:11; 21:15–17). Under an open heaven, the walls are down, the fences have been removed, and the curtain is split open. Now we have divine access. Jesus has opened a way for us to enjoy the benefits of a perfect and complete sacrifice. Entrance to the Most Holy One is ours 24/7. We can approach Him with faith and confidence. A new depth of intimacy with God is now possible, one transcending the intimacy even Moses experienced (Eph. 3:12; Heb. 10:19–22).

God Has Broken In Permanently

Something that was previously closed, or opened only temporarily, is now opened for good. God has finally answered the desperate prayer of the prophet Isaiah: "If only You would tear the heavens open and come down, so that mountains would quake . . . [and] nations will tremble at Your presence" (Isa. 64:1–2). The prophet regarded the firmament above as a barrier and a cause for great calamity.[15] If there is no opening, the enemies of God's people will have their way. Wolves will rule the forest.

But now, heaven and earth have intersected. The enemy will not have his way (Luke 11:22; 1 John 3:8). Both Jacob and Nathanael experienced mystery, but what Jacob saw vaguely, Nathanael sees with greater clarity. Jesus has intruded into human reality, bridging from one realm to another in ways God never has before. Nathanael and those who follow Jesus will behold His glory. "Come and see" will expand to mega-proportions.

We Will See Expanded Supernatural Possibilities Emerge from the Permanent Opening

The Son of Man has become the means by which new "beyond the physical" realities of heaven are brought down to earth in an ongoing way.[16] This contradicts a worldview that assumes the world is a closed system outside of which there is nothing.

An open heaven means that earth is now the place where God's world and our world meet. Though our senses cannot readily perceive His presence and His ongoing activity, His reality is more real than the physical realities surrounding us.

Hence, Jesus forces us to understand the world differently than we have before. Jesus will tell His mother her view of time must expand to Spirit time (John 2:4), inform Nicodemus that there's a different way to enter God's kingdom (3:5), prepare the woman at the well for a day when worship will expand to "in [the] spirit" (4:24), enlarge Martha's understanding of what resurrection means (11:25), press His disciples to see that they can do even greater things (14:12), and show

Peter that His life and death have reframed the meaning of mercy (21:15).

Divine Activity Has Intensified

The angels of God, last witnessed tending to Elijah, are again active on earth. They are ascending and descending to earth using the Son of Man as a bridge, doing the work of messaging, serving, and showing the incomparability of Jesus. They maintain the link between heaven and earth, though we do not easily see their fuller movements. They are too absorbed in the light of His revelation.[17] They are the mighty winds that can blow at any time and the fiery flames sent out to serve those who inherit salvation (Heb. 1:7–14). Their movements "symbolize the whole power and love of God, now available for men."[18] They "bring transcendence to our attention," as Eugene Peterson puts it, serving as messengers who signal that "there is more here than meets the eye."[19] They affirm that the long silence is over. Earth is no longer left on its own. God is revealing Himself in ways He never has before.

Along with the angels, God's presence and power have taken on a more obvious force. Luke's announcement that the heavens have opened affirms that the three persons of the Trinity have crashed into the calm. The Son of God comes in the flesh, the heavens open and the Spirit descends, and the Father speaks words that are now audibly heard on earth (Luke 3:21–22). God is now on the loose, announcing the kingdom, loving on people, and plundering the strong man's house (Matt. 12:29). The signs in John are the evidence of His authority and His deliverance. There is the dawning of the new covenant. Jesus brings God's promises to fulfillment, coming as the last Adam, the new Moses, the true Israel, the Son of Man, and the ultimate prophet, priest, sage, and king.[20] "He will mediate a greater revelation than Abraham, Jacob, Moses, and Isaiah," or anyone else (John 8:58).[21]

This is God declaring that He is not some distant moral influence (as if He ever was). Jesus cannot be "locked into an abstract and theological system," Andrew Purves asserts, "like a fossil trapped in amber."[22] He doesn't sit on the sidelines of the cosmos, cheering us on. Under an open heaven, Jesus is God in person, active in the life of the world. It's not WWJD but WIJD (what is Jesus doing?). John is not interested in merely revealing who Jesus was; he shows us who Jesus *is*.[23] Nathanael will see the evidence of God's continuing interaction with humanity through Jesus's acts and through His conversations.

And if we're looking, we hopefully see similar divine presence and power in our lives.

God Has Opened a Way for Jesus to Ascend and the Spirit to Descend

Nathanael does not yet realize it, but when Jesus ascends to heaven, the third person of the Trinity will come and indwell and empower the hearts of believers in a way the world has never seen before, enabling them to do greater things than ever (John 14:12–17).

In His coming, the Spirit will indwell us and bring Christ to us, mediating His ongoing presence. Where two or three gather, He will be there (Matt. 18:20; 1 Cor. 5:4). We aren't working out our salvation alone; He's at work in us, both to will and to work for His good pleasure (Phil. 2:12–13). More than imitating Christ, we are participating with Him. It's not merely imagining the unimaginable; He's able to do the inconceivable through the power of the Holy Spirit now working in us.

Eternal Life Is Both Future and Present

Life is a major theme in the gospel of John. There are sixteen clusters of references to life in John.[24] Some speak of life in the present, others of life after this life. What we commonly associate with life in heaven—love, joy, peace, purpose, rest, healing—is actually ours to taste in the present. We don't have to wait for heaven. A new way of being human has been launched. Jesus is life (John 1:4). He has come that we might have *life* in all of its fullness, beginning now (10:10).

This destroys any assumptions that life is to be simply endured like "lifeless" people waiting in line at a DMV office. Jesus has come so life can be more varied and mysterious than we've imagined. What the greatest saints of the Old Testament had as a foretaste is now the believer's present and ongoing meal. Jesus is our Bread of Life (6:51). The Spirit is our power. The Father is our worship. We can live with anticipation, knowing that God the Father, Son, and Spirit are constantly on the move. Who knows where They might break out next?

It might be on a morning walk, reflecting on His Word, and we sense an affirming voice behind the printed page telling us He has a future for us (Prov. 23:18). Fear gives way to hope, and new possibilities open, even amid our mundane activities. Maybe in the act of taking Communion, when we long for something beyond mere memorial, we find ourselves suddenly entering into a fellowship with the bread and the cup (1 Cor. 10:16). In this act, the Spirit has mediated the presence of Christ. He may reveal Himself in a dream, a vision, or other supernatural interventions. He may simply breathe something of His power on us, and life takes on otherworldly, robust dimensions. It might even be a carbonated-soda-out-the-nose moment!

Under an open heaven, there is light that exposes the darkness: life as God intended before the darkness of sin was embraced in the garden; life where some things don't have to be justified by their usefulness (like eating ice cream, paddling under waterfalls, and riding elephants). We find ourselves nudging the borders of eternity to experience a hint of heaven. Like Jabez, we petition that boundaries be constantly expanded (1 Chron. 4:9–10). An open heaven asks, "Why not?"

C. S. Lewis captures something of this life in one scene in the Chronicles of Narnia. The White Witch turns the inhabitants of Narnia into lifeless, winter stone. But Aslan, the Christ figure, jumps into the stone courtyard. He pounces on the statues and breathes into them the life and light of spring.

The courtyard looked no longer like a museum; it looked more like a zoo. Creatures were running after Aslan. . . . Instead of all that deadly white the courtyard was now a blaze of colors . . . reddy-brown of foxes . . . and crimson hoods of dwarfs. . . . And instead of the deadly silence the whole place rang with the sound of happy roarings, brayings, yelpings, barkings . . . songs and laughter.[25]

Jesus came to turn this world from a stone yard into a garden.

THE VISION ISN'T PERFECT

Under an open heaven does not mean life no longer has its challenges. This is no realized eschatology. To the degree the kingdom of God has not been fulfilled, it cannot be lived out; hence life under an open heaven is limited in its scope and effects. Things are partly completed. Symphonies remain unfinished. We cannot expect perfection in things we do. We are not fully redeemed and fully outfitted for eternity, so we must be careful of idealized expectations.[26] We do not have in the present everything God wants to give us. We see glimpses of His glory, but not the glory yet to be beheld in heaven (John 17:24). After Christ's death and resurrection, the ruler of this world was dethroned, but he continues to create havoc. Heaven is open, but creation still groans. Illness, grief, and death are part of our experience. We have overcome, but the world still hates us and aims to overcome us. Forgiveness and grace are still necessary.

Even so, as N. T. Wright puts it, "There is no reason why we should not pray and work for signs of that new world to be born even in the midst of the old age, of the world that is still, as Paul says, 'groaning in labor pains.'"[27] Though the fullness of our hope is still to come (14:1–3; 16:33), the whole awesome power and love of God are now available (Heb. 6:4–5). We can see the greater things—do the greater things. We are invited to contemplate a whole new realm of reality.[28] So step out! A great door has swung open in the cosmos. The heavens are no longer closed. We have been liberated from assuming we are alone amidst the predators and life is up to us.

QUESTIONS

1. What are some of the "wolves" circling your life? How are you dealing with them?

2. In what ways does skepticism creep into your thoughts? How do you combat it?

3. Which of the permanent realities created by an open heaven impacts you most?

2

LIFE IS ABOUT EXPERIENCING GOD'S SUDDEN SHIFTS

A Conversation with Mary

JOHN 2:1–12

> *When the wine ran out, Jesus' mother told Him, "They don't*
> *have any wine."*
> *"What has this concern of yours to do with Me, woman?"*
> *Jesus asked. "My hour has not yet come."*
>
> —JOHN 2:3–4

"IT'S A WATER-TO-BEER MIRACLE!" THIS HAD TO BE WHAT HALDIS Gundersen was thinking when she stuck her mug under the water tap. Lo and behold, out spouted beer! She shared the miraculous moment with reporters in her western Norway town. Alas, it turned out to be a slipup in the plumbing. Someone downstairs at the Big Tower Bar had hooked the beer hoses to the water pipes to Gundersen's apartment. When asked if the turning of water to beer was a blessing, she responded, "The beer was flat and not tempting."[1] It turns out nothing had really changed.

But things changed in Cana of Galilee. There was a water-to-wine miracle. Unsuspecting guests were about to gain a taste of life under an open heaven. In a moment of time, stone vessels for ritual washing were transformed into wine barrels for celebration. It was all by divine design, and the wine was anything but flat. The guests rave. God saves the best for last.

IT'S A WHOLE NEW PARTY

Water to wine is the first of seven signs in the book of John (temple cleansing, healing a son, healing a lame man, feeding a multitude, healing a blind man, and raising Lazarus are the other six). There are many others, but John does not record them (John 20:30). Miracles aren't the main point of the book; they are not what Jesus is about. He is not into wowing a crowd with supernatural phenomena. Jesus is not impressed with people who withhold faith until they have seen some wonder (4:48). In most cases, they will still disbelieve (12:37).

He does not bless churches that use snake handlers or hot-coal walks or spirit barking to advertise or entertain. Lots of false messiahs can still perform their tricks but leave deadening disillusion behind.

As Eugene Peterson writes, "The miraculous is no proof of truth or reality."[2] Those who insist on miracles are likened to adulterers (Matt. 12:39). Adulterers reduce love to sex; spiritual adulterers diminish a relationship with God to spectacle.

Nonetheless, signs are a part of Jesus's ministry. While pointing to His authority, they serve as signposts telling the approaching guest the skies have opened, so proceed at your own risk. Each miracle is embedded in a conversation intended to draw people to Jesus and prompt them to affirm His messiahship. And enter His party!

THE PARTY JESUS CRASHES

The storyteller tells us the water-to-wine miracle occurs on the third day (John 2:1). Is this simply a historical account, or is John creating suspense? Short answer—yes. There is something about the third day. The third day is a traditional day for Jewish weddings. The third day in creation was the day of seed bearing (Gen. 1:11–13). It is the one day God doubly blessed what He had made. But there is also this: the resurrection occurred on the third day (John 2:19).

Oh, and there is this. The story immediately follows Jesus's announcement to Nathanael. John's initial readers would have recognized these things. Hence, he builds a certain anticipation; something significant, even miraculous, is about to happen. God is preparing us for His glory which is about to go onstage. We are about to see one of the greater things He promised Nathanael (1:50). We are about to see the evidence that God has transcended the heaven-earth divide.

This sounds so dramatic! But the setting is fairly innocuous. A man and a woman have chosen to enter into nuptial bliss. The bride has been escorted to the groom's home to the accompaniment of singing and dancing. They are now into the festivities. Jesus and the twelve, it may seem, have decided to crash the party. Actually, they have been invited (2:2). Jesus has to be here. This is a family occasion, and Jesus has certain duties as the older brother, the head of the family. His presence is expected, for "Jesus' mother was there" (2:1). Enough said.

Weddings require a certain order. Considerable planning is necessary. A venue is determined, menus are planned, food and beverages are ordered, and invitations go out. The guests arrive, ritual washings occur, and a prescribed script is followed. I tell my students that there are two occasions that, as pastors, you can't screw up—weddings and funerals. But things do not always go as planned. Emotions get out of line, brides are overwhelmed with details, parents are suddenly overcome with a sense of loss, best men lose the rings, members of the wedding party are no-shows, the candles do not light, and pastors forget their words.

JESUS, THE GO-TO PERSON

In the case of this wedding, the family has not calculated carefully. The problem is the wine supply. It has failed. Obviously, there has been a miscalculation caused by God knows what. Maybe it was the unexpected guests or an unforeseen collection of heavy drinkers. Maybe the merchant got the order wrong, a barrel ruptured, or a thrift-conscious parent cut things too close.

Mary is the first to take notice: "They don't have any wine" (2:3). John writes this in the present tense for a reason. He is inviting us into the action, as if we are right there at the table sitting in front of an empty pitcher. Mary foresees that guests will soon notice that pitchers aren't replenished. Things are getting a bit uncomfortable. I imagine a wedding reception in my church where the punch bowl is empty and people are still waiting in line for the buffet. If no one comes to the rescue, the festive spirit will be disrupted.

At first, Mary's comment seems nothing more than an observation. They are now into the festivities, which may have been going on for some time. A Middle Eastern wedding celebration could last one to two weeks (a needful diversion from the daily grind). But consumption is beginning to exceed expectation. In a culture where hospitality is everything, this is a major faux pas, a misstep, a misjudgment, a gaffe—take your pick. If not corrected, the wedding will fall flat, the joy will vaporize, and in an honor-shame culture, the host family will fall in disgrace.

Mary is doing more than making an observation. In an indirect way, she is urging Jesus to employ His power and act.[3] Mary is also doing what most women love to do—be helpful. My wife loves to do the same thing. "Our son has no money." "Have you called your mother?" "The neighbor is laboring with a garbage can. She needs your help." (There's a reason Genesis 2 refers to Eve as a "helpmate." Men would be "help-less" without them.)

Someone must revive this rapidly withering party. And Mary knows just the go-to person. From the very beginning, she has had these glimpses of divine activity. The skies appear to be on the verge of cracking open. She is aware of her son's propensity to fix things that are broken. He is good at crafting furniture, and He fills the things that become empty. He is especially good at creating out of nothing.

Why else would she turn to Jesus? She anticipates something extraordinary. Meeting the disciples and hearing their excitement that Jesus is the long-awaited Messiah only confirms her confidence. Jesus is *the* go-to person. He will do what is expected—chase away the clouds, spur people to action, open doors, crash parties, and relieve us of our pains—and carry them out in a timely manner.

This would also be a wonderful way to introduce Jesus to others. Everyone around the table has been talking about their kids, exaggerating certain accomplishments. Parents, especially of the proud sort, like to parade their children and inflate their importance. "My daughter is an honor student." "My son is studying to be a doctor." "My son is an engineer." At a social event like a wedding, where there is generally a bit of "sniffing" going on, it has to be tempting for Mary to say, "My son has grown up to be the preexistent and eternal Word of God, enfleshed as the Son of God! The sun more than shines on Him; the heavens have actually opened to announce His appearance." Or at least hope for a situation in which this suddenly becomes apparent.

JESUS CAN BE SO OPAQUE

But Jesus is not so concerned with parading His wares before a wedding audience. He responds to her words with a question intended to give pause to any assumption that He is there to respond to human expectation. "What has this concern of yours to do with Me, woman?" (John 2:4). Literally, Jesus is asking, "What is it to Me and to you?" Even in modern, sassy America, this sounds like back talk.

What does this mean? The phrase is familiar. It was a common Semitic expression used to establish relational distance (1 Kings 17:18). It was also used in ancient secular Greek. It was a way of saying to others, "What do I have to do with you?" Or worse. In Mark 5:7, the demons used this same phrase to, in effect, say to Jesus, "Butt out! Mind your own business."[4]

Is this what Jesus is saying? Referring to His mother as "woman" only reinforces the interpretation that Jesus is rudely belligerent or, at best, impassive and indifferent. Without hearing the verbal tone, and without seeing the facial expression, we are left to imagine. Words alone are inherently ambiguous.

This explains why, in an age of emails and tweets and texts, we misunderstand and are often misinterpreted. Eugene Peterson, who works with words like an artist works with paints, describes the difficulty of simply reading words. "They are never exact: . . . the attentiveness or intelligence of the listener affects how they are understood; place and weather and circumstances all play a part in both the speaking and the hearing. The more we are 'in context' when language is used, the more likely we are to get it."[5]

Moving deeper into this setting, it may still be hard to get. Throughout John, Jesus's emotions tend to run on a flat plane. It's hard to argue with R. Alan Culpepper, who makes the observation that Jesus's conversational language is often enigmatic, confrontational, and oblique.[6]

In our own day-to-day conversing with Jesus, we can find His responses hard to read. His answers to our prayers can seem ambiguous. Is He really saying no or wait or yes? He seems to be speaking through circumstances, but the leading of the Spirit seems to contradict. Is He testing my faith? Does He feel the weight of need like I do? Does it really matter to Him?

When I lived in the Netherlands, I discovered that the Dutch love certain phrases, phrases that are sometimes difficult to interpret. One of them is *"dat kan niet"* ("it is not possible"). This irritating expression is heard in conversations 18,537,243 times a day (just a guess). On the surface, it appears to indicate there is no way forward. The door is closed, the request is unfeasible. End of discussion.

But this is not necessarily what the words mean. In actuality, things may be possible. In some cases, the responder is buying time. In other moments, the one saying this is testing the other's resolve. Do you really want to do this? (Or it could be the person is simply messing with you.) Is Jesus saying something like this to Mary?

Perhaps His words reflect Someone who is simply put off. Maybe He was in a conversation with a guest about the gospel of the kingdom, the inauguration of Satan's reversal, or the judgment to come. Possibly, He didn't want to be at this party in the first place. Jesus is, after all, into things "above" (John 8:23). And certainly merrymaking with heavy drinking is not a place for holy men who are better suited for time away in the wilderness. Why should Jesus and His followers be wasting time with these lushes when they could be fasting with the monastic community in Qumran?

Or maybe in the whole scheme of things, with the weight of the world's needs on His shoulders, this dilemma is sooo inconsequential!

Days into my first pastorate, a woman whom I can only describe as a perpetual whiner called to say, "I have no Pepto-Bismol." Like Mary, observing something missing at the table, this woman realized something was missing from her medicine cabinet. And she expected an immediate response. Things did not change when I moved to a pastorate in Europe. Parishioners would call, wanting to know if I could find a good pecan pie recipe. Are these people taking me with any degree of seriousness? I took seriously this call to enter ministry and see lives transformed.

Jesus came to save the world. Is this how Jesus felt? Is this how He sometimes feels after hearing our prayers that the whip cream will last until the last dessert is served? Or that the dealer we plan to buy a car from has it in the right color?

Or perhaps the impenetrable coolness of His reply may have simply been a way of saying that this is *their* problem. Mary is acting like Martha, obsessed with all things prim and proper (Luke 10:40). He might have been thinking, "Why are you involved, and why involve Me? Are you the self-appointed wedding coordinator who is still trying to direct traffic? Are you expecting Me and My disciples to make a beverage run over to Nazareth, hoping to procure some cheap wine? Shouldn't the wedding party deal with their failure to plan adequately for *their* party? *Does this party really need to continue, anyway?*"

JESUS CAN BE SO ENGAGED

Of course, none of these interpretations fit the true person of Jesus. In the first place, as the disciples were discovering, Jesus loved to be at social events. He seldom turned down a party. The first responsibility of discipleship, as John tells the story, is for His followers to attend a party. In his chapter "Party Person," William Willimon makes the point that Jesus "was no ragged renunciator of this world."[7] He loved to mix it up with the crowd, eating and drinking, and getting in trouble with the religious police (Mark 2:15–16).

Jesus had no problem with wine. He even likened Himself to it— wine in its tumultuous phase of fermenting. He used the metaphor of a vine dedicated to producing wine to describe His relationship with us (John 15). He invented and mandated feasts and provided the wine to gladden the heart. At times, He likened His earthly journey to a groom at a party (Luke 5:33–34). He urges us to rejoice and delight in the things of life, for present happiness is practice for happiness (and partying) in heaven. He will one day rejoice over His bride, the church. He will turn up the music and make a feast of "well-aged wines strained clear" (Isa. 25:6 NRSV).

Furthermore, Jesus is anything but indifferent to life's issues. If He were, He would not have left heaven to move into our neighborhood. He would not have fed the five thousand—on His own initiative—when there was no food to be found. He would not have become a symbol of hope to lepers, the blind, epileptics, the poor, and the dispossessed.[8] Instead, He intimately engages and experiences our personal difficulties, no matter their size. He cares about our needs more than we care about our own. If the way of a sparrow matters to Him, then He feels the weight of a job loss, the loss of a loved one, and the pain of life's embarrassments (like running out of beverages). I could go on here, but I would only add to my shame for not picking up the Pepto-Bismol and searching for that pie recipe.

Finally, He is more than able. He is too aware to ever be unaware, too immense to ever be measured, and nothing but wise and caring in everything He does. To change water into wine is nothing new; it's an annual practice for God. He turns water, soil, and sunlight into juice, and He makes the microorganisms that eventually turn the juice into wine.[9]

The Maker of the universe is incredibly engaged in day-to-day life. And under an open heaven, the presence of His power to do the impossible is available to us.

If anyone knew all of these things, it was Mary. She experienced angelic activity up close, sensing heaven was breaking in (Luke 1:26–28). She knew Jesus's status. She understood something of the magnitude of Jesus's joy and compassion and power. She lived with her son for thirty years. She saw how He cared, how He loved to laugh uproariously at the dinner table. She must have witnessed over and over His generosity as well as His ability to take on every challenge.

She knew He was more aware of the need than she was. And she knew He was sensitive to a mother's wishes. There never was a question of honoring family.

JESUS CAN BE SO FOCUSED

Mary expects something extraordinary, but she recognizes there is mystery. Under an open heaven, there are many things she has not been able to explain. Her observations are not necessarily His observations. Her timing is not always His timing. Jesus is at once "haunting, disturbing, and [intensely] attractive."[10] He tells her, "My hour has not yet come" (John 2:4). Earthly expectations are governed by divine parameters, including timing. Once Jesus reveals His identity, He will be pressed to solve family problems, heal illnesses, exorcise demons, and still storms. The will of the Father and the timing of the Son trump everything. This is what is being played out in Cana. What it is to Mary and what it is to Jesus are different. For Mary, it's about meeting an immediate expectation. For Jesus, it's about remaining focused on following and fulfilling the purpose of the Father. It is always about single-minded submission and devotion to God's schedule.

This is not the first time family expectancies collide with divine boundary markers. When Jesus went missing as a young boy, family members were beside themselves. They assumed Jesus was with the caravan returning home. But He wasn't, and after several days of searching, they found Him in the temple in the confines of the Father's will. One can hear the frustration in Mary's voice when she asks, "Why do you do this to us?" Apparently it has been a pattern. But Jesus's response, even as a young son, makes it clear that His first obligation is to His heavenly Father and His mission (Luke 2:49).

This tension will increase as Jesus's ministry grows beyond Cana and impacts others. Things will become progressively strained at home. Clearly, "Jesus's ministry is not a family matter."[11] The family will again have to look for Jesus. They will want to gain control and even attempt to "restrain" Him (Mark 3:21). Religious experts will want to do an intervention. Gradually, Jesus's earthly family will find themselves on the outside looking in (John 7:3–8). Jesus must be about His Father's will, and only those who are of the same mind are His true mother and brothers and sisters (Mark 3:35). Family relationships are not the ultimate determining factor in Jesus's decisions. They should not be in ours either.

In a subsequent conversation, Jesus will tell an anxious crowd that He has not come to do His own will, but the will of God who sent Him (John 6:38). His occasional journeys to the wilderness to be with His Father are all about establishing divine will. Fulfilling the purpose of the Father is what sustains Him (4:34). He will not be distracted by another's expectations if they conflict with the overall mission.

We must not be distracted either.

Jesus's words affirm that He lives by His Father's timetable. Life is not measured so much by chronology as by turning points. Each of these timely (*kairos*) encounters points toward a date to be kept, a target to be reached, and an hour that will come (7:6–8; 11:9; 16:4).[12] His ministry will have its time. In the perfect moment, He will begin to reveal His identity through the miracles He performs, the divine activity He unleashes. They will bring a crisis of messianic belief in the audience. These will prompt investigators to be dispatched. Religious leaders will be threatened. Individuals will be forced to decide. Jesus will be arrested, go to the cross, and rise on the third day. He will eventually host His own wedding, and wine will drip from the mountains and flow from the hills. But not until the Father gives the go-ahead and says, "Now!"

The wedding conversation between Jesus and Mary appears to end. Mary shifts the conversation to the servants, "Do whatever He tells you" (2:5). On the surface, Mary seems to be pressing the issue, insisting, ever so subtly, that her will *will* be done. Did she really hear Him? Is she like the Canaanite woman in Tyre who will not be deterred by Jesus's hesitancy to help (Matt. 15:27)? As far as she is concerned, is the time now?

Maybe. But these words might also reflect a mother who has given the matter completely over to her son. She has shifted from expectation to expectancy, from "what I would like now" to "whatever and whenever He says." It will be right, it will be generous, it will be timely, and it will be wise. This is not aggressive parenting nor apathetic resignation but a humble correction that acknowledges, "He's in charge and He knows what time it is."

It may be we need the same attitude of trust.

JESUS CAN BE SO GENEROUS

As Mary's voice fades out of the story, Jesus sets His sights on six water jars used for ritual purification. They are a necessity in a devout person's home. In the day to day, there is always the risk of becoming unclean, be it eating with unclean hands, consuming the wrong foods (lobster bisque, pork ribs), dealing with a skin disease (psoriasis, pimples), contacting a dead animal (roadkill), or experiencing an involuntary genital discharge (it happens). No doubt these guests are in constant need of ritual cleansing, for the laws regarding contamination are strict and penalties severe. But Jesus has something else in mind for these jars, and so He speaks and acts as if He is in charge, because He is. He is about to replace the symbols of religious ritual with something far more life-giving.

Jesus commands the wine be drawn out "now." The whole sequence seems rather strange. In one moment Jesus appears to say, "Now is not the time." In the next, Jesus says, "Now is the time." How do we resolve this? Maybe we can't. We are bound by time, but God is not. We think in sequence (*chronos*); He operates in the opportune instant (*kairos*). Jesus will wait for the Father's perfect moment, which may mean months or years—or seconds. In God's kingdom, time is compressed; "there is a tremendous sense of urgency about action in the present."[13] There are these sudden shifts. How else does one explain such incidents as the one in John 6, where Jesus gets in the boat and the disciples are immediately on land (v. 21)? There is a breathless pace in which God's campaign is unfolding. Hang on!

As the Cana wedding party is winding down, the master of the banquet is brought a cup of wine and is startled to sip a wine of incredible intensity and exceptional length. It surpasses the best Cabernet Sauvignon. He is so stunned that he calls aside the bridegroom, puzzled because most hosts serve the cheapest wine at the end of the feast when people are too smashed to tell the difference. But this bridegroom has saved the best for last (2:10). "Jesus as God's Genesis Word continu[es] to speak creation into existence."[14] Let there be wine! And in this moment, the miracle serves as a signpost pointing to the divinity of Jesus. It evidences Jesus's statement to Nathanael that the heavens are open, and divine activity is at work (1:51). The best has come at last!

Other signs will foster division over Jesus's person, as they prompt a response of either faith or rejection.[15] The wedding party, however, has no response. The guests are too consumed with consumption to see that the visible representation of God, the one who holds all things together, is right before their eyes. The angels of God are anonymously at work as well, providing and protecting and serving. Only the servants are aware there has been a miracle. The headwaiter knows something strange has occurred, and he compliments the bridegroom for setting aside 180 gallons of superb wine. That's 907 bottles. This is God's extravagance, though the hapless groom seems to be all too willing to assume the credit.

Those around the table have completely missed what has happened—"a top-to-bottom rearrangement of the ordinary into the extraordinary of which the miraculous rearrangement of water into wine is just the beginning."[16] They lose meaning in His presence.[17] They miss that He too is a bridegroom (3:29; Rev. 19:7–9) who has given the guests a foretaste of life in heaven, where purification pots will be replaced with flowing wine. They may realize the wine and the wedding feast are images of the coming age (see Amos 9:13–14), but they are too earthbound, too focused on the predictable to notice.

This will be a recurring pattern with the other signs (John 5:18; 9:16; 11:46). Unbelieving Israel will be oblivious to divine presence and impervious to Jesus's miracles. They will also miss the fact that a generous God, too, has saved the best for last ("For the law was given through Moses, grace and truth came through Jesus Christ," 1:17). The good wine of the messianic age has been saved until now.[18]

John 2:11 ends the account saying that Jesus has displayed His glory—His splendor and His honor. It is fitting. The third day is all about glory. It is a glory that is consistent with His other acts—acts that are often quiet, behind the scenes, and often unnoticed by others. He uses our requests to express something of His weight and worth and splendor—as well as give evidence of an open heaven. And when we get a glimpse of this, as the disciples did, we believe.

WE ARE INVITED TO TASTE THIS GENEROSITY

So where is this going? What does this story have to do with us? Like Mary, we also come to God with our expectations. I find myself telling God that things are not as they should be. Jesus should fix what is broken and replace what is missing. Desperate pastors, realizing it is Friday and their sermon preparation is "failing," tell Jesus "they have no sermon." Parents, surveying the poor choices of their kids, lament, "God, they have no future." God has to do something now!

It's not that we should come to God without expectations. Mary certainly had expectations. And God commands us to come to Him with our needs like persistent widows (Luke 18:1–8). He delights in dogged, stubborn prayers and can accomplish what must be done. Seek, and keep seeking; ask, and keep asking. Persistence pays off. It builds our faith and enables us to be ready when God responds. Tenacity separates the wheat from the chaff. Mere whims give way to deep-seated desires. Like the woman with the issue of blood, we are encouraged to not let go of the hem of the garment. The question He leaves us with is this: "Nevertheless, when the Son of Man comes, will He find that faith on earth?" (v. 8).

But sometimes our expectations are *our* expectations, expectations that must meet *our* anticipated outcomes. Steve Jobs, cofounder of Apple, went to church in his early years. But it all changed one day when he was thirteen. Staring at a picture of starving children in Biafra, he confronted his pastor. Hearing that God is all-knowing, he asked, "Well, does God know about this and what's going to happen to these children?" When his pastor failed to give an answer that met his expectations, Jobs announced that he did not want anything to do with God anymore.[19]

Ultimately, any expectations of God must fall in line behind what God expects of us. Like Mary we need to say, "Do as He says." As missiologist Lesslie Newbigin puts it, "Jesus cannot become the instrument of any human purpose"; we are the instruments of His will.[20] It is not heaven responding to earth; it is first earth responding to heaven. Better to come with expectancy.

There is something else in this conversation that provokes me, and it gets to the point of the book. Am I conscious of the fact that the heavens have opened? Are my eyes seeing the greater things, or am I completely oblivious? Those at the wedding seemed to hardly notice that God had broken in. Do I? Do you?

Reflecting on this story, more and more questions surface:

How many times have we enjoyed the gifts of God without ever really noticing—let alone acknowledging—their source?

How many times do we assume that we have made things happen?

Are we attentive to miracles? Do we notice when God has served up the new wine, saving the best for last?

Have we noticed that, in the span of a moment, He has replaced the cheap with something precious?

As substitute gods gradually come up short of their promised benefits, do we discern that Jesus has filled the gap with His abundance?[21]

Are we sensitized to His unpredictable movements?

Can we tell when He has filled our emptiness with the Spirit's fullness?

When two or three have gathered together in His name, have we
noticed that He is suddenly present?
When He generously supplies for the party, will we know?
Will we acknowledge Him and will we give thanks?

In my college years, I was at full press. Involved in athletics, studying international relations, and leading campus ministries, I was often
more full of myself than God. Too often I missed what He was doing
right in front of me. One day, I came across a little booklet entitled
My Heart—Christ's Home. In it, Robert Boyd Munger describes the
human heart as a house with many rooms. Christ fills all the rooms,
but there is one room He has chosen to manifest His particular presence—the living room. Each morning, He makes a fire and waits for
us to meet Him. He has prepared a table. He has poured His wine. But
in our hurry, we often miss that He is there.

Munger exposed, and continues to expose, my tendency to race
through life and pass by where He is and what He is doing. It may be
true of you. Too often we are like these guests in Cana, wrapped up
in their socializing and wine, and missing what God has just accomplished. Missing that the heavens are open. And maybe like Mary,
missing that He too notices and acts when the time is perfectly right
in ways that transcend expectation.

QUESTIONS

1. *How would you contrast expectation with expectancy under an
   open heaven?*

2. *Are there situations in your life that seem opaque and confusing?
   What might God be doing in those situations that you are
   completely oblivious to?*

3. *Signs reveal God's glory. What does this mean? Where have you
   seen evidence of His glory?*

3

LIFE IS ABOUT MOVING WITH THE SPIRIT

A Conversation with Nicodemus

JOHN 3:1–15

The wind blows where it pleases, and you hear its sound, but you don't know where it comes from or where it is going. So it is with everyone born of the Spirit.

—JOHN 3:8

"What do a Buddhist, a biker couple, a gay-rights activist, a transient, a high-tech engineer, a Muslim, a twenty-something single mom, a Jew, a couple living together, and an atheist all have in common?" asks Pastor John Burke in his book, *No Perfect People Allowed.* It isn't a trick question. Answer: they are tomorrow's church.[1]

At first, they will come as seekers. They will be on the perimeter, watching, investigating, and asking, "Is this Christian faith genuine? Is Jesus worth following?" When they discover He is and experience the mysterious moving of the Spirit, they will begin to discover what life under an open heaven is about.

A similar conglomeration of seekers came after Jesus: disciples of John, a noted teacher of Israel, a woman of disrepute, a crowd longing for a king, and men who ranged from fishermen to former terrorists. Who could ever build a church with that lot? As New Testament scholar R. Alan Culpepper puts it, "The Wizard of Oz with its tin man in search of a heart, its lion looking for courage, and its little girl who just wants to go home is no more incongruous."[2]

When Jesus sees this odd mix looking for him, He turns and asks, "What are you looking for?" (John 1:38). (He knows, of course, but wants them to think about their motives.)

At other times, Jesus is the seeker. He finds Philip and says, "Follow Me" (1:43). He goes out to meet a woman drawing water at a well and invites her to drink (4:10, 13–14). He seeks a lame man in a crowd and, oddly, asks if he wants to be healed (5:6). He sets His eyes on a man needing sight and challenges him to see with faith to believe (9:35). Throughout the gospel, "God's reckless love is on the prowl, willing to crash through our distance and crush down our idols to get to our heart."[3]

Under an open heaven, it's a mutual pursuit. All of us are the hunters *and* the hunted.

AN UNLIKELY ENCOUNTER

Nicodemus is one of the hunters (3:2). He is also one of the more mystifying characters in the gospel. Unlike some biblical conversations where people remain anonymous, this man is clearly identified by name and profession. He is a Jewish leader and an apparent seeker. We generally associate seekers with the irreligious, but Nicodemus is just the opposite; he is the epitome of religion.

It's not immediately clear why he has come to Jesus. Has he come out of simple curiosity? To check out the competition? Is he searching for something less constrictive than the religion he has grown up with? Is he attracted to Jesus and His gospel and thereby open to belief? Or has he come on a mission to challenge, even undermine and undercut, the person and work of the Messiah?

The reader would like to believe Nicodemus is on a journey of faith. We want to see him make the same profession as Nathanael: "Rabbi, . . . You are the Son of God! You are the King of Israel!" (1:49). It would be great to see a man of his stature come to experience life under the open sky. But while it is difficult for us to ascertain the motives of Nicodemus, it's not a mystery to Jesus. John makes this clear in the closing words of chapter 2: "for He Himself knew what was in man" (v. 25). The statement frames this second conversation. The man coming to discover Jesus is already uncovered in the eyes of God.

The first thing John wants us to know is that "There was a man" (3:1). It's an intentional link with the last word of the last verse of chapter 2—"man." Nicodemus serves as a test case of what is in man.[4] He will confirm Jesus's practice to not place His trust in the words and actions of men (2:24). But Nicodemus is not just any man. John tells us he has significant rank. He is a member of the Pharisees, the most devout group in Israel. These were the intellectual guardians of the law, and Nicodemus is the chief warden. He is also a ruler, a member of the highest national body in charge of Jewish affairs, the Sanhedrin.

This establishes him as part of the inner circle and a member of the upper social strata.

We can picture an impressive figure standing before Jesus in all of his fashionable wear. Here is Nicodemus, distinguished by his silk threads, enlarged phylacteries, exaggerated tassels, impressive head-dress, and a seal that defines his ring. He is a member of the City Club. No wonder there is an aristocratic lilt to his voice. He is both pious and privileged, a part of the white-flannel set. He has an executive suite at the stadium where he can schmooze with other highfliers. He has it together; his world is tightly ordered. He is the "strings" men try to pull as they jockey for position. It is a major score to be on his guest list. Sycophants are always seeking to try to flatter him, curry favors, and write books where they can refer to him as "my friend." But he is about to meet a Man who is not so impressed with these sorts of things. Even to this man, Jesus will not entrust Himself.

Nicodemus comes in the night. Whatever his motives in coming, he knows he must be careful to protect his position. To be too public with Jesus would cost valuable political capital with the rest of the suits. If others caught wind that he, whose name means "conqueror of the people," was hanging out with Jesus, it would be potentially embarrassing. He would lose prestige. It might suggest something is missing in his life. What will his peers say if they hear he is a Jesus seeker? Surely, seminary-credentialed God experts do not seek help from untrained carpenters turned wannabe itinerant preachers! But Nicodemus seems to do this.

The disciples are not mentioned in this story. In John's gospel, they are often silent when Jesus is interacting with others. But it does not mean they are absent. In this situation, they might have shrunk into the background like neophyte Catholics intimidated by an unexpected visit from the pope. Why has this exalted leader come? Men of such high and holy rank do not mix with the hoi polloi, fraternizing with spiritual amateurs. Their crude and unsophisticated ways tend to be a real put off to the Jewish clergy.

Lingering in the spectral shadows, John and James and Peter are surely suspicious. It makes no sense that Nicodemus suddenly shows up. Is he doing surveillance? Pharisees are masters at this (Luke 14:1). Maybe he is a spy for the Sanhedrin—a dangerous lot—though as yet they have no inkling that the Sanhedrin will become the driving force to get rid of Jesus.

A SEEMINGLY SIGNIFICANT OPPORTUNITY

Fear might also be mixed with a sudden rush of excitement. If curiosity turns to commitment, Nicodemus will be quite a trophy, like marquee athletes and entertainers. His newly acquired Jesus jewelry will lend instant credibility. He might run interference with the establishment. Even influence the choice of the next court appointee.

We can only speculate what the disciples are doing. Maybe they anticipate a crash course in seeker evangelism, silently taking notes as Jesus talks to Nicodemus. To be effective, Jesus will have to make His gospel message attractive, impressing Nicodemus with teachings that are largely narrative, inductive, and relevant. He will need to be real, talking about His own failings as a member of the clergy, admitting that not all of His sermons have been home runs. People have even grabbed their things and walked out in the middle of His first point (John 6:66).

The Scriptures don't tell us what was going on with the disciples because that isn't where the conversation is. So let's listen in on Jesus's actual encounter with Nicodemus. Let's look for what John is showing us about life under an open heaven, where the unexpected upends the expected. It is here we will discover how one gets in.

The conversation begins well enough. Amidst some initial awkwardness, there are the usual pleasantries (John 3:2). Nicodemus addresses Jesus as rabbi, an honorary title for those in a rather exclusive theological club. He follows up with, "We know that You have come from God." He wants Jesus to know he is a man in the know. He and his associates are paid to keep up with what is current. Nicodemus was there in Jerusalem observing Jesus during the Passover, witnessing His signs and His growing popularity (2:23). Has this piqued Nicodemus's curiosity? Does he sense that something of God's anointing is on Jesus? After all, when the Messiah comes, everyone knows He will perform miraculous signs (7:31).

Can it be that Nicodemus is envious? Jesus seems to be the talk around town. He carries Himself with a certain gravitas, even in His lighter moments. Nicodemus has witnessed Jesus's zeal for the house of God and possibly said to himself, "I wish I had the guts to do that." He knows the money changers and sacrifice dealers have slowly, intentionally moved their businesses from outside the gates to inside, compromising sacred temple ground. For inexcusable reasons (unless bribery is viewed as credible), the religious caretakers have looked the other way. Not Jesus! With the force of holy conviction, Jesus recently did what others feared to do.

It may be that Nicodemus is simply baffled. Jesus may be a man of God, but He is full of inconsistencies and contradictions. He is a rabbi, but where are His formal rabbinic credentials? From what seminary did He graduate? Has He published anything? Has He read Karl Barth? True, He is a capable communicator, but how did He acquire such homiletical skills?

Is Jesus a fountain of truth or a seedbed of heresy? Messianic claims have been around almost as long as the Jews have been a nation. Now people are throwing the *Messiah* word about, associating it with Jesus. Could this be the real thing? There are things He does that hint at messiahship. Yet, all in all, this Man does not do the things one with any theological sophistication would expect.

It is like an experience I had years ago in San Antonio. I wanted to stop to see the historic Alamo. The road map told me I was in the right place, but all I could see was a small structure, a play fort that appeared to be an advertisement pointing ahead to the real thing. *But it was the real thing!* Wait, John Wayne could not have fought here! Jesus can't be the Messiah. He is too small and unimpressive.

Maybe He is a trailer to the real movie coming soon.

There are all of these contradictions. Jesus does teach the Law with amazing exegetical skills, but He appears to be more interested in upstaging rather than serving in the temple.[5] He teaches religion within its halls, but worse than bringing coffee into the sanctuary, He trashes it! He has a holy deportment, but there are rumors He parties with prostitutes, hangs out with tax thugs, and says nice things to Samaritans. He heals, going against all Sabbath protocol. He has never dated. Is He gay? Nicodemus has to find out for himself who Jesus really is, *for Jesus does not fit his categories.*

Does He fit yours?

Perhaps Jesus is just another up-and-coming emergent leader whose popularity is affecting attendance patterns and threatening the offerings of churches like Nicodemus's. Families are leaving their comfortable pews for shifting outdoor venues. One can only hope they will come back once Jesus flames out. Jesus is just another shooting star, isn't He? He connects with the thirtysomethings, with His appeal for social justice (check out His latest Sermon on the Mount podcast). They like Jesus's kingdom theology and exile language. They love that He rips into established religion and leans toward a more egalitarian style (though it would be great if He addressed climate change, gun control, and immigration).

But Jesus will eventually implode. Like other blowhards, the love of power will get its grip on Him. Nicodemus is certain this growing following, this mix of the sane and psychopaths, will lead to success and seduction. Jesus's video venues, His established franchises, led by these twelve misfits, will soon be a forgotten fad.

Still, His church is experiencing "off the charts" growth. Who is He? What are His methods and His message? He attracts large crowds and offers free food (organic, gluten free, and made on the spot). Nicodemus has to scout out this threat to the established Jewish church. As Eugene Peterson notes, "Leaders, if they are to maintain their influence, have to stay ahead of the competition, have to keep up with the trends, know what sells best in the current market."[6] Their students must know they stay current.

How does Jesus respond to this impressive seeker?

JESUS UNIMPRESSED

While Nicodemus is polite, Jesus gives no special welcome. There seems to be a deafening dearth of excitement. Jesus doesn't appear to thank Nicodemus for taking an evening from his demanding schedule to come to see Him. There is no small talk, no use of time to get to know Nicodemus, hear about his past, learn about his family, and make him feel special. No comparing notes on Grammy Awards, favorite movies (what did you think of Russell Crowe as Noah?), or books (yes, I've always found Grisham to be a page-turner).

Jesus responds, but not in the same way He responded to John the Baptist's doubts. When John was in prison and wondering why things were not adding up, he sent a note to Jesus asking, "Are You the Expected One? Are You really the one come from God who's worth staking my whole life on, because I didn't expect to be here?" Jesus gave reassurance, along with compelling evidence (Matt. 11:3).

He could have done the same with Nicodemus. But John is a disciple and a witness. Nicodemus is neither. Rather than provide some divine guarantee, Jesus begins to draw lines and point out Nicodemus's refusal to acknowledge or move with the Spirit.

Jesus can see that this is less an inquiry and more of a show of wits.[7] This is less a seeker service and more like a drama played out before an audience. There is conflict from beginning to end.[8] The Hellenistic world had a long tradition of dialogue as the vehicle for teaching. This informal debate between two main characters, protagonist and antagonist, appears to follow this pattern.

Nicodemus Needs to Start Over

This encounter is also part of a larger encounter. Human authority ("we know") meets divine authority ("truly, truly"). The ultimate representative of the Jews squares off with the ultimate representative of God. The teacher of Israel goes head-to-head with the Teacher of the universe—"from below" is clashing with "from above"—darkness colliding with Light. This explains the following discourse:

> Nicodemus initiates—You can't do these signs unless You are from
> God (John 3:2).
> Jesus responds—You can't see the kingdom of God unless you are
> born again (v. 3).
> Nicodemus reacts—What nonsense! No one can be born again
> unless one reenters his mother's womb (v. 4).
> Jesus declares—You can't enter the kingdom unless you have
> experienced spiritual rebirth (v. 5).

As the conversation moves back and forth, the scene becomes more confrontational and more tense. And somewhat inexplicable. These sentences seem to be placed next to one another by connections that can only be understood through chaos theory.

From the beginning, Nicodemus has assumed he is in charge of the exchange. He is confident, for he and his peers know divine protocol. They know God has chosen them to lead. They know the Scriptures. As Scot McKnight puts it, Pharisees were the "home Bible study movement," the ones who interpreted the Torah for the less knowledgeable to follow.[9] But over time, their purist concerns gradually stiffened into morbid scrupulosity. They mastered every jot and tittle, but they ended up straining gnats and swallowing camels (Matt. 23:24). Their standards were rigid and unrealistic, so much so that they could not even live out their rules. The world of Nicodemus lied to itself so often it couldn't pass a polygraph test. Still, how dare this newcomer come onto their turf and try to push His way into leadership of their people!

But it is Jesus who is really in charge, who has always been in charge, and He turns the conversation into a classroom. He begins with the basics. There is a kingdom that is not merely future—it is present. There has been an inbreaking of God's rule, and though its coming can be compared to lightning (Luke 17:24), one must have the eyes to perceive it. There is a heaven that is wide open, but one must gain sight to see it. It is through rebirth that one is awakened to the sight (John 3:3). We're talking redemption. One must be born again.

Again, Jesus has a way of breaking through to our mind-already-made-up brains. This "from above" language is beyond the realm of Nicodemus's present perception. His refined mind is flummoxed. Nicodemus lives in a "flatland world."[10] He is oblivious to the rolling hills, the majestic mountains, and the stunning vistas of life under an open heaven. He cannot see beyond the now, the everyday, the Law.

It may be that our perceptions have similar limitations. There is a covert side to this kingdom, one that is alive on arrival (Matt. 13:31–33).

"Born again" is about spiritual changes. We're familiar with the phrase; it is church language. The words are code for praying the sinner's prayer. It's what separates real Christians from all of the rest. The irony of ironies is that Jesus says these words, "you must be born again," to a religious man. He will not use these words with the lost woman at the well or with the unreceptive crowd living for their bellies. He will not even use this language when speaking to His unbelieving brothers or when confronting the pagan Pilate. These words are reserved for a righteous man of the cloth, supposedly knowledgeable about spiritual matters, faithfully carrying out the Law, as well as following the added 613 rules and 1,521 emendations!

As they spar, Nicodemus is becoming more confused. This was not the conversation he envisioned. What has he stepped into? If there was music to complement this setting, it would be the score for Alfred Hitchcock's *Vertigo*.

This is not relational—it is not even rational conversation. It has the feel of my first day in Statistics 101, a required course taught in college by a French professor whose English was barely intelligible. We listened for one useful syllable. What is going on? Where am I? How did I get here? How can I escape?

This is supposed to be a theological discussion, but Nicodemus cannot believe that Jesus is using gynecological language (John 3:4). One can almost hear Nicodemus's derision: "You're telling me that to be in God's kingdom, I have to turn the clock back, climb up the birth canal, and reenter my mother's uterus?"

Nicodemus assumes Jesus is speaking of something physically impossible. It is beginning to seem that Jesus might be what whisperers are saying—He's a lunatic! Oh yes, this is the same one who claimed He could build the temple in three days (2:19–20). Crazy, loony—completely batty.

Jesus, however, is purposefully deconstructing the faulty foundation on which Nicodemus has built his faith. His Israeli citizenship papers, Jewish heritage, synagogue education, and Pharisaic status are not enough to enter God's kingdom. Nicodemus is beginning to realize that Jesus is telling him that he must start over. It's like telling a five-star general, with his uniform weighted down with medals and ribbons, that he must meet with a recruiter and start back at boot camp.

It is telling a contractor near the end of a project that the plans were flawed and it will be necessary to tear it all down and go back to the footings.

Nicodemus Needs to Get in Step

Nicodemus is stunned. But Jesus doesn't back off. He tells Nicodemus to stop being surprised (3:7). One can hear Jesus asking, "Are you not acquainted with the messianic texts? Have you not heard of the Spirit? Didn't the prophets speak of a coming day when God will send His Spirit?" (see Isa. 64:1; Jer. 31:31–34; Ezek. 11:19–20; 36:25–27). Surely religious leaders understand that flesh gives birth to flesh, but only the Spirit can give birth to things of the spirit. This rebirth and regeneration are about the Spirit rushing in, leaving a path of radical heart change. It transcends a religion of works and rules—powerful evidence that the heavens have opened.

Jesus doesn't pause to give a "sorry, it's okay" pat on the back. Behind the verbal sparring is a Savior who loves Nicodemus the same as He loves the world (John 3:16). But Jesus will not tell him what he wants to hear. He tells Nicodemus what he needs to hear. He says absolutely nothing to affirm this hard-charging, self-made man who has grown up in a world of active verbs. Jesus is not impressed with his accomplishments, any more than He is with ours.

Maybe you noticed that Jesus uses the passive voice with nearly every verb in His conversation with Nicodemus. It is intentional. Something outside of Nicodemus will have to happen, something from above, something radical—and something by someone else! Nicodemus, for all of his performance, his accomplishments, his affiliations, and his board memberships, has to be born from above. He will have to submit to the mysterious workings of the Spirit who may disrupt all of his labeled and sorted "neat piles."[11]

We, too, must learn to receive the movements of the Spirit, the changes God wants to fulfill in us. And like Nicodemus, it may shift our neat piles, blowing a fresh wind into stale places in our lives. Welcome to life under an open heaven!

Nicodemus Needs to Get Educated

The adversarial sparring moves on. Nicodemus is mystified by where this is taking him. "How can such a strange birth happen?" Jesus turns the tables on Nicodemus and asks him to explain it: "You be the teacher" (see v. 9). But Nicodemus can't, and Jesus feigns amazement at Nicodemus's obtuseness: "Aren't you supposed to be *the* teacher of Israel, the right reverend doctor?" Jesus appears to extend deference, but in reality He is exposing pretense and ignorance. He is pointing out the irony that here is an "enlightened" man who comes in the night and is completely in the dark.

With all of this discussion about God's Spirit, Nicodemus should have realized it just might be that the kingdom is near and the King is here. He and his tribe lived with the hope that God's rule would appear someday. He was a trained professional when it came to spiritual matters and the Spirit's movements. A theological expert should have recognized the brilliance of God's plan, a plan laid out as far back as Genesis 3:15. He should have grasped that the heavens have opened. But Nicodemus seems to have skipped a required course, Prophetic Literature 101. One can almost hear Jesus asking, "Did you simply audit correspondence courses, or worse, did you buy your degree from some diploma mill?" Jesus has a way of exposing those of us who think we know everything as those who know next to nothing.

But Jesus focuses on something deeper inside Nicodemus. This isn't so much an intellectual issue as it is a heart issue. Confusion and rigidity are both at work. Jesus again uses "truly, truly" to call for full attention: "What *We* have known *We* are speaking, and what *We* are perceiving *We* are bearing witness to, but *you* do not accept *Our* testimony" (see John 3:11). The plural is used to declare that the whole Trinity has been summoned onstage to speak to Nicodemus. The full weight of divine authority confronts this teacher of the law.

But Nicodemus refuses to accept Jesus and instead stubbornly clings to what he has learned. He already has God and His movements down to a science. At least he thinks he does. In Nicodemus's mind, God must move in unbending obedience to the Jewish religious understanding. Nicodemus is seeking to conform Jesus to his own messianic assumptions, but he can't. He cannot commandeer the Spirit of God's presence any more than he can manufacture, systematize, and control life with his religious codes. The Spirit is too elusive and disruptive. People born of the Spirit live lives of unpredictability.

In effect, Jesus says: "Get over your religious credentials. You're not that good!" As with all people, Nicodemus's efforts and all of his impressive works must be consigned to trusting and receiving. You can manipulate the law and control people, but you cannot direct God. Life under an open heaven is not some reward for those who have the proper pedigree, the appropriate credentials, and have met the key performance indicators.

Nicodemus Needs to Get Saved

If Nicodemus is unresponsive to divine changes, how will he believe Jesus's words about heaven and grace and redemption (vv. 12–15)? How will he have the spiritual sense to see that Jesus is the one who ascends and descends through an open heaven (v. 13)? How will he get it, that just as Moses lifted up the serpent in the wilderness, so He will be lifted up, making salvation possible for everyone who believes in Him (vv. 14–15)? How else will he have eternal life?

Unfortunately, in his hardness, Nicodemus is unwilling to commit. He thinks he knows the Word, but it does not abide in him. He does not believe in the One the Father has sent (5:38–39). In the end, Nicodemus fades back into the religious conformity whence he came. Back to where things are closed rather than open; back to where he can't feel the wind. The unpredictable, intrusive ways of the Spirit are much too threatening.

This is Nicodemus's MO throughout the rest of John. He will maintain a closet faith of a sort, playing the middle where he can. He will attempt to come to Jesus's defense, but with the mocking response of his peers, Nicodemus will pull away and recede into the background (7:51). He recognizes the authority in Jesus, but he does not want to lose club privileges. He prefers the praise of men over the favor of God (12:42–43). In the end, Nicodemus will pay his respects at the grave of Jesus (19:39), bringing a massive amount of spices, perhaps to assuage his guilt. Most likely, this visit will also be in the night. There is a position to uphold, a control to maintain. He is, after all, the teacher of Israel. One can only imagine the life he could have lived!

Soon it will be Nicodemus's peers whom Jesus will engage. These conversations, too, will be confrontational: "You say you believe in Moses's writings, but you really don't" (see 5:47); "You have memorized the Law, but the Word does not abide in you" (v. 38); "You receive glory from your peers, but you seek not the glory that comes from God" (v. 44); "You say you are Abraham's descendants, and yet there is no resemblance to him" (8:39). These men have the law but nothing of the Spirit.

Sadly, like most seekers, Nicodemus and his buddies weren't far from the Light. Nicodemus came "out of" the night, drawn to the Light. But he is "not yet able to leave the darkness."[12] In the darkness, his deeds can remain hidden (3:20). He remains in his blindness, not realizing this impedes his steps. "If anyone walks during the night, he does stumble, because the light is not in him" (11:10).

WE NEED TO GET IN THE FLOW

So what does this third conversation in John reveal about life under an open heaven? If we have something of the same rigidity as Nicodemus, prepare for God's pickax to work at breaking the hardness. Prepare to be brought back to the beginning. You cannot possibly hold tight to your own preconceived ideas about God and still experience the Spirit flowing through an open heaven. You will need to be reborn.

If you have experienced rebirth and are part of today's (and tomorrow's) church, then open your eyes to see that the kingdom is here to be experienced in the present (3:3). It has broken in and is remaking the world. Live the life you are expected to live. Anticipate the Spirit's movements. Open wide and taste something of the powers of the age to come (Heb. 6:5). And hang on! The presence of Jesus and the moving of the Spirit affirm God's inbreaking. This divine wind blows where He will, and this is both exhilarating and unnerving. God is a wind whose intensity depends upon the context. His impact may be as gentle as a breath or as forceful as a hurricane. Just as the Spirit compels Jesus to go to the wilderness to meet the Devil (Mark 1:12), He may throw us into situations that will test our convictions—but also widen our horizons.

Some seekers prefer a God they can figure out and manipulate. But God is a mystery that cannot be explained, a wind that cannot be traced or tracked. At any given moment, the Spirit gives birth, enlivens, inaugurates, initiates, guides, lures, speaks, convicts, woos, influences, restrains, purifies, illuminates, fills, anoints, intercedes, gifts, mediates, empowers, and inspires. For the watchful, He opens our eyes to new skylines and new possibilities. Life under an open heaven is anything but predictable, it is certainly not boring, and it looks nothing like what the religious elite expect.

My wife and I occasionally escape to a wilderness place near the Canadian border. Halcyon days can be interrupted by sudden micro cells, these powerful rushes of the wind. Everything loose better be tied down, or it may be floating down the Pend Oreille River.

So with the Spirit! Ever since Pentecost, all bets are off. Like Philip, born of the Spirit and filled with the Spirit, we may be snatched away (Acts 8:39–40). We may find ourselves at Azotus (or The Hague, Dubai, a rural village outside of Jos, or a new neighborhood across town). If we release ourselves to trusting God, life under an open heaven will be a ride. An amazing rebirth!

QUESTIONS

1. *What's your take on Nicodemus? A sincere seeker or a man determined to put Jesus in His place? In what ways are you like Nicodemus? In what ways are you different?*

2. *The only time Jesus uses rebirth language is with a religious Jew. Why do you think that is the case?*

3. *Describe a time in your life when the Spirit moved in a way that was entirely different from what you expected. What did you learn from that experience?*

4

LIFE IS ABOUT DISMANTLING BARRIERS

A Conversation with the Woman at the Well

JOHN 4:7–26

He left Judea and went again to Galilee. He had to travel through Samaria, so He came to a town of Samaria called Sychar near the property that Jacob had given his son Joseph. Jacob's well was there, and Jesus, worn out from His journey, sat down at the well. It was about six in the evening.

A woman of Samaria came to draw water.

"Give Me a drink," Jesus said to her.

—JOHN 4:3–7

I AM ABOUT TO DO WHAT IS QUITE POPULAR THESE DAYS—RIP INTO the established church. I admit I am often on the defensive when other people do this. I have, after all, given most of my life to the church. I have pastored a midsize church in one of the rougher parts of east Portland and an international church in the strategic area of The Hague, Netherlands. And I have devoted these last sixteen years to leading a large multicultural church on the west side of Portland. My identity has been closely attached to each one. So when someone attacks "organized" faith, it can feel personal.

Nonetheless, some disparagement is warranted. Too many churches, pastors and parishioners alike, are exclusionary. They preach an inclusionary gospel, directing the message to those largely like themselves. This is a failure to see the greater things God intends us to see. We build walls between others and ourselves, between the God we've been commanded to share and those He wants to reach. This is not what life under an open heaven is about.

THE WALLS WE BUILD

For some churches, exclusivity is in their DNA. They began as ethnic communities (e.g., German Baptists or Korean Presbyterians) hoping to preserve and protect their cultural heritage, their customs, and their language. It is in their mission to maintain their traditions, their identity.

Other churches have intentionally created monocultures out of a church-growth theory that says "like attracts like." They go out of their way to target people like themselves (same tastes, same economic status, same interests), and in many cases the growth stats affirm their utilitarian strategy. Their success stories are showcased in church conferences and written up in Christian-centric publications.

Other churches exclude because of bigotry. There is an obvious bias against any who are different in age or ethnicity or affluence. They do not welcome those who are unlike themselves. You would think they have never heard of Jesus's ministry to those who are different. Are they familiar with Jesus? The congregants of these churches are written up in books like *The Help* by Kathryn Stockett.

And then there are some churches where discrimination is far more subtle. One experiences this at the door of a church, where the greeting is contrived and manufactured. It is obvious you are not part of the club or a member of one of the tribes. It plays out in the lobby, where people gravitate to people like themselves. Meanwhile, over by the information table, there is the new visitor left to fend for himself, trying to figure out where the entry points are. Is it necessary to get a club card with a bar code to gain entrance and enjoy the perks?

In such places, singles and single parents, divorced or widowed, can find themselves left out of the conversations. Some of the elderly, those who can no longer make a "meaningful" contribution with their resources, are treated as nice but no longer significant. And in some groups, guilt and condemnation work to shun or at least keep to the margins those who have committed moral failure. This can extend to those of different education or economic status or intellectual capabilities—those who don't measure up.

THE PAIN WE CREATE

At a recent staff meeting, one of our pastors shared a troubling note from a teen who had just visited the youth group (the names are changed to maintain privacy):

> Hi Steve, my name is Jennifer. I attended the high school youth group last night, and I wanted to share my experience with you. I came last night already really scared. I know you understand how I felt because you shared your story with us. First off, my mom was concerned for me when she dropped me off (because

I knew no one and we have only been going to this Village for a little while), so she saw a couple senior girls and introduced me and asked them if they could help me and make sure I felt welcome tonight. But the minute my Mom left they started looking at me and skootching away. They just ditched me. I couldn't believe these Christian girls behaved the way I would expect girls at my high school to act. So after that I just decided to stand by the wall because I was afraid to talk to anyone. I tried to stand by people, working up the nerve to say something, but before I got the chance, I would get a mean look, or someone would look up and down my body, then turn away. As I said before, I came to the youth group scared and this was definitely not helping. There were only a couple of leaders who talked to me, but that was it. Eventually I just sat down by myself. You mentioned that you talked to the leaders about making sure people felt like they belonged, but I think your students need to know that too. I didn't feel like I belonged. I felt like an outsider. I was hoping that I would feel more included last night. I went home and cried because it was difficult and stressful to get through.

I am emailing you because I feel you need to know this and I want to feel comfortable and welcomed to the youth group. I would like to be able to go to Wednesday night groups accepting that I may not know anyone, but I won't feel like I can't talk to anyone or they won't talk to me.

Sincerely,
Jennifer

This young woman came looking for Jesus and the in crowd elbowed her out of the way.

These stories and their painful experiences underscore why the church in America continues to be one of the most segregated communities on earth. Take race. Only 5 percent of churches are comprised of racially mixed congregations. Martin Luther King Jr. was fond of saying, "At 11:00 on Sunday morning when we stand and sing and Christ has no east or west, we stand at the most segregated hour in this nation."[1] Instead of reaching across barriers, too many of us prefer working within familiar categories and social lines.

This kind of bigotry not only dissuades an emerging culture from identifying with the church; it robs the church of any credibility to preach reconciliation. It denies the church of its most compelling witness—that people of great diversity (age, ethnicity, economic class, marital status, etc.) can live together in community because of the radical love of Christ. It disfigures the message of grace; it hollows out the church's essential, unified identity; and it demystifies the mystery of the gospel (that Christ's redemptive work makes diverse people coheirs and partners of the promise; see Eph. 3:6). Most of all, it misses what life is intended to be under an open heaven—the inauguration of a new order of life. Inclusive has replaced exclusive.

THE WALLS JESUS TEARS DOWN

Jesus comes to change all of this. He is an includer. Open heaven translates into open hearts. He is always unlocking closed doors and crossing boundaries, and John records His conversation with the woman at the well to make this point. Following His encounter with Nicodemus, Jesus is on His way to Galilee. There is a woman He wants to meet, and He will cross all lines to reach her. John 4 is one of the longer conversations recorded in the book. As with the rest of John, "dialogue rather than action carries the scene."[2]

One of the first observations is that John has positioned this conversation right after the conversation with Nicodemus to create an antithesis:

- He (Nicodemus) is a seeker—she (the woman at the well) is sought.
- He is a named man—she is an unnamed woman.
- He is Jewish—she is Samaritan.
- He has seen signs—she has seen nothing.

- He is city—she is rural.
- He has a noble heritage—she has a shameful past.
- He has it together—she is broken.
- He is powerful—she is powerless.
- He is connected—she is estranged.
- He is clean—she is unclean.
- He is orthodox—she is a heretic.
- He is an insider—she is an outsider.
- He is an insider (who becomes an outsider)—she is an outsider (who becomes an insider).
- *He is unwilling to believe in Jesus—she believes.*[3]

The two conversations are juxtaposed to show irony. In John 3, a religious ruler goes out of his way to protect his reputation; in John 4, the Ruler of the universe goes out of His way to *ruin* His reputation. Jesus travels to the other side of the tracks (vv. 1–4). Given the shorter distance, this is a preferred north-south route travelers take. There are other options, but Jesus has to travel through Samaria (v. 4). This is a "must" mission determined by Committee, one comprised of Father, Son, and Holy Spirit. Jesus never operates independently: He submits His schedule to the Father's timetable (2:4), He yields His itinerary to the leading of the Holy Spirit (see Matt. 4:1), and He sifts every decision through the filter of compassion and eternal purpose.

Jesus models what He expects of the church: "Be My witnesses in Jerusalem, in all Judea and Samaria, and to the ends of the earth" (Acts 1:8). This is more than a statement about starting local and going global. Samaria underscores that the Great Commission includes going to adverse regions. It is going to marginalized people, like Matthew the tax collector (Luke 5:27–32). It is having a meal with men like Zacchaeus, the sort people disdain (Luke 19:5–7). Again, Jesus *must* stay at his house, because Jesus is driven by the precision of eternal purpose. He must also come to Sychar to declare that things have changed now that the skies have ripped open.

The Wall of Prejudice

On the surface, it makes no sense to come to Samaria. It is not so safe. One must keep the windows up and the doors locked, even if it is unbearably hot. It would be akin to present-day Jews driving through Bethlehem. Best to keep a low profile, for as John explains, "Jews do not associate with Samaritans" (John 4:9). These are people groups who are not on friendly terms. Going to such places will involve risks. In going directly north, Jesus ignores five hundred years of prejudice and hostilities and tears down the barrier between these two people groups. For the disciples, it will be another heart-pounding moment. It's bad enough they are already under surveillance (v. 1). Who wants to be a victim of violence?

Jesus is unusually calm (but when is He not?). The suspicion, fear, prejudice, and distance are all familiar territory. Jesus knows what it's like to be on the other side. In His early years, He was displaced, a refugee without a home in Egypt. Eventually, He returned home, but He did not return to attend private schools. He grew up in poverty. His hometown had a history of being dismissed by both the elite and the common. To be a Galilean was to experience prejudice. To be a Samaritan was to experience animosity and hate. Exclusion is familiar territory.

Nonetheless, given that Jesus has only three years to carry out His public ministry, isn't a journey with possible stopovers in Samaria getting Him off course? There are conferences to speak at, book signings to attend, healing services to perform, and leaders to pour into. Why take a side trip to a region most people try to avoid? Isn't the clock ticking? Is Jesus an underachiever?

Sadly, I ask these questions as a type A who insists on nonstop flights. My family has had the pleasure of going on trips with me where restaurants and rest stops and historic sights are viewed from a car going seventy miles an hour. But we do make good time. In this story, Jesus not only stops; He stays for a couple of days (John 4:40). He is more interested in finding the people behind the wall and hanging out with them than in making good time.

Perhaps Jesus is on some holy-site tour. Maybe this trip has something to do with historical interests. After all, Samaria is part of "holy geography."[4] With His Lonely Planet guide, Jesus is on a pilgrimage, going to the place where Israel's story began. This is the first region to which Abraham came, then called Shechem (Gen. 12:5–6). The map shows that Jacob's well is here. John tells us this town, now called Sychar, once belonged to the Old Testament patriarch Joseph (John 4:5). This is where he was buried (Josh. 24:32). Imagine the inspiration generated for the next blog post.

But clearly sightseeing had nothing to do with this stop. This was no quest inspired by glamorous brochures. Samaria is not in the promotional materials of any Jerusalem travel agency. Expedia.com returns "no search results" when "hotels, Samaria" is typed in. Travel advisories warn against purchasing tickets. Remember, Jews do not associate with Samaritans. There are too many bad memories.

Samaria represents the northern kingdom, where the likes of Jeroboam and Ahab once ruled, men who were evil and reprehensible. It is the kingdom that was judged by God for its idolatry. Those living in the late 700s BC were defeated and deported to Assyria. Pagan cultures came with their gods and settled, and those Jews too unfit to be exiled eventually intermarried. Over time, Samaria became the breeding grounds for half-breeds and dangerous cults.

The kind of prejudice that radicalizes an orthodox Sunni Muslim to attack the heretical Druze sect gripped the ancient Jews.[5] They saw the Samaritans as heretics. This was the place where religion got screwed up. Interbreeding and syncretizing paganism with Judaism led to a strange brew of beliefs. The Samaritans ended up with a revised Bible, a different expectation of the Messiah, and a different place of worship. Jews considered them "menstruants," the epitome of uncleanness.[6]

In the second century BC, the Jews burned down the Samaritans' temple in retaliation for allowing the Greeks to use Samaria as a base to control Jewish territory. Nearly a century later, the Samaritans returned the acrimony, denigrating a holy site in Jerusalem. On the eve of Passover they scattered dead bones over the landscape of the temple. Years later (AD 527), the Samaritans burned the estates of the Jews in Scythopolis.

Samaria is still dangerous to this day. This is the West Bank, the other side of the tracks, the place on the other side of the wall. Tit for tat still goes on.

As a holy Man, Jesus could have chosen a different route. There is a way to Galilee that the "pious" always take. There are historical sites to see in Galilee as well. But Jesus heads straight for Samaria, crossing geographic and ethnic boundaries. There is work His Father has called Him to do, and doing the Father's will is opportune—it is what sustains Him (John 4:34). There is a woman to see, and in coming to her, He crosses deep cultural lines. He is showing us the way things are under an open heaven.

The Wall of Misunderstanding

It was outrageous for a Jew to cross into Samaria, but it was just as scandalous for a Jewish male to engage in a conversation with a strange woman. Men in this culture refrained from even making eye contact with women. Respectable Jewish males, *especially respectable Jewish Messiah males*, do not associate with foreign women. But Jesus does, shocking His disciples (v. 27).

Jesus initiates the conversation: "Give Me a drink" (v. 10). This is less a demand and more of a request. The Creator of the universe, the Holy One of Israel, places His needs before a Samaritan woman. The angels who are actively engaged with Jesus must have shaken their heads! "Necessary Existence" yields to "the shifting contingencies of ordinary, natural life."[7] The incarnated Son of God drinks from her bucket. There is only one reason—Jesus intends to get down to our level so that we might rise to His.

She is stunned by Jesus's request. Men do not do this, certainly not Jewish men! Jesus has crossed the kind of barriers that leave her suspicious. Is He after something more than water? Her straight black hair, her attractive features. She is used to advances from other men, especially in this setting. Wells in ancient times weren't just for fill-ing pots. They were social contexts, places like laundromats or local hangouts where people showed off their fitness trackers and com-pared fuel-burn scores, discussed minivan mileage or argued over political hacks. They were also places to pick up women.

In John 3, John seems to be using the background of Greek drama to set the conversation between Jesus and Nicodemus. Something similar is going on here. There are two characters on this Samaritan stage, but the backdrop is a typical Old Testament betrothal scene (think Abraham, Isaac, Jacob, and Moses). Paul Duke sketches the familiar story line: a man is traveling in a foreign land; he goes to a well; he meets a woman who is a virgin; water is drawn; there is the gradual and inevitable movement of two characters toward one another; the woman runs home to tell her family; the man is invited to stay; they get married.[8]

There are parallels here, but things also break down. The woman Jesus meets is not available, and she is definitely not virtuous. Her standoffish posture, vacant eyes, suggestive clothing, and the needless makeup (she seems to have applied it with a trowel) reveal a woman who has long ago lost all innocence. Eventually, she will run home to tell her friends and family, but she does not realize at first that He is from another realm, where gender, economic status, age, and ethnic distinctions are irrelevant. Holiness is what defines relationships. She does not grasp that Jesus is already engaged to someone else. Her name is the church. But the woman will eventually take His name, and ironically, Jesus will take hers. She will be "Christian"; He will be referred to by others as "Samaritan." It will be her blessing. It will be His curse (8:48).

The Wall of Fear

When Jesus asks her for a drink, she assumes everything is one way. It's all about meeting this Man's needs, and who knows if it stops with water. What she doesn't realize is that Jesus has engaged in this con-versation because He's actually the one with something to offer her.

"If you knew [which you don't], ... you would ask [which you won't]" (4:10). She does not yet realize that the God of the universe, the one who creates and owns everything and is rich beyond measure, made plans in eternity past to travel to her neighborhood. He has come to give her a taste of life under an open heaven. He has come to quench an aching thirst that H_2O cannot slake! He has come to offer her the drink of choice of open-heaven citizens—living water (7:37–39).

It's an incredible shift in the dialogue. As Dale Bruner writes in his commentary, "Jesus's little conversation has gone in about six seconds from a Death-Valley thirst to a Mount-Everest fountain."[9] But this is all rather incomprehensible to her. It is all words, which are making no sense. It is obvious He has nothing of substance to offer. He doesn't even have a bucket (4:11).

Like Nicodemus (and all too many of us), this woman is limited by her earthbound imagination that fails to penetrate the deeper meaning of Jesus's offer of water. She has no awareness she lives under a heaven that has recently opened up, creating a world that is about receiving. She cannot see the gifts of God.

Can we? Are we aware of what He might be serving up in this moment?

She is unimpressed with what Jesus offers her (v. 12). Her prejudice presses her to religious comparisons: "You aren't greater than our father Jacob, are You?" In other words, "If this is about some claim that your water, or your religion, is superior to mine, then here's what I want to say—'Your water isn't any better than Jacob's water. And by the way, you are no Jacob!'"

One cannot help but wonder what the tone sounded like. Is there teasing going on? Is she flirting? Does she think He is? Is this offer of living water a reference to something sexual, something she intends to exploit? As Peterson notes, "maybe *she* is on the hunt."[10] More likely, she is speaking with an edge in her voice. She has been made to feel inferior all of her life. Those Jews who pass through Samaria are usually dismissive. They never say please or thank you. Anything they have, including water, is always better. There is an arrogance that says they are a purer race. To walk in their cities and ride on their buses is to face signs saying "Jews Only." There are constant reminders that you are not like them. One can get no further than the outer court. It is a religious caste system that can move outsiders to hate themselves. So it's understandable she is defensive. She will let Jesus know He is not so great—at least on her turf!

But Jesus will not get sidetracked. Though one greater than Jacob is here (1:51), He will not get into an argument over ancestry or H_2O claims. He will not be baited into a conversation that gets stuck at the mundane, physical, or prejudicial level. This is not market research comparing the properties of bottled water versus tap water. This is not two mayors comparing the superiority of what comes out of their taps, any more than it is two breweries comparing the water they use with their hops. And this is not a Jew trying to prove He is superior. This *is* the Son of God speaking metaphorically and spiritually (as with Nicodemus) of a gift that, if internalized, will satisfy one's most profound thirst. This is God in the flesh, under a rolled-back sky, extending love and acceptance—as well as new life. She is seeing what Jacob could only see vaguely.

Jesus knows that the yearning to find that which satisfies the soul, that which turns our spiritual wilderness into an extravagant spring, is what drives her and everyone else (4:13–14). But whatever we consume from this world, whoever and whatever we chase, never completely satisfies, be it water or riches or career or relationships. We always wake up with a renewed thirst, a vague letdown, and a resentment toward that which we thought would be so fulfilling. Something is missing.

Something of eternity is placed in the human heart (Eccl. 3:11), and it has ruined us—in a good way. We have been created with a deeper desire that transcends this world—which only God can satisfy. It drives us to Him, and when we meet Him, we are able to see the things of this world in proper perspective. We reduce our expectations so that people or things no longer live under the weight of unrealistic hopes.

Jesus has crossed the lines to fulfill the promises given to the patriarchs, including Jacob. He has come to bring about events foretold by Old Testament prophets—the coming of a Savior, the proclamation of forgiveness, and the presence of the Holy Spirit in power and glory. "He never concerned Himself with the rules of defilement."[11] This is God who accepts a prostitute's anointing with gratitude (Luke 7:37–38). But the woman at the well is unaware. Her eyes cannot see beyond the immediate; she does not realize the heavens have ripped open. With John's typical irony, she is defending Jacob, even though the ladder Jacob saw in a dream is standing in front of her. The Lord is in this place, and salvation is being offered. Greater than the obstacle of prejudice and discrimination is spiritual dullness.

Nonetheless, there are signs of change. Her heart begins to open. Fear relaxes and defenses begin to go down. She begins to inquire. Using the same tone of an earlier request by Jesus, she asks: "Give me this water" (John 4:15). But she is still at groundwater level. She wants what He offers so she will no longer have to make these bone-wearying trips to the well.

Jesus does what He sometimes must do with us, especially when we become absorbed in the here and now. He moves us from our mundane, earthbound petitions. He exposes the true cause of our thirst. He points us to what we should be really asking. Even if she is to drink water that permanently satisfies her physical thirst, she will still languish. She will still be dry. Something has to change. Gently, but firmly, Jesus commands the woman to bring her husband to Him (v. 16).

The Wall of Shame

With these words, Jesus exposes the reason she is the one who is in need. It is not God who is found wanting. We are the ones who are desperate. She is desperate. This is a story of the Loose Samaritan. She has a shadow side. She has sought to satisfy her thirst through men, but her choices in life have left her parched and ashamed. Hers is a life of self-condemnation. It is part of the reason Jesus has come to her.

But like us, she is good at deflecting, for "shame can't tolerate transparency."[12] "I don't have a husband" (v. 17). She must be wondering, *What does this have to do with drinking to one's content? Is this man trying to discern my marital status? Is He interested? Has He heard something?* But Jesus knows her story as completely as He knows ours. He knows she doesn't have a husband; she has a string of failed relationships and is currently in an illicit affair with another (v. 18). And she knows this, that she is a five-time reject living with the wounds of guilt and estrangement and emptiness.

Jesus's reply exposes her life, her guilt, her shame, and her need. This is life under an open heaven, where what is hidden behind the wall is exposed to the Light (8:34–38). But the Light does not merely expose our sin and guilt. It penetrates deeper to expose the dehumanizing life we often suffer and shows us a way out. The woman at the well lives out a nonsatisfying, nonfulfilling cycle of filling and emptying water jars, marrying, divorcing, and remarrying. He sees the wounds, scars, and profound sadness that come from a relationship focused on one's personal gratification.

All of us have been used and abused to some degree; He also sees the same in us.

The signs of this woman's injuries were already there. There can only be one reason Jesus meets her in the scorching heat of the day. There's only one reason she draws the water alone. She's a moral outcast. And if you are marginalized by other Samaritans, you are *really* outside! Jesus has gone to the far side.

The Wall of Religion

The conversation is increasingly uncomfortable and embarassing. She reacts in the same way most broken people react under the light of holiness—she shifts the conversation and changes the subject (vv. 19–25). Let's go back to theology. That is much safer. What else explains her attempt to bring up temple controversies, disputes that have been raging for centuries?[13] Or is she attempting to recover some respect?

Like Nicodemus, she wants Jesus to know that she is religious. It's like people I meet on a plane, who suddenly realize I'm a pastor. On the heels of consuming a second Jim Beam and eyeing a flight attendant, they promptly turn their heads and talk about their spiritual heritage. They bring up theological questions. They want me to know they never miss Easter Sundays.

She wants Jesus to know she has gone to church. She knows her Bible. Samaritan synagogues existed in her day and still remain to this one. She knows that there is a messiah, He is coming, and (thank God) He will explain everything (v. 25). After all, so much of life makes no sense!

In this moment, Jesus gives the most powerful demonstration of His grace-filled inclusive heart: she, a Samaritan woman and serial fornicator, is the first person in the gospel to hear the words: "I am" (v. 26). No accompanying descriptions—He simply shares His personal name, identifying Himself with Yahweh in the Old Testament, and makes it clear He Himself is the Messiah (this is the first of the absolute "I am" sayings in John; see also 6:35; 8:23, 28, 58; 13:19; 18:5–6, 8). The Anointed One has come to extend His kingdom of grace and mercy. She has met her seventh husband, and He is the perfect bridegroom. And just as abruptly as the conversation ended with Nicodemus, it ends here. A seed is planted, and unlike Nicodemus, doors are opened, and people believe (4:39).

She experiences a taste of life under an open heaven, where renewal and forgiveness and hope reign. And after a short stay, Jesus moves on. There are other outsiders, others who are marginalized, and others who experience prejudice and shame and know nothing of life under an open heaven. Jesus goes to them.

He still does. And so must we.

ANOTHER STORY WITH WALLS

There's one more conversation with a marginalized woman.[14] Like the woman at the well, the woman of John 8 also has experienced deep moral failure. She also knows shame. But in this case, she is brought to Jesus, dragged in after the religious elite caught her "in the act of committing adultery" (v. 4).

As we have noted, those most proficient at shaming others tend to be the religious. Over time, people of the Word can allow their learning to curdle into pride, creating a distinct us-versus-them stance. Belief systems can mutate into smug superiority; spiritual shepherds can turn into religious police; self-righteous congregants can become good at showing disdain for the less devout. There's a reason one of the episodes of *The Simpsons* has Bart asking his born-again neighbor Maude why she has been gone. Her answer: "I was at Bible camp. I was learning how to be more judgmental."[15]

Jesus begins this conversation not by drawing water but by drawing on the ground (v. 6). Whatever the words were, it caused those who love to shame others to drop their stones and leave. They are overwhelmed by a force comprised of mercy and righteousness and divine conviction. With their departure, Jesus directs His conversation to the disgraced woman. And as with the woman at the well, He lifts her out of her shame and calls her to live as God intends her to live.

For these two women in John 4 and John 8, Jesus is the first man to break down the walls and reveal their incredible worth. Pure holiness reaches out and speaks into ungodliness without heaping on shame and guilt. These two conversations highlight with a permanent marker that it is in Jesus's nature to reach the unattractive and undeserving. He welcomes those the world leaves out. He looks for the kid who didn't get chosen at recess; He comes alongside the student who didn't get invited to the dance; He is with those voted off the island, those who sit in economy class, and those not invited to be part of one's Snapchat.

Others may create barriers—Jesus tears them down. There are no racial, cultural, gender, theological, or moral barriers that Jesus is unwilling to cross to engage in conversation. There is no place for exclusivism under an open heaven. This is the gospel, the good news! And through these conversations, He is telling His church to do the same.

THE INCLUSIVE LIFE WE ARE CALLED TO LIVE

In his chapter "Welcome One Another" from his book *Love One Another*, Gerald Sittser tells the story of the Elephant Man. He was a hideously deformed creature, a freak show in a circus. He was also a man by the name of Joseph Merrick. One day, he was rescued by a compassionate doctor named Frederick Treves who took him under his care. But real transformation did not occur until he had an encounter with a widow. Sittser notes what Merrick later told the London physician: "This was the first woman who had ever smiled at him, and the first woman, in the whole of his life, who had shaken hands with him. From this day the transformation of Merrick commenced and he began to change, little by little, from a hunted thing into a man."[16]

We who claim to follow Jesus must listen for the same compulsion that led Jesus to Samaria. Under the light of an open heaven, we are enabled to see the world differently. The Trinity will, on occasion, urge us to leave for parts we may not choose on our own. It may be overseas, sitting in a tent in the Bekaa Valley with a Syrian refugee. It may be next door, to the neighbor other people shun. Or it may be across the lobby, to the mother whose son is a reject so she is considered a failure. It will surely be beyond the safe walls of our social groups (or social media, where so many hide today).

Like this story, we are called to engage flesh to flesh with a different ethnicity; we are compelled to reach out to those facing the pain of moral failure. In following Jesus, we will likely be led to places remote, inconvenient, costly, and unattractive in order to reach the marginalized, the ostracized, and the outsiders—*and take their hand*. We will be called to do battle every time a condescending thought whispers, "Look at her, a loser." We must be bold enough to say to God that we will go—and to demeaning thoughts that they have no place.

There is no racial bias, gender prejudice, nor generational arrogance with God. To be inclusive is our undeniable witness of God's deep love and God's mighty presence under an open heaven. How can we speak of an open heaven and close our hearts to those who are different? To look beyond our differences is, as Paul puts it in Ephesians 3, the mystery of the gospel!

A few years ago, our church was given a diversity award for our efforts to be a multicultural community. At the brief ceremony, I was given an opportunity to speak. I told these public officials that none of this was motivated by a desire to be politically correct. Rather, it is a way of saying the gospel is true. Jesus has come, torn down the walls, and asked us to cross the barriers our society has constructed. Reaching out, especially to those on the margins, affirms that divine activity is at work. There really is a work of uniting that mystifies the watching world. And these torn-down walls will attract the most unlikely of folks.

QUESTIONS

1. *What barriers exist in your world? Which of them have you crossed?*

2. *What walls are still standing that you are unwilling to tear down?*

3. *Describe the grace God has shown you under this open heaven.*

5
LIFE IS ABOUT LIVING EXPANSIVELY

A Conversation with an Invalid
JOHN 5:1–15

> *One man was there who had been sick for 38 years. When*
> *Jesus saw him lying there and knew he had already been there*
> *a long time, He said to him, "Do you want to get well?"*
>
> —JOHN 5:5–6

In her book *Quiet*, Susan Cain tells the story of a young man growing up in the middle of nowhere—Harmony Church, Missouri. Ironically, there is not much harmony in his spirit. He is all but destined to a small life. His father is a pig farmer, and worse, he is bankrupt. Timid, skinny, and anything but athletic, he dreads the likelihood that he will follow in the poverty-stricken footprints of his parents. But all of this changes.

One day a man with impressive communication skills comes into town and breaks into his world. Dale listens, and he begins to see a world of possibilities. He sees the value of developing the skill of public speaking. After some training, he sets up as a public-speaking teacher, and his class is an overnight sensation. He publishes his first book, *Public Speaking and Influencing Men in Business*. Eventually he writes a best seller, *How to Win Friends and Influence People*. Maybe you know his full name. It is Dale Harbison Carnegie, and his books on self-improvement, salesmanship, and interpersonal skills continue to change the world.[1]

JESUS SPEAKS INTO OUR DESPERATE CONDITION

Like the man in Dale's story, Jesus also breaks into the world of a man seemingly destined to an insignificant existence. Jesus habitually goes to unexpected destinations. He does not hobnob with the rich and famous. He is not enhancing His reputation by mixing it up at happy hour with the movers and shakers of the city. He is again with the marginalized, and again He is revealing that heaven has opened.

This means everything has changed—and is changing! Life is to be different. It is a messianic world we now live in. Life has come to life, meaning "lives can be transformed from top to bottom."[2] Life as we know it can be more expansive! But not everyone buys in.

There is a feast, and Jesus makes His way back up to Jerusalem. He has a divine appointment at the Sheep Gate, located at the northeast corner of Jerusalem near the pool of Bethesda (John 5:2). The gate likely received its name from its use for bringing the sheep through it for sacrifice. It's fitting that the One identified at the beginning of John as the Lamb of God (1:29) would choose this entrance to do His work. Here at Bethesda are the down-and-out, the weak, the blind, and the withered. They have come to find healing, not realizing that the Lamb who has come to be sacrificed—enabling our healing—is in their midst. They sit and wait with hundreds of others in an area as large as a football field. It is a fellowship of suffering.

Any who have traveled, especially to desperate regions of the world, can picture the wretched scene. Beyond the physical suffering, there is the vacancy in one's eyes, the sense of desperation, and the resignation in one's will. Here are countless stories of heartache and disappointment. What makes it worse is that there are no medical clinics. There is no social care—no governmental assistance, Obamacare, pharmaceutical cures, nor nonprofits committed to the ministry of compassion. Frustrations pile up daily.

For the people on the outer perimeter of Jerusalem, the only hope out of a confined world is an occasional stirring of the spring-fed waters, a myth that endures for years. Ironically, it promises to reward the healthiest, those who have the advantage of strength and movement to move to the front and get into the water first. But like the water in Jacob's well, this water has its limitations.

The upper class—especially those committed to maintaining ritual purity—avoid this place. It is potentially contaminating. Those from the adjacent Antonia Fortress watch for any disruptions. It's not the ideal duty station for those called up. But Jesus is here, and He is up close. Jesus spent a fair amount of time healing people who were lame, blind, deaf, paralyzed, in the grip of leprosy, and weakened by ongoing bleeding. His compassion for the lowly, the needy, and the sick—those confined to small worlds—required this. It is His nature to work against the effects of sin. These are the ones invited to His future banquet (Luke 14:21).

Jesus steps into Bethesda to speak to one man (John 5:5). If there are others, John does not tell us. We are not told the man's name. We are not even told the specific need. All we know is that he has been unable to move for a long, long time. In his weakened condition, he has been confined to a four-by-eight-foot world. He has been there nearly forty years, as long as Israel wandered in the wilderness. There is little that attracts. His grubby bandanna has a faded peace sign, his hand-me-down T-shirt reads "Seven Days Without a Pun Makes One Weak," and his scraggly beard has not been trimmed in months. His only companion has been the occasional stray cat. Had we been there with Jesus, we too might have been drawn to his plight. We might have been stunned as we learned of his perseverance.

This man's condition has defined most of his life. It's probably how he earned his living. It's definitely what he is used to. Knowing this is the case, we might have also wondered—does he really want to be healed?

Despite the fact that Jesus asks the question, "Do you want to get well?" Jesus doesn't need to be informed. God is aware of everything there is to be aware of in our lives. He knows the answer to the questions He asks. He knows the motivation behind our answers, for He knows our hearts perfectly. He knows this man. He has been drawn to him from eternity past. *Why* He is drawn is not so clear. This is the third conversation Jesus has initiated. In the first, the one with Nathanael, Jesus begins with a statement; in the second, with the woman at the well, Jesus begins with a request; and in this context, Jesus begins with a simple question. *Do you have the will to be whole?* It echoes a conversation in Mark 10:51. On that occasion Jesus asks the blind man, "What do you want Me to do for you?"

The question is mystifying. If all you have ever experienced is a painful past and a disappointing present and a hopeless tomorrow; if your life has been confined to a small space; if each day is a series of bedsores and unpleasant issues with personal hygiene; if all you have known are people fending for themselves at your expense; if you have been excluded from society, from worship, and from most all relationships; and if you have never been able to work, travel, make love, cook, care for kids, chase after dreams, and participate in sports—*would a desire to be healed even be a question?* In this case—yes.

The paralytic finds it difficult to answer Jesus (John 5:7). Maybe he is annoyed. Passersby say some pretty ridiculous things. Yes, given he is at Bethesda says something. If he didn't want to be healed, why would he hang out where healings happen? But he is unable to give a simple answer. He does not impress us as a man with any vein-popping intensity. Over the years, it's easy for minds to become blank slabs of black asphalt. He makes excuses: "The pushy people, the paralysis, the timing. Do I want to be healed? Have you noticed? The rule here is 'every man for himself.' There are no lifeguards on duty, no monitors to keep everyone in line, and no 'take a number.'" He can see no other means to healing than someone carrying him to the pool when the stars align and the angels come, but for the last 13,870 days no one has volunteered to do this. Unlike the paralytic in Mark 2, there are no men to pick him up and bring him down. There isn't even one!

The ailing man here in John 5 cannot get a foot in edgewise. The only means of healing is the moving water, but this has turned out to be a hopeless venture, a pipe dream. He has forgotten that it is God who breaks through heaven to heal (Deut. 32:39). Malevolent spirits do not have ultimate control of human life.[3] And now, like the woman at the well, he is too unaware to notice that heaven has opened and the Living Water is right next to him, and he is suddenly in the front of the line. Jesus has brought the stirring, living water right to his pallet.

Maybe the man's response is a smoke screen. He has exercised no imaginative approach to his dilemma. Maybe this man is not so sure he wants to be healed. Not everyone wants a remedy for their malady. Not everyone wants change, even if it means an expanded world. Some will have to be dragged in, with heel marks visible on the floor. Maybe he is quite comfortable in his small world. He does not beg to be healed.

Suddenly, through the sheer force of grace, Jesus removes every excuse this man has. Like He will do with Lazarus, Jesus commands him to rise and leave his small, former world of pain and death (John 5:8). Unlike the disciples, who were told to drop their nets and follow Him, this man is ordered to gather up the world he has known and be on his way. Years of limitation abruptly vanish. Life under an open heaven begins! Muscles, nerves, and joints explode into life. A skeletal frame is suddenly made firm and called into action. Atrophy is served notice. And the nearby crowd must have suddenly become dumbfounded. A man who simply took up a small space can now do so many things that a moment ago he could only imagine doing.

This story forces us to rethink our theology of healing. We are inclined to believe a miraculous recovery is predicated on meeting certain conditions. If we pray and fast; if we work to erase any doubts in our minds; if we call the elders; if we make some pact, some vow with God; if we confess every remembered sin—then Jesus will heal. But sometimes, as this story indicates, healing occurs without any stipulations (see also Luke 13:10–17).

I can't help but ask why Jesus goes to this man. Surely there are others at Bethesda who are more deserving. At least more responsive. The story drives home the point that healing is not the guaranteed right of those meeting certain conditions; it is God's surprising work for different people in different times. The reasons lie within God, whose grace goes against claim and calculation.[4] This has been my experience in ministry.

If only this story of healing went somewhere good. But something gets in the way. Like being in a room where the power goes off, something short-circuits this narrative. John interrupts this nice story with the ominous words, "Now that day was the Sabbath" (John 5:9). This is where the perceptive reader begins to suspect things will not end well—*that all hell is about to break loose.* And it does. Jesus's command places this man on a collision course with the regulations of his day. The conversation shifts from Jesus to the legal experts (v. 10), which leads to a lengthy discourse on the Sabbath and so forth (vv. 16–47). They tell this man it is the Sabbath. The tense implies repetition. They need to keep making the point, for this is an affront to established procedures. The tension in the air is palpable. And we can't help but ask—really? After thirty-eight agonizing years of begging near the temple, this is the first reaction to a man who has suddenly been liberated?

Like impassive policemen writing tickets, these religious authorities pull this man over to inform him that he has broken Sabbath law, specifically M. Shabbat 7.2 and 10.5 of the religious code (the Mishnah). It forbids the carrying of any goods, particularly "empty beds" on the Sabbath. This is, therefore, no mere misdemeanor. Going back to the Law (Exod. 31:14), this is a Class 1 felony. They want to get to the bottom of this. They need to know who has interfered with their authority, contradicted their laws, *and ruined a perfectly good legalistic day.*

These rigid, doctrinaire, uncaring, blind guides of the blind cannot see the miracle before them. They have their own impairment. They remind me of contemporary keepers of sacred sites, places like the Dome of the Rock or the birthplace of Jesus. These legalists are trained to look for any religious infractions—exposed shoulders or pockets concealing Bibles—creating a blindness to sacred moments. The Jews in this story fail to see that they live in a world smaller than the four-by-eight-foot world of the paralytic. They are blind to grace. They have no clue what Sabbath really means. It is when the day-to-day activities are set aside to enter a different time, a time to contemplate God's promised future.[5] Sabbath points forward to the time when time will be fulfilled, when heaven comes down.

The irony is that Jesus's healings on the Sabbath announce that heaven is open, and something of God's future rest has arrived in the present. It's the time they were looking for. Divine mercy is at work. The kingdom of God is at hand. The forces committed to disrupting creation have been put on notice. There's no better time to celebrate healing than on the Sabbath—the day of the Lord.

But all they can see is illegal activity. They teach a "love of the Torah," failing to teach a "Torah of love."[6] They will not relent until they find out who is the healed man's accomplice (John 5:12). They are legalists doing what legalists do: reducing life to technicalities.[7] They use their codes and their holy days to rain on the celebration. Their laws are not intended to enhance holiness or expand worlds. They are "cruel instrument[s] of oppression."[8]

But this restored man has his own dullness. His way of survival has been to look out for himself. His circumstances have shoveled defined ruts and built a fence around him. His life is now disrupted. If anyone is to blame, it's Jesus: "The man who *made me* well told me, 'Pick up your mat and walk'" (v. 11). If there is anyone to arrest, it is this man! You can almost hear him saying, "I was a law-abiding citizen minding my own business until He came and caused me to run afoul of the law."

He is right about one thing. Doing what Jesus commands generally gets a man in trouble.

The Pharisees need more information. Knowing the perpetrator is an adult male does not help. To complicate things, Jesus does not hang around to continue the conversation. Jesus does not heal to amaze the crowds. He does not pause to win applause; He knows that "miracles [do] not readily convert into life-changing faith."[9] As suddenly as He appears, He disappears.

We should not be surprised. Sometimes, Jesus "disappears" on us. At least it feels that way. He upends and expands our world and leaves us to sort things out. He may be testing us. Do we really believe in Him? What will we do with our new wellness? What will we do with this new opportunity? How will we handle a second chance at life? Will we acknowledge that, apart from Him, we can do nothing—that unless the Lord builds this house, we labor in vain? Will we give Him the glory? Will we step into our enlarged boundaries to gain a greater glimpse of an expanded life under an open heaven? *Will we scream and leap for joy?*

The healed man does none of these. He does not make any effort to seek Jesus, let alone express any gratitude. He is inclined to hang with those who live reduced lives (vv. 13–14). He is too familiar and too comfortable to live beyond small worlds. Maybe he gives them a brief sketch. Maybe they are able to get fingerprints, do a DNA analysis. All *they* care about is that there is a fugitive on the loose; all *he* cares about is covering his rear (v. 15).

Jesus, however, has not completed the conversation. There is unfinished business. As Frederick Gaiser notes, "Illness is never only a physical reality."[10] Under an open heaven, more healing is possible— and necessary. Jesus again finds him, for He knows where to find him. Jesus is very good at tracking all of our steps.

Again, Jesus initiates the conversation with a rather odd statement: "See, you are well" (v. 14). He again speaks to what is obvious to us, but it is not so evident to this man. I imagine Jesus saying something like this: "Look at yourself. Something profound has happened. You have become whole." The perfect tense of the verb "to be whole, well," implies a wellness that has ongoing results. "Your upside-down life has turned right-side up. Grace has been extended in a powerful way, and it is flowing. You now have an appetite. There is a renewed energy that is available today and tomorrow. You can see from a height higher than ground level. You no longer have to be a dependent. Do you realize how well you are and how this has changed everything? But this does not mean everything is okay. Not everything is well."

JESUS DOES NOT GIVE A PASS TO SMALL LIVING

This former paralytic is more physically "whole" than he might realize, and ironically, more sick than he knows. As with the woman at the well, Jesus must address a deeper healing. Like his illness, something else must come to an end. The healing "work of Jesus is an attack upon the whole power of evil which manifests itself both in sickness and in sin" (see Luke 13:16).[11] But unlike the paralyzed man in Mark 2, who receives immediate forgiveness, the paralytic is told to "stop sinning!" Jesus addresses a pattern of behavior that is ongoing. His command is a necessary complement to "get up." This is why James connects healing with confession (James 5:16). One must be willing to address the whole of one's life. *This is what matters to God.*

For Steve Jobs of Apple, one of the more impressionable times in his early life was watching his father work. He noticed that his father gave the same attention and detail to the inside of cabinets and fences as he did to the outside. "He loved doing things right. He even cared about the look of the parts you couldn't see."[12] He took this same approach to the technology he created.

Jesus is not finished. It's the other side, the inside of this man, that matters most.

With the same discernment of Jesus, we have to have the courage to turn to the inside and ask ourselves and others who have come to us for help—are there things we are harboring in our hearts? Are there misbehaviors we are hiding from our families? Are there sins in our past we have left unconfessed? Are we using our situation to manipulate?

In the context of healing, we have to have the nerve to say, "Stop sinning!" But too often, we turn the healing ministry into a medical report. We want to know the latest findings, as if we are attendant physicians ready to give a second opinion. We pray for God to do a physical miracle, overlooking that the greatest work is a changed heart.

In His command against sinning, Jesus does not give any details except to say there is a deeper sickness, a more severe paralysis at work. And if it is not addressed, there can be more severe harm (John 5:14). One must be careful with application, but there are occasions where personal sin has a direct relationship to our physical health (Ps. 38:3; Acts 5:1–11; 1 John 5:16). There is the persistence of some evil in this man's life. There are behaviors that must cease! Gambling? Porn? Theft? Envy? Sloth? These do not seem likely. Maybe the sin is less obvious.

Maybe it is not identified because the conversation goes beyond the healed paralytic to us. The unnamed paralytic, like other unnamed characters, serve as a type in the church.[13] The language allows us to put our own sin in the story. Any of us may be physically healed in the present. And if we experience such grace, we can still be unwell. There can be a sickness in the soul that is far more deadly than any cancer, any heart disease, and any impairment. There are numerous possibilities.

Perhaps Jesus is addressing the sin of ingratitude. Like the nine lepers, there is no expression of thanks. The first sin of Adam and Eve was a failure to be receptive and grateful. Gratitude is the first and the most important step in overcoming the practical atheism that besets our everyday lives.[14] God's grace selected him out of a crowd and redeemed him out of despair into a life of possibility, from the badlands to the highlands. But there is no appreciation in his voice, no God in his life.

For sure Jesus is addressing the fundamental sin—unbelief. In the upper room, Jesus defines sin as unbelief (John 16:8–9). There is no evidence of belief in this man. He retains "a worldview that looked for healing in water or magic ritual rather than in God."[15] He exhibits no trust in Jesus. *His sin is the sin of the world.* Nothing indicates he has any interest in God. He never reached out to touch the hem of His garment. His worldview has no room for an open heaven. He prefers to live under a predictably closed sky. Maybe this is why Jesus calls this man out and severely warns him that if he does not change, life may take a more severe turn.

In the end, there is nothing really attractive about this flat character—at least to me. Unbelief and ingratitude are their own ugliness. You would think he would be over the moon; he would be seeking some way, any way, to demonstrate his gratefulness. Like the blind man healed, he would be searching for a way to believe

(John 9:36). Like the demoniac, he would do anything to get into Jesus's boat (Mark 5:18). How can he be so thoughtless? Maybe he believed that any healing was deserved. God owed him big time for thirty-eight years of suffering.

My judgmental temperature rises when I picture this man. But then I realize there are moments, many of them, when I have missed the opportunity to thank God for some extended grace. I have my own moments of unbelief. I too am good at sitting and complaining like Jonah (Jonah 4:5–9).

There are other things surely at work. Perhaps his disordered soul wants to hang on to his brokenness. He does not want to pay the price of wellness. After thirty-eight years of absolute dependency, this man sees himself as a victim. His heart has turned in on itself, and he sees no one else but himself. He has no awareness of others and their needs. All that matters is self-preservation. Everyone else is secondary; other people's needs are inconsequential. Sometimes we can get used to being the center of sympathy and attention, the sort that come when one has been dealt a bad hand.

Maybe the sin Jesus sees in him is the sin of avoiding responsibility. In some strange way, sickness can become the sick person's haven. Confining as his small world was, he was freed from many of the daily obligations that confront those who are well. Maybe as Michael Card writes, "he clings to his disability like a lifesaver because it saves him from life itself."[16] He can avoid the demands of a changing world. Jesus is warning any of us who prefer to stay in our comfort zones—be it under fig trees or on our sofas—that settling for a life of mediocrity, passivity, and mere existence is sin. It is time to step up!

Every spring, commencement speakers go onstage before an audience of graduates and share their wisdom. They try to show the world as it is and will be. They inspire grads to go after a more expansive world. They too give their warnings. Ben Bernanke, former chairman of the Federal Reserve, in a 2013 address to students at Bard College, gave this advice: "During your working lives, you will have to reinvent yourselves many times. Success and satisfaction will not come from mastering a fixed body of knowledge but from constant adaptation and creativity in a rapidly changing world."[17] He was making it clear that whatever disciplines you have sought to master, don't be surprised if a hyperculture makes it obsolete. You will have to be willing to change, reinvent, and repristinate with an ever-expanding world. And if you don't, life will pass you by.

Maybe the sin Jesus warns this man to stop committing is the sin of missing his moment. If he does not seize it, life will pass him by. Is life passing you by?

Whatever the sin, here was a man missing the opportunity to step into the life God restored him to live. There are words to describe such a condition: a dullard, a drudge, a drone, a taker, a user, a man only out for himself. Such soulless men live their lives repairing nets rather than throwing them out into the deep. They are right down there with others who have lived flat, hollow lives: the ten spies who could only see the giants, a wife of David too bound in resentment to dance with him, and a Jonah too confined by his exclusivism to see the generous, redemptive grace of God set before him.

My first pastorate was in a church planted in a tough part of Portland. It is still known as "Felony Flats." People came regularly to the door for help. Tragically, all too many were simply looking for resources to maintain their addictions. Many were cons, for churches can be easy marks. There were exceptions, but many had no desire to hear the gospel and change. Rarely was there gratitude. Like this man, most preferred their small worlds.

We want this conversation to end on a better note. We want to see this partially healed man become whole. He has languished for thirty-eight years. We want to see him join the discipleship team and be the special guest speaker at the next evangelistic crusade. We want him to write a best seller like Dale. We hope he will chase after it with what time is left. We want him to stand in the Hall of Faith with other expansive souls. He is in the third third of life. There is no time to lose. Behind the severity of the command, he must have heard a tone that said, "Come live the abundant life. Go past the jetty!" But he is not interested in the white water. The harbor with its pollutants will do. Jesus has upset his world and violated his space. He prefers the rule keepers rather than the Ruler of the universe.

Jesus breaks through our handicaps, our insecurities, our small visions, and He grants us wide vistas of possibility. Like this man we often miss the kind of expansive, no-limits life that an open heaven makes possible.

QUESTIONS

1. *Few of us experience life-narrowing disabilities like the paralytic man, but we all have things in our lives that paralyze us. What are the areas in your life that hold you captive?*

2. *What do you imagine the man's sin was that Jesus asked him to stop committing? Are there sins in your life that prevent you from living the expansive life God intends for you? What are they?*

3. *Is God asking you to step out of your comfort zone to do something for him? How will you respond?*

6

LIFE IS ABOUT CONSUMING THE BETTER FOOD

A Conversation with the Crowd

JOHN 6:22-71

When they found Him on the other side of the sea, they said to Him, "Rabbi, when did You get here?"

Jesus answered, "I assure you: You are looking for Me, not because you saw the signs, but because you ate the loaves and were filled. Don't work for the food that perishes but for the food that lasts for eternal life, which the Son of Man will give you, because God the Father has set His seal of approval on Him."

—JOHN
6:25-27

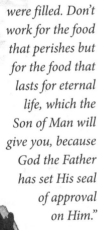

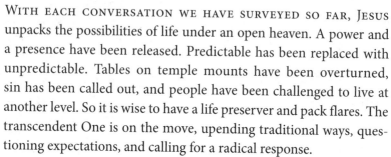

WITH EACH CONVERSATION WE HAVE SURVEYED SO FAR, JESUS unpacks the possibilities of life under an open heaven. A power and a presence have been released. Predictable has been replaced with unpredictable. Tables on temple mounts have been overturned, sin has been called out, and people have been challenged to live at another level. So it is wise to have a life preserver and pack flares. The transcendent One is on the move, upending traditional ways, questioning expectations, and calling for a radical response.

The problem is, we prefer things conventional and safe. We look for nonthreatening people and pain-free environments. Even on college campuses, Greg Lukianoff and Jonathan Haidt describe a growing movement to make these institutions of higher learning "safe spaces." Words and ideas that cause discomfort are increasingly scrubbed from lectures. One must be careful in conversations. Asking an Asian American about one's birthplace is considered to be a "microaggression"; it might imply that he or she is not an American. Words that bring up painful memories, like "violate," are off-limits. According to cultural experts, much of this is attributed to an emerging generation of students who suffer from a fragile psyche.[1]

I am guessing Jesus would not have had a long career at most contemporary universities. He would have never made tenure. He had a penchant for being offensive. He began His preaching in His hometown, and the application of His sermon so upset the hearers that they took Jesus to the edge of a cliff to shove Him off (Luke 4:28–29). He drove people out of the temple with a whip and likened the religious leaders to rotting bodies under polished tombs (Matt. 21:12; 23:27). He sat down to preach His Sermon on the Mount, proposing facial mutilation as a way of dealing with lust (5:29). Coming down from the transfiguration, He castigated the crowd for being perverse, wondering aloud how long He must put up with them (Matt. 17:17).

It was so bad, dinner parties sometimes turned into near riots (Luke 11:37–53).

Somewhere along the journey, Jesus's words have probably offended you as they have me. He humbles us when our egos get the best of us, exposes our worries as nothing less than mistrust, and checks our motives with merely a word. Life under an open heaven isn't always safe and pleasant. Jesus, full of grace and mercy, is also full of "shadows and mystery."[2] John underscores this in almost every chapter of his gospel. It is "part of its power and its fascination."

THE JESUS WE WANT

Still, most of us desire a kind and gentle Jesus. We shy away from books like Mark Galli's *Jesus Mean and Wild* that suggest we have "become soft around the middle."[3] We prefer pastors who preach lovely sermons, who have been domesticated over time and trained to be nice. Eugene Peterson, contrasting persecution in American culture with other cultures, writes: "Our culture doesn't lock us up; it simply and nicely castrates us, neuters us, and replaces our vital parts with a nice and smiling face."[4] This leads to a "therapeutically correct" ministry that comforts congregants by telling them Jesus has come primarily to meet or needs, heal our hurts, and coddle our minds. Were it not for the intervention of pastoral theologians in the late '80s, most of our pastors would be little more than trained therapists. But this does not represent Jesus. Indulgent He is not.

The crowd in John 6 assumes Jesus has come to meet their needs. He moves about, casting out demons and laying His hands on suffering souls. They see Him as a sort of Benny Hinn, there to bless and heal—and be perfectly safe. The wine miracle in Cana, the buzz in Samaria, the healing of a high official's son, and the healing of a paralytic have nurtured their hopes. They may hate Him in Jerusalem (7:1), but up here in the north, in the more rural regions of Galilee, Jesus has become a regular folk hero. Galileans like to go against the flow. They like being known as rebels who ignore the more liberal cities and their city-council regulations. It's a badge of honor when their voting precincts do not align with Jerusalem County.

Jesus is up here with His disciples seeking time alone (6:1–3). Both the rejection in Jerusalem and His growing popularity in Galilee are draining. Rhythm calls for retreat, but it is difficult to escape. Eventually, Jesus's fame will evaporate under the heat of unsafe words. But for the moment, it is creating a logistical nightmare.

There are five thousand adult males not to mention the women and children (v. 10). People with everything from never-ending migraines to malignant tumors are pressing in on Jesus no matter where He goes. It's not a stampede, but it is close to a crowd crush. It is becoming a struggle to take another breath. Compounding all of this, it's late in the day and people have gone without food. Babies are screaming and teens are complaining. Concession stands have not had time to materialize; food carts like Pastrami Zombie, Mama Hummus, and Jook Joint are nowhere to be found. And no one is willing to go home, let alone lose one's place in line.

John is setting the context for the next conversation. Jesus will, with graphic and unsafe language, talk about life under an open heaven, and it will not go well. John hints of this with one more detail: "Now the Passover, a Jewish festival, was near" (v. 4). These words are not simply adding color; they are heightening the tension. In every encounter, the cross is always in the background. Though now back to Galilee, Jesus is always headed, ultimately, to Jerusalem. He has not come to fulfill our will but the Father's, and this must go through Calvary. Popularity will eventually give way to animosity. He has come to be our Passover Lamb.

Jesus queries the disciples as to what food stores remain open. Philip should know; he is from nearby Bethsaida, the "house of fish." But Jesus knows. His question serves as an instructive moment; John tells us it amounts to a test (v. 6). Jesus wants to know if they really believe they are living under an open heaven, where a new age is dawning and the power of God is present. But these men are slow to grasp what Jesus promised Nathanael (1:50–51). Rather than lay the desperate need before His feet, they shift into problem-solving mode. Given their fiduciary responsibilities, the disciples convene an emergency board meeting and do what boards have a propensity to do—confine their discussions to what is humanly possible. Philip calculates that the costs will be in the thousands just to give each person a scrap (6:7). Even at thrift-store prices, there is not enough money in the deacon fund to cover the need. Alternatives are proposed. Questions are raised. Should they pool resources and order a large takeout? Does Meals on Wheels have a hotline? Andrew notices a backpack in the vicinity with food enough to feed a family. (Philip likely again calculates—this will meet 0.0002 percent of the present need.) In the end, the board sends the problem to the stewardship committee for further study. This is a convenient way to avoid problems, stall for time, and save money.

It's time to intervene. Jesus has everyone sit, and He gives thanks for the small portion. Good luck if you are sitting in the back. But Jesus demonstrates His authority over nature and begins to feed everyone from these very loaves (vv. 10–11).

Something is going on that must not be missed. The miracle is transpiring as the food is distributed, and it is obvious this is no Costco sampler. Jesus does not pass out token wafers nor fish pieces skewered with toothpicks. People are eating as much as they wish (v. 11). Jesus keeps providing, and the food keeps coming, until they are filled to the full. All that is missing is a rock band and other forms of entertainment.

As happens when Jesus provides, He makes too much (v. 12). He did the same thing with the wine at Cana and the fish haul at Lake Gennesaret. It is "a standard element in these stories."[5] Under an open heaven, Jesus has come that we might have life in abundance (10:10). His ample food and drink declare that the kingdom of God is unleashed.[6] God may be mystifying, unnerving, and confounding— but one thing He is not is cheap! There's good reason to pray, "Give us each day our daily bread" (Luke 11:3).

John tells us this was another sign of divine power (John 6:14). This is big! Apart from Jesus's resurrection, it's the only miracle recorded in all four Gospels.[7] The people suddenly realize that Jesus must be a prophet. This happens at other moments when Jesus displays His supernatural power (as with the woman at the well and the blind man), but the language here suggests that they see Jesus as more than a prophet. He is "*the* Prophet who was to come into the world!" (v. 14). The phrase has messianic overtones. It is language going back to Deuteronomy 18:15, a passage promising a future prophet like Moses, an end-time figure who will come and reveal God and provide. There has been an opening in heaven. Consequently, a messianic fever is setting in and infecting the crowd. Like an earlier generation in Israel that rose to anoint their king (1 Sam. 11:15), this crowd decides it is time to sign Jesus to a contract and make Him their new prophet-king. Who needs primaries and a convention?

Jesus is becoming their idol, and this is dangerous. As Galli warns, "The greatest danger—and the most tempting idol—is to imagine that God is the servant of our desires, who meets all our needs and is there for us in crises in exactly the way we need him to be there for us."[8]

People are getting the wrong idea about what life is under an open heaven. We saw this in His conversation with His mother (John 2:1–12).

THE JESUS WE NEED

Jesus will have none of this. He is not going around the countryside drumming up support like some politician in Iowa. In fact, Jesus is not so impressed with crowds. He is leery of sycophants and brownnosers chanting "Jesus is the One." He is wary of those who gravitate to signs and wonders (John 2:24). He knows that witnesses can get caught up in the moment. He will not deliver Himself over to their will for His life, any more than He did to those in Jerusalem. He knows what is behind their enthusiasm and their flattering words.

He also knows what is in our hearts; He realizes there is a human tendency to go after things that attract, stimulate, entertain, and provide for the self. It seldom lasts. *To go after is not the same as to stay with.* Like the crowd that will shout "Hosanna!" (12:13), these people will stay until something better comes along or things with Jesus are no longer safe.

Solomon speaks to our transient ways in Ecclesiastes. He tells the story of a young man who has risen to fame. Against impossible odds, he emerges to lead a nation. He has captured the hearts of the masses, and he thrives on the adoring crowds who chant his name, carry his signs, and release their balloons. But just as swiftly as they run after him, they shift course and run after someone else—someone younger, more attractive, and more promising.

The sage is giving his wisdom: time and familiarity have a way of taking their toll. Today's hope is tomorrow's call for change. Today's hero is tomorrow's discard. Today's inaugurated president is tomorrow's disappointment. Followers have this tendency to fail their leaders (Eccl. 4:13–16).

Jesus will not allow this crowd to use Him to further *their* ends. He will not be reduced to their fickle desires, and He will not allow Himself to be seized by their force. "He doesn't let anybody handle or control his identity and mission, which he has received from his heavenly Father."[9] We must not either. Pleasing people nullifies service to God (Gal. 1:10). It compromises divine purposes. It short-circuits what life is to be under an open heaven.

So He immediately sends away His disciples to nearby Capernaum before they are caught up in the confetti, and He withdraws to the mountain again to be alone (John 6:15). It's not that Jesus is disinterested in people coming after Him. He came to call the world to Himself. But something else is going on, and the conversation brings this out. They are not really interested in the Messiah spoken of in the prophets. Many in this region want the militant, political messiah of their imaginations, one who will free them from oppression. They want an earthly king who promises benefits—someone who will connect with their rage, address present needs, and implement the policies that are popular. They want a builder to construct the home that they want.

But Jesus is an architect who comes with His own plan.[10]

In removing Himself from the temptations of power and conformity, Jesus teaches us that there are times when *popularity can be just as dangerous as hostility.*[11] There are times when He removes Himself from us *until we learn to accept Him on His terms, not ours.* Until we wake up—

> *Do you ever wonder just what God requires?*
> *You think He's just an errand boy to satisfy your wandering desires*
>
> *When you gonna wake up, when you gonna wake up*
> *When you gonna wake up and strengthen the things that remain?*
>
> —BOB DYLAN[12]

There are times we also need to open our eyes. Forces may be at work to conform us to someone we are not. Situations may come that we have no business entertaining. Time alone will help us distinguish the necessary from the trivial and "filter the essential information from the nonessential noise," the legitimate from the illegitimate.[13] We need to be like Jesus, an essentialist who recognizes the motives, discerns the Father's will, and determines a prudent way forward.

(Memo to evangelists and pastors who go for crowds and cave in to their demands: Jesus is not impressed with attractional ministries that raffle off cars and draw big numbers. Those caught up in all of this might consider escaping to the mountains, where they will find solitude and space, and maybe find themselves and Christ once again.)[14]

Someone Who Mystifies

Jesus's departure leaves everyone confused. Mysterious provision is followed by His mysterious withdrawal. People awaken and are asking themselves, "What just happened?" He was their write-in candidate, but He failed to show up at the convention to receive the nomination.

A posse is sent out to hunt Jesus down, and He is apprehended in nearby Capernaum (John 6:22–24). This is déjà vu all over again (see Luke 4:42).

What follows is an extended conversation. People need answers: "When did You get here?" (John 6:25). A more expected question would be, "*How* did You get here?" His disciples had left the night before without Jesus. There is no way He could have made the journey by foot.

In typical fashion, Jesus does not answer their question. As Culpepper notes, "Jesus seems to be congenitally incapable of giving a straight answer."[15] Just ask Nicodemus or, later on, Pilate. It's not that He is stonewalling. He is not oblivious to our queries; Jesus is far more interested in going below the surface, to the unverbalized question behind the question. When we fail to realize this, we misinterpret His silence as someone removed and uncaring. It's not that He doesn't hear us. He is listening for and answering the true question.

Here is what they really want to know: "*Why* did You leave us?" Why would Jesus spurn their advances? Why is He not throwing Himself into the crowd with full abandon? Is He insensitive to their will? Is He missing God's will and failing to seize His moment? Is Jesus an introvert who runs from people? Maybe He needs time to think this over. Becoming king is a lot to put on someone after one gathering. The crowd is still with Him. Polling numbers remain high, but people are getting a little nervous. They are also getting hungry.

Someone Who Exposes

Jesus quiets the crowd. His use of "I assure you" (or "truly, truly") is, once again, a way of calling for their best attention (v. 26). Maybe they expect a small speech before the next meal, an announcement explaining when He arrived, and then, who knows what small lunch sack will turn into another plentiful feast? But something has changed. There is an edge in His voice, one more prophetic than pastoral. It has been all smiles and photos and small talk, but bluntness is about to shove congeniality aside. This is Jesus unsafe.

As Galli puts it, "There are times in John that Jesus plays percussion when we expect strings."[16] He tells Nathanael that his belief is superficial, tells His mother to back off, mocks Nicodemus for being a theological neophyte, calls a loose woman out, and tells a healed man to quit sinning. He will tell His brothers to get a life and warn professed believers that their father is the Devil. And here, He tells a crowd they live by their glands (v. 26). When Jesus shoots, it is always straight.

Imagine a rally and a Billy Graham type saying to those who have come forward: "I know why you are here. It's not the Word you are interested in. It's the attractions—the action sports, the fireworks, the music, and the pop stars we brought to this event. Your motives are operating only at base level. Stop living for things that are temporal. Start seeing life from an eternal perspective!"

This is what Jesus does. He calls them out: "Don't work for the food that perishes but for the food that lasts for eternal life" (v. 27). In effect, He says, "Go after something more substantial than the things that mold, sour, rust, decay, decline, erode, and fall apart. Don't settle for a mere cycle of survival! Invest in things eternal. Pursue ventures that will have endless rewards. Don't live to satisfy your bellies; they will only scream for more. Don't come after Me simply to be healed. You will still die. And while we're on this topic, stop viewing Me as a health-and-wealth Jesus. I am not some 'meal-ticket messiah,' a wonder chef, a supernatural healthcare provider. I am not your temporal king here to take on the Romans and create a nanny state. Life under an open heaven looks much different."

His words force each one of us to ask hard questions of ourselves. What is the fundamental principle of my existence? Is it food? Material possessions? Is there more to me than my appetites? Am I truly aware that there are deeper dimensions to life than the physical? Would I be more shaken by a famine of Word or a famine of food? Am I simply living out what my culture has chosen to label me—a consumer? Do I want Jesus only for what He can give? Do I want the life an open heaven gives—and requires?

Just as physical hunger was a test of faith for Israel in the wilderness, so this crowd's present hunger is their test. Do they get it that "man does not live on bread alone" (Deut. 8:3)? Jesus is testing, probing, and exposing, and people do not generally like to be outed. There is enough offense in Jesus's words to thin out this crowd, but while some may have marched out the door and tore out of the parking lot, others are not quite ready to end the conversation.

Someone Who Will Point Us Beyond Ourselves
Jesus has the Father's seal of approval (John 6:27). The Father and the Spirit teamed up to affirm Jesus as He came out of the waters of baptism (Luke 3:21–22). The crowd wants a similar affirmation, only they want to pin it on their own efforts: "What can we do to perform the works of God?" (John 6:28). Where is the program we need to sign up for, and when does it start? Is it a ten-step or a forty-day plan?

They do not realize that life under an open heaven is not about works. It's not about fulfilling a Pharisaic to-do list. It is about belief.

It is here, as Michael Card puts it, that Jesus "begins talking like a madman."[17] "Believe in the One He has sent" is Jesus's response (v. 29). Belief occurs when one is "sufficiently assured of that person's trustworthiness."[18] Jesus is calling them to pursue Him—not for the bread they have received, nor for the government they hope He brings, but for the relationship they can enter into with God. Entering into relationship is their work of faith; it is likewise our work. It's the day-to-day responsibility of those living under an open heaven. But He knows they refuse to pursue God and learn to trust Him, and their unbelief is the major roadblock to finding the eternal, tasting the real bread, and experiencing the life Jesus has come to offer.

The belief Jesus speaks of is more than intellectual assent. True belief includes a decision to change course and leave old ways. It is a resolve to follow Him, to hunger for Him more than anything else. It requires everything of us. But this is apparently asking too much from those who are left. They will need more evidence if they are to buy into this life under an open heaven.

During my years in seminary here in Portland, Oregon, I would often run to the top of nearby Mount Tabor in the afternoons. It was a way of decompressing after time spent in a classroom discussing pluperfects and infralapsarianism and protocol for doing weddings. One day, I noticed a man sitting, with legs crossed, enjoying the panoramic view of Portland. Being the evangelist I am (and given it was a class assignment in Ecclesiology to lead someone to Jesus to pass the course), I asked him if he knew God. To my surprise, he informed me that he was God. My first instinct was to question his stability. My second was to ask for a sign—like changing my semester grades to As.

The crowd also wants a sign. They want proof. It's all beginning to sound like an earlier Israel in the wilderness: tired, grumbling, and hungry. And just like the renegades crossing the sea from Egypt, they have seen an amazing work, but it is not enough. They need more indicators if they are to buy in. "What sign then are *You* going to do so we may see and believe You? . . . What are *You* going to perform?" (v. 30).

Those in the crowd have their performance expectations as well (v. 31). To paraphrase, "If you expect us to believe that You are God's gift to humanity, we need more to work with. You will need to perform at a level that puts You in the Moses bracket. Moses fed more than five thousand people, and he did it for forty years. You have only fed us once. How about another meal, and if it's okay, add dessert. Give us a bigger-than-Moses's-size miracle, and then we'll talk!"

Any pastor who builds his ministry on crowds, on being more attractional than incarnational, knows he has to come back with something bigger and better next week. *Earthly appetites are never satisfied.* He must make sure the gospel demands are softened so as to not offend. Preach topically. Be relevant. Be safe. Add humor. Bring in a Christian movie star or professional athlete to verify the claims of the gospel. Deliver amazing music. Use the pulpit to demonstrate one's incredible abilities to perform. And outperform the week before. Otherwise, they will be off to the next show, chasing the next fad in town.

Jesus will not perform to get people to make a decision. He made this clear to His mother (2:4); He will impress this on His brothers (7:6–8). Jesus is not at our beck and call. He is not obliged to meet our expectations. He will not satisfy the Tempter, who is always seeking to seduce Jesus into doing something to impress the crowds. Jesus knows that the excitement generated by miracles does not readily convert into an open heaven or a life-changing faith. They attract crowds but do not lead to repentance. They amass onlookers, but they do not lead to belief.

The woman at the well wanted Jesus to know He is no Jacob; this crowd wants Jesus to know He is no Moses. They are both right. Jesus is far more. Jacob provided a well for water; Moses simply passed on instructions for gathering food. Jesus *is* the Fountain that satisfies one's thirst; He *is* the Bread that fulfills one's hunger (4:14; 6:35). He will repeat these words about being the bread that comes down from heaven two more times to make the point, for it is obvious their hearts are dull and their minds obtuse (6:48, 51).

With each statement, Jesus is forcing them to come to terms with who He really is—and who they really are. He continues to extend the invitation to come to His table. He is breaking and passing out the better food; He is offering to them a foretaste of eternity under an open heaven. But the distance between Jesus and the crowd only widens. Skepticism has replaced enthusiasm; support has shifted to antagonism. One can sense a divine hardening at work. They are closing the door on life under an open heaven and throwing away the key.

I have witnessed this in ministry. A needed correction can lead to a hardening, where any hope of receptivity is gone. Sometimes a deep antagonism can lead to divine judgment (see Isa. 6:9–13). The ability to hear is lost. Early in my first church I reproved a man for his coarse behavior and rude language at a business meeting. From that day until the day he died, he sat in services, his cold demeanor set in stone. I am pretty certain he never received a word I preached after our confrontation.

There appears to be a similar divine work going on here. These who are left, who now challenge Jesus in the synagogue (John 6:59–66), are not the recipients of the Father's prevenient work; unless they are drawn by the Father, they will not come (v. 44). This is a repeated theme in John (10:29; 17:2, 6; 18:9).[19] It's another way of underscoring that we do not determine our lives. God does! But this crowd assumes that they are in control. At every point, the crowd wants to set the terms. They want *their* king. They want Jesus to perform. They want proofs. *They want food!*

Someone Who Will Point Us to the Better Meal

A palpable antagonism is growing to a breaking point. Jesus's tone becomes more severe. He shifts to language that could be best described as "crude forcefulness."[20] Eating the flesh of Jesus and drinking His blood amount to a direct encounter, an intimate presence, and a willingness to believe. It is the necessary step to abiding (6:56). Regularly feeding on Him is what leads to the abundant life He promises (v. 57). It is what creates union. It's language Jesus uses to say He wants to be experienced, not as a religion, a church, a moral philosophy, an impersonal king, a formless life force—but as the Son of God who is invited into the deepest textures of one's being.

Yet this crowd prefers to have a childish tea party, drinking their tea from empty cups and nibbling cakes made of dust. They are far more interested in having their physical needs met rather than their spiritual needs. They prefer the old Moses to the new Moses. They want God, as long as He provides, as long as He is safe, and as long as He keeps at arm's length.

Søren Kierkegaard once told the story of an auditorium where there were two doors. "Above the one door was a sign labeled 'heaven.' Above the other door was a sign labeled 'lecture about heaven.' And people flocked through the door labeled 'lecture.'"[21]

Under an open heaven, we are invited to enter through a door labeled "abide." This is "the basic mode of Christian existence."[22] Upon entering, we find a heavy-laden table of the Jesus we need. Here we draw life and sustenance from Him. We move from the sterility of knowing *about* God and His law to an experiential knowing *of* God and His person. But most prefer the other door, "lecture about abide." They are content with their empty cups. Or in the case of this conversation, "loaves and fishes" is preferred over "Bread of Life." Things intensify. As Jo-Ann Brant notes, "Verbal shoves become verbal punches."[23] Rejecting the Bread of Life amounts to choosing death (vv. 57–58). There is no room for compromise when it comes to following Jesus. More and more leave. There is no longer a passive crowd but an active and agitated core (vv. 60, 66). This is Jerusalem and its acrimony all over again. Many are unable or unwilling to process spiritual realities. The words are too hard, rough (note the Greek term *skleros*). Ironically, this fibrous conversation has created a sclerosis of the heart. The call to consume Him, and all the implications of masticating, chewing, drinking, assimilating, internalizing, and metabolizing Jesus, are repulsive to them. It also hints of sacrifice. They are unwilling, and unable, to incorporate Jesus into the bloodstream of their lives.

As in other conversations, Jesus declares that He is the one the Scriptures point to. His deeds (such as feeding the five thousand and walking on water) affirm what His words say like "many streams converging into a mighty river."[24] But as N. T. Wright notes, "most of his contemporaries had in mind a different kind of river."[25]

Someone Who Will Risk Popularity to Declare Truth

This has been a long, laborious, and intense conversation. By most standards, it turns out to be a monumental disaster. The morning-after headlines might have read, "Bread of Life Speech a Huge Letdown," or "Graphic Words Offend Receptive Crowd." Those political pundits analyzing the returns might have noted that Jesus failed to connect with His base. His words are too disruptive. His political advisors could do a better job marketing Jesus to the masses. He has command of the material, but His figures of speech are way too difficult. The #NeverJesus crowd will not be won over if this is not changed.

But Jesus is no politician. And in a rather un-nice way Jesus is serving notice to anyone interested in following Him that nominal adherence is not enough. He is not interested in groupies. He is after followers.

Like many conversations, this one draws a line in the sand. Are you willing to give up the Jesus you want for the Jesus you need? Are you willing to expand your appetite for the table He has prepared for us, one even better than the table the psalmist envisioned (Ps. 23:5)? *He invites us to eat Him up*—to get Him and His Word into our gut, into our nerve endings, our reflexes, and our bloodstream such that He naturally flows out of our lives in acts of love and holiness, healing, evangelism, and justice.[26] This is resolute feasting, the central act of the soul. Not pecking around the margins. Not nibbling as you would a snack.

It can be risky. This graphic language points to the cross, and with it the sacramental meal.[27] Eating His flesh and drinking His blood is to enter into covenant with Him (Matt. 26:28). It is to contemplate His death, and our own. Even in the partaking, there are certain table rules that, if ignored, can lead to severe consequences (1 Cor. 11:27–30). Sounds like "microaggressive" language. It is.

The language of consumption also speaks to the day-to-day life under an open heaven, where we are invited to dive in and consume something of what we will have in full in eternity—grace, peace, joy, hope, love (the list could go on). Every moment of life is an opportunity to internalize Jesus. But as lavish as God is in the present, it all amounts to hors d'oeuvres before the heavenly banquet. He gives us in the present a foretaste of the goodness of God's Word and the powers of the coming age (Heb. 6:5).

QUESTIONS

1. *If Jesus allowed the crowd to crown Him as their earthly king, how would life on earth be different? Why didn't He accept the position?*

2. *What does it mean to consume Jesus as one consumes bread? What would doing this look like in your life?*

3. *What is your motivation for chasing after Jesus?*

7

LIFE IS ABOUT SOMETHING TO LIVE AND DIE FOR

A Conversation with His Brothers

JOHN 7:1–9

Jesus told them, "My time has not yet arrived, but your time is always at hand. The world cannot hate you, but it does hate Me because I testify about it—that its deeds are evil."

—JOHN 7:6–7

AT DIFFERENT JUNCTURES OF LIFE, WE FIND OURSELVES ASKING KEY questions:

- *Twentysomethings* ask, "What am I becoming? What will I do with my life?"
- *Thirtysomethings* ask, "How do I prioritize these demands made on my life? How can I fulfill my life purpose? What will I stand for? What was I made for?"
- *Fortysomethings* ask, "Why are limitations beginning to outweigh options? What would it take to pick up a whole new calling?"
- *Fiftysomethings* ask, "Why is life moving so fast? How do I deal with my failures and successes? How can I reinvigorate my relationship with my spouse—and my work?"
- *Sixtysomethings* ask, "When do I stop doing the things that have defined me? Do I have enough time to do all the things I still dream about?"
- *Seventy- and eightysomethings* ask, "Is anyone aware of what I once achieved? Is my story important to anyone? Can I still contribute? Will I be missed? Has my life been impactful or irrelevant?"[1]

Okay, I left out the *ninetysomethings*. It's just a guess, but maybe some of them ask, "What was the question?"

The opening words of John 7 suggest that a thirtysomeone by the name of Jesus is at a critical juncture in His life. Maybe you are there and you find yourself asking some life-defining questions. One can't afford to drift, but Jesus seems to be drifting. Things appear to be at a turning point. Life is conspiring against Him. His last sermon on the north side of Galilee caused a mass exodus (6:66). He is facing an increasingly hostile world down south in Judea (7:1). His picture is up in the local post office in downtown Jerusalem. There are orders out for His arrest. Religious leaders seethe when His name comes up in conversations. And some of His strongest supporters up in Galilee are among those who have just walked out.

The Twelve are still in (6:67–68), but some, like Nathanael, might be wondering if the greater things promised are short-lived. If heaven has opened and angels are ascending and descending, then where is the divine activity? Just how much opening is there, and what difference is it making?

These may be our questions as well.

THE LONELY SIDE OF A PURPOSE-DRIVEN LIFE

Jesus is walking (7:1). The tense of this verb suggests protracted action in past time. Jesus is walking and walking and walking. He is also avoiding. For the moment, Galilee is the safer place (v. 1). John does not add that Jesus is preaching and healing, or anything else. There appears to be no straight-line development. Where is He going?

This walking is different than His other travels. In the previous stories, Jesus "decided to leave for Galilee," "had to travel through Samaria," "went up to Jerusalem," and "went away to the other side." If you want to follow Jesus, you need to get in step. He is on the move. There is a reason the early church was referred to as "the Way" (Acts 9:2). The disciples are following Someone with the precision of eternal purpose.

But there is no defined way here. After leaving the synagogue in Capernaum, there appears to be no destination. At best, He seems to be going "intently haphazard."[2] Is He at a crossroads? Is He asking the kinds of questions thirtysomethings ask? Is He wondering, "Where do I go from here?" But then, does God ever ask questions He doesn't know the answers to?

If I were increasingly hated by the culture and abandoned by those I led, I would be asking some huge questions, beginning with my sense of calling. If leadership is defined as "one who has followers," am I still a leader if people are abandoning me? Is God finished with me? Is there something everyone seems to recognize but me? I know I would ask these because I have. I have had these seemingly aimless walks. Most leaders have.

There was a season in the Netherlands in which I felt I was losing the support of my board. I was in a terrible conflict with my board chairman. We saw ministry differently, and he was suspicious of my pastoral authority. Several influential congregants were troubled that I chose to preach from Ecclesiastes, wondering what place a book written by an obvious narcissist has in a Christian pulpit. They were no longer following. My staff were under severe criticism, and my health was beginning to be affected. And it had been one of those long Dutch winters.

I found myself walking alone for long stretches among the dunes along the North Sea. Walking and walking and walking. I was a fifty-something pondering my identity, questioning the will of God, and trying to figure out my next steps. Sometimes I looked deeply into the expansive sky, wondering if the heavens had closed on me.

For Jesus, the opening words of John, "He came to His own, and His own people did not receive Him" (1:11), are coming to fuller expression. Token opposition has shifted to rejection. The plot is being played out. He longs to gather His children under His wings, but they are unwilling (Luke 13:34). All roads are leading to the cross and complete abandonment. He moved into the neighborhood to clean up things and put to right the wrong. He left heaven to rescue people from legalistic structures that constrict and destroy. He came to offer an alternative to life dominated by one's appetites and addictions. He came to pay the price for our failures. He came to pull back the curtain of heaven and give us life abundantly. But most people like things as they are.

I spend part of my summers in the wilderness of northeast Washington, kayaking near the Canadian border. Year after year I come into town, and nothing changes. I'm learning something about certain rural parts. People tend to be set in their ways. They like things as they are. It's okay that unsold homes remain unsold, main street still looks like main street, and the local grocery still smells like fried chicken. Change agents are viewed with suspicion—even if the intention is to simply organize a Lions club, clean up things, or bring salvation.

I know I am lingering over these opening words that establish the setting of this next conversation, but I believe they serve to give us pause. The road is an important part of Jesus's ministry. Things happen on the road. Some of God's best work happens on the road. I imagine Jesus's walk to be a mix of quiet pondering and heart-to-heart conversing with the Father. If only people would look up to see what is breaking forth.

This is a hinge point for His disciples, and I am guessing that, though they are not mentioned, they are walking alongside. Perhaps they are wondering what they have gotten themselves into. Is Jesus and His ministry going anywhere? Nearly six months have gone by since His bread sermon, and John records nothing of this season. We have to go to other gospels to fill in the space (see Luke 7–9). There are parables, occasional encounters with visiting Pharisees (who are always stewing for a fight), amazing healings, and a mind-bending transfiguration—all evidence that heaven has opened, but John leaves them out.

Eventually Jesus begins to head from Capernaum, away from the sea. It is a familiar route, one they have taken many times. They will move southwest, going through a pass and climbing some 2,100 feet. But why here? Why go back to Nazareth? Wasn't it here that people also walked out on Jesus's sermon? More than walked out—they responded to it by trying to kill Him (Luke 4:29).

It may be that John is again writing this scene like a script for a Greek theater. Hellenistic culture seems to have trained him to see things through a cosmic drama. Actors enter the stage, and things move in a suspenseful way between protagonist and antagonists. The plotline plays out in a perilous way. This happens in the next conversation.

Jesus, the central character, enters walking, and it might be that the narrator wants us, the audience, to visualize ourselves in this "walking" scene. As the whole John story progresses, one conversation to the next, we are also asking some hard questions:

- Why does Jesus get people so upset?
- Why does He seem to constantly live somewhere between condemnation and alienation?
- Why do Judeans have a warrant out for His arrest?
- Why do Galileans no longer want to follow Him?
- Did He just miss a great opportunity?
- Are His demands too harsh?
- What happens next?
- Is life under an open heaven all it is cracked up to be?

THE MISUNDERSTOOD SIDE OF A PURPOSE-DRIVEN LIFE

Enter the antagonists onstage (John 7:2–4). Jesus has returned, but His younger brothers would prefer He leave. No doubt His earlier Isaiah sermon in the local synagogue alienated just about every Nazarene, and no one has forgotten. People do not like to hear that they are a lost cause, and most are still wondering how He mysteriously escaped the moment they attempted to hurl Him over the cliff (Luke 4:30). What if word gets out this wannabe prophet, this persona non grata, is back home? Jesus's brothers could lose their jobs. They have already lost their family honor (not to mention it has messed with their dating).

Everyone is getting ready for the Jewish Feast of Tabernacles. The brothers point out that Jesus should be getting ready. He should go where He is needed (John 7:3). Have you noticed how people love to give God suggestions? We feel it is our duty at times to advise Him. Sometimes, when things are not adding up, we find it necessary to inform God and tell Him what would be the better direction. Like most parishioners, we love to share "our concerns."

The scene reminds us of a similar one in John 2. Jesus's mother also encouraged Jesus to reveal His power. Her sons have similar advice for their brother: "Show Yourself to the world!" (7:4). Make a public display of Your capabilities! But unlike Mary, who knows who Jesus is, His brothers do not. They do not believe (v. 5).

One can hear the sarcasm in their voices. They have heard the threats, the pushback Jesus is receiving, and so each one eggs Him on: "Time to go big time!" "Show Yourself to the world that will soon gather in Jerusalem!" "Those who claim to be the Light of the world do not hide their light under a bushel." "You can't make it big in the way You are seeking to be big if you stay in the small confines of a backwater town like Nazareth."

As Dale Bruner observes, "It sounds like a call to Hollywood or Broadway rather than to Golgotha or Bethany."[3]

The Feast of Tabernacles was associated with eschatological hopes. It was the mother of all feasts. So in their minds, this was the perfect moment. Like merchants who decorate their stores for the Christmas rush, this is the optimal time for messiahs to come out of their closets and parade their wares. Again, one imagines words like—"At the very least, go over to Jerusalem and drop a few pearls of wisdom. A message akin to Coach Wooden's 'Pyramid of Success' might win detractors. You might be able to recover Your losses, reverse Your fortunes, and win back those who were offended by Your bread sermon."

Jesus's brothers join a long list of other unbelievers wanting Jesus to prove Himself and do something big to satisfy their curiosity. The crowds often hounded Jesus to perform more signs. And all of this was driven by an adversary whose initial temptations included jumping off a temple pinnacle to wow the masses (Matt. 4:6). They all want Jesus to exploit His relationship with the Father for His benefit—and theirs.

Familiarity has a way of breeding contempt, even when your brother is God! Jesus found little receptivity in His back yard, acknowledging that "no prophet is accepted in his hometown" (Luke 4:24). Proximity and familiarity have a way of blinding people. Maybe it is more than resentment. Maybe His brothers are jealous of His glory, remembering the wedding at Cana. Maybe there are too many memories of living with a perfect brother who never did anything wrong. Or maybe they are embarrassed by the reported scandals, the recent parties with the prostitutes, the associations with the tax mafia, and the recent defection of the disciples. In a shame-honor culture, they may have felt another miracle might recover some of the reputation that has been lost, especially if it's in the big city. Maybe the family name can be restored.

It is amazing that Jesus's brothers can grow up in the closest proximity to divinity and be so obtuse, misunderstanding His purpose. But then I think about the church. Not everyone who grows up with Jesus gets Jesus. Over time, familiarity in this context can breed its own contempt. People know all of the Bible stories. They have the language down, the hymns memorized, and they know how the story ends. Once the preaching concludes, they express appreciation for the reminder, as if there is nothing more to discover. The name of Jesus, once met with joy and reverence, is met with a collective yawn. No wonder Jesus warns that any exposure to Him under an open heaven requires senses wide open, ready to receive. If not, whatever we have will be taken away (Mark 4:21–25).

THE TIMELY SIDE OF A PURPOSE-DRIVEN LIFE

Jesus can see what is going on in this conversation. He hears beyond the words. He knows their intent. He knows where it is going. Jesus can see our motives as easily as He can see our inclinations. He can see into the deepest part of our hearts. He has made our hearts, so He understands everything we do (Ps. 33:15). He can read His brothers' hearts, and He has a perfect response.

Jesus responds with the same coolness, the same seeming indifference as with His mother at the wedding in Cana. Once more, He must clarify that He does not need His family's counsel, any more than He needs ours. He is on a mission perfectly timed and perfectly carried out. He is never surprised. There is nothing He has not anticipated. Jesus is not here to conform to anyone's wishes other than His Father's. He is not moved to satisfy sibling expectations. He is not directed by family pressures, let alone self-interest or fear. In due time, people will see His glory. It will become evident that God is becoming king on earth as He is in heaven. He may be walking, but there is rhythm to all of His work.

The language of John 2:4 ("My hour has not yet come") and 7:6 ("My time has not yet arrived") makes the same point—Jesus lives by divine parameters. Jesus's only obligation is to the mission of the Father. He takes His cues from Him, not from the world. He has an inner ear for the Father's purposes, all of which are perfect. In everything He does, it follows an intentional plan that is worked out in time. But it is an itinerary that is not His own. The Son can do nothing of His own accord (5:19). Hence, contrary to perceptions, His steps are calculated, measured, ordained, and precise. They reflect a God who knows what time it is (Jer. 8:7). And the divine moment, the purpose for which He has come, is not yet. He is not on the clock. Jerusalem and the cross will have to wait until the Father says, "Now!" In the meantime, Jesus has been sent to Nazareth. All of this adds to the suspense.

It is here that Jesus differentiates Himself from His brothers. While His time is "not yet," their time is "always at hand" (John 7:6). It is a way of saying their time is always ready. What does this mean? Is this a compliment? Are they receiving a merit badge for being prepared? Steve Mariucci, former head coach of the San Francisco 49ers, was once asked why he did not wear a watch. His reply: "I never wear a watch, because I always know it's now—and now is when you should do it."[4] Is Jesus marveling at their opportunistic ways? Differentiating His tendency to be cautious in contrast to His brothers' tendency to play hard and fast? Is He acknowledging a certain divine procrastination, while His brothers live with impressive urgency? Is Jesus commending them or condemning them?

This is what He is doing: Jesus is teaching His brothers, and us, something about one's approach to time under an open heaven. Time is more than mere duration (*chronos*), the ordinary events of buying and selling, eating and sleeping. Time includes opportune moments (*kairos*), moments we should respect when God says, "Not yet!" and seize when God says, "Now!" Jesus is present to the Presence. He lives on "redemptive time," where time is not about human deliberation; divine decision is what matters.

Jesus's brothers are oblivious to both redemptive time and divine decision. "In *kairos* time you ask, not 'What time is it?' but 'What is this time *for*?'"[5] What am I to do in this next chapter? How do I fit in this divine narrative? This life is really a redemptive event and thus is bound to the time fixed for it by God.[6]

Jesus is telling His brothers that, as far as they are concerned, any time will do. Their time has no special significance from a divine point of view. They live as if everything is determined by them. When or where things happen doesn't really matter. Because their hearts are unbelieving, they can go wherever and whenever. In the end, their movement is rather aimless and confused; they are like men who run around with fire extinguishers in times of flood. What they are doing serves little ultimate purpose.

It reminds me of a man I once met, sitting on his porch overlooking the Pend Oreille River. As he sat with his can of beer, gazing out into the distance, I knew this was going to be a deep conversation. I asked him, "So what is life up here in the wilderness like? How do you spend your time?" He told me that he gets up to watch the river. I asked, "Anything else?" "No, not really" was his bland response. He struck me as a man whose time is always at hand; his mission had all the patina of banality.

Ronald Rolheiser gives us a warning worth heeding: "When we fail to distinguish among the different seasons of our lives and how these interface with the challenges and invitations that God and life send us, we are in danger of hurting ourselves in two ways: first, by trying to take on too much when we are not ready for it, and second, by not taking on enough when we are ready for it."[7] Jesus's words here suggest the latter. Their time is always at hand. They may be ready, but they take nothing on.

It follows, as Jesus notes, that His brothers cannot be hated (7:7). Inconsequential and untimely lives provoke little response from the world. This also differentiates them from their brother. Unlike Jesus, they do not disturb the comfortable. Because they have no real convictions, the kind that change the world, they do not alienate. They pursue what the world pursues. If they have any core principles, they keep them to themselves. It is far more important to be accepted and liked.

Memo to the church: When you have no sense of timing, of mission, of core convictions, you are not a factor in the world's destiny. You make no ultimate difference; you change nothing. You merely shamble through life, eliciting little to no response. Be wary of congregants who have no sense of urgency (and committees that exist to avoid decisions). Avoid communities that simply want to be loved by everyone. Stepping into your divine moments and living and dying for Jesus and His teachings will create tension. It will eventually cause some relationships to go crosswise, even within the church. Certainly within an unbelieving culture.

Because Jesus is guided by the Father's time and the Father's will, He is consequential. Jesus has a message that declares, "all have sinned and fall short of the glory of God" (Rom. 3:23). In the fullness of time, He stepped into our neighborhood to serve notice to evil (Gal. 4:4–5). He came to call it out. He came to destroy the works of the Devil (1 John 3:8). Wherever the Light of the World went, He exposed this alternative kingdom, drew it from the shadows, disrupted establishment protocols, and confronted prejudice, greed, hatred, injustice, and sexual misbehavior. He likened the most pious establishment to "whitewashed tombs." They "appear beautiful on the outside, but inside are full of dead men's bones and every impurity" (Matt. 23:27). He claimed to be greater than Moses (John 5:46–47), called people to eat His flesh and drink His blood (6:53), and claimed to be the only way (14:6). Consequently, Jesus was hated.

Whether Jesus's brothers knew this or not, nowhere is Jesus more hated than in Jerusalem. To step into this city amounts to a death sentence. There would be no avoiding this, but it would come at the Father's call, when the time has fully come. Jesus therefore turns the exhortation around and tells His brothers, "Go up to the festival yourselves" (7:8). Enjoy the festival and pass the time in small talk, discussing your small ways. Talk about your favorite Starbuck's beverage, obsess about your favorite team's draft, or compare your latest colonoscopy results. Go through the rituals and come back to your small worlds.

Here, the conversation ends. Like the conversation with His mother, John gives us only a part. As R. Alan Culpepper notes, the scenes in John "can be fitted into about two months of the two-and-a-half-year period" of Jesus's complete narrative.[8] So much more could have been written about Jesus and His conversations with His brothers. Much more space could have been given to just about everything Jesus did on earth (21:25). Unlike anyone else who has ever lived, Jesus was (and is) bigger than the size of history. But we only get a brief glimpse.

Did Jesus's brothers ever come around? Did they find their divine purpose or did they remain attached to the world? When the Jews at the feast were inquiring as to where Jesus was (7:11), did they offer information? The crowd was clearly divided. Where did His brothers land? Did they join in and pick up stones (8:59), or did they come to a place where they realized this truly was God in the flesh? John gives no clues. Like Nicodemus and the paralytic, we do not know if their irrelevant drifting was transformed into an intentional, purpose-driven journey.

THE SATISFYING SIDE OF A PURPOSE-DRIVEN LIFE

Stepping back, I am aware that this conversation can be misunderstood. Jesus might come across as someone who attaches little value to small things. His words can sound like a holier-than-thou older brother who has long been impatient. On the surface, the language suggests that Jesus disdains family members who waste their moments on the normal things of life. Could His words have provoked a "here we go again"? Did He come back to Nazareth only to (one more time) put down people as lost causes?

As I write this book, I can become wrapped up in things of kingdom importance. I want these words to build up the church. I want people to open their eyes to see what life under an open heaven can look like. But then my daughter pokes her head in the room and asks about the weather forecast and if I like what she has chosen to wear. Oblivious to my missional focus, she asks, "Are we having leftovers tonight?"

Obviously, her time is always at hand. Doesn't she understand that there are more important things than choosing fingernail polish? Is she not picking up my disinterested posture? Hasn't she read this conversation in John 7?

But all of this would insinuate that the ordinary things of life don't matter to God when, in fact, they do. If they are not important, why would He give such attention to designing butterflies? Or spending time with children (which frustrated His mission-centered disciples)? Or insisting that we take Sabbath moments to do nothing but rest and ponder? The reality is that most of life is composed of routine tasks and small talk. If we belittle them, we misrepresent God and the gospel.[9]

Still, this conversation with His brothers serves as a corrective to those who routinely squander their time. Scripture is the account of men and women who missed their moment. One thinks of Israel and its failure to seize the open door and enter the land; Saul sat under a pomegranate tree while Israel was paralyzed in fear (1 Sam. 14:2); and Jonah never seemed to have understood his moment. But others were keenly aware of their opening. Moses was confronted at a bush with the command to lead God's people, and he went out and led. After the seventh lap, the priests were told to blow the trumpets, and Joshua stepped into the reason for which he was made. Jonathan crossed over to the Philistine garrison and scattered an army. And at a critical instant, Esther realized she could no longer be silent. And when the moment passed, all surely heard the words, "Well done!"

Living under an open heaven, where Christ rules as the ascended Lord and the Spirit indwells us with His power, time has been reconfigured. We are no longer marking time, but making time. We are no longer watching the river; we are in the flow of divine purpose. There is a power to receive, an authority to exercise, and a purpose to live out 24/7. There is a Savior and King to identify with and a kingdom gospel to proclaim. And our use of time is a core indicator of how conscious we are of God's intentions for us. It matters whether we are squandering or redeeming the time.

Such a life, sensitive as it is to divine purpose, will upset the status quo. The deeper our identification with God's redemptive work and the message He has called us to declare, the greater the potential for animosity. This is what Jesus is telling his brothers. Those who call out sin are hated. Shining light on the darkness has a polarizing effect. Speaking against injustice and empty religion, and telling the ungenerous that it is not their money but God's, will not earn us favor. There is a cost for declaring that our bodies are not our own because they belong to God. Not everyone embraces God's design for marriage or God's will for purity and covenantal relationships. Some may change, but the majority will hate us (John 15:18–25). Fulfilling the will of God under His open heaven is to live dangerously—not aimlessly. It is to live life to the full, to live a life that counts.

In a small town on the Sea of Galilee, Magdala, there is a chapel with these words over the door—*Duc in Altum*. They refer back to Jesus's command to Peter to put out into the deep (Luke 5:4). They inspire worshippers to go further out, to avoid staying in the shallows. They tell twentysomethings—like Jesus's brothers—that it is time to live with aim.

QUESTIONS

1. *What kept Jesus's brothers from believing in Him?*

2. *Are you seizing your divine moment? If so, what are some specific ways you are living out your opportunities? If not, is it because you are not recognizing it when it comes, or could it be you are running from it?*

3. *Have your convictions led to a certain resistance from the world? What are you facing? Are you overcoming them, and if so, how?*

8

LIFE IS ABOUT BEING SET FREE

A Conversation with Unbelieving Believers

JOHN 8:30-59

> *As He was saying these things, many believed in Him. So Jesus said to the Jews who had believed Him, "If you continue in My word, you really are My disciples. You will know the truth, and the truth will set you free."*
>
> —JOHN 8:30-32

ANDRE AGASSI GAVE PRACTICALLY HIS WHOLE LIFE TO TENNIS. HE dominated the game, earning the rank of number one in the world. At his retirement, some described Agassi as the biggest worldwide star in the sport's history. You would expect him to love the game. But in his autobiography, *Open*, he begins *and ends* the book screaming, "I hate tennis, hate it with a dark and secret passion, and always have."[1] How can this be?

The first clue is found in the opening page. He begins his book with a quote from the Dutch Postimpressionist painter Vincent van Gogh. In a letter to his brother in July of 1880, Van Gogh wrote: "One cannot always tell what it is that keeps us shut in, confines us, seems to bury us, but still one feels certain barriers, certain gates, certain walls. Is all this imagination, fantasy? I do not think so. And then one asks: My God! Is it for long, is it forever, is it for eternity?"[2]

What a scary thought! Unfortunately, Van Gogh could never escape his sense of entrapment. Ten years later, he walked into a wheat field and shot himself.

Agassi obviously resonates with Van Gogh. He too feels trapped and wonders if he will ever get out. He is handcuffed to a racquet by an abusive father and terrorized for most of his formative years by a demanding ball machine. He grows up confined to a court and its four walls. It has been ingrained in him that no matter how much you win, if you're not the last person to win, you're a loser. There is no escape.

THE RELIGIOUS TIE THAT BINDS

All of us have experiences that confine, close us in. Jesus steps into a similar world when He comes. Humanity is walled in by sin. An open heaven is the first signal that release is at hand. Things once closed are now open. But some prefer the walls, while others are oblivious to the cells they inhabit. In John 7, Jesus's brothers are unaware of their own self-imposed restrictions. They are bound to a purposeless existence. John 8 reveals a similiar, if not deeper, bondage.

Ironically, they head to a festival commemorating their freedom. Jesus waits, and then secretly follows (v. 10). We're not told if they again connect. As Jesus makes the long journey south, He is surrounded by other pilgrims. There is anticipation as they make the long climb and hear the sounds of celebration in the distance. The three traditional feasts are full of ritual, but the Feast of Tabernacles is the ultimate party. The agricultural year is over, and now they can relax and enjoy the harvest. There are festivities and processionals in which people are doing the wave. Women are comparing their ethrogs and lulabs, and men are sizing up this year's sukkah designs. Teenagers are checking out the new crop.

If you can get past all of the noise and clamor, you might also hear the sound of chains. There is the feel of confined spaces, not because of traffic gridlock or population density. People are squeezed in by rules and regulations of a religious type. There is the ubiquitous presence of religious police (v. 11). Jerusalem is the epicenter of Jewish religion. Over the years, religious leaders have become "small-minded, obsessively concerned with all the minute details of personal behavior."[3] It's impossible to escape their intimidation and legalism. They are an ominous presence, keeping people under watchful surveillance.[4] With a word, they can expel one from the synagogue, the heart of Jewish community life (9:22). Living within the four walls of a tennis court seems expansive in comparison.

Jesus has come into this oppressive scene to declare that the heavens have opened and the prisoners have been set free. To use the language of Jabez in the Old Testament, a man who longed for a more expansive life (1 Chron. 4:10), the boundaries have been extended. Are we aware of this? Over the coming days, He will encounter the legalists (aka the Pharisees and scribes) as well as those who make up a broader segment, the crowd. John places all of them under the category "the Jews." They advance the plot in this ongoing story; they are a dark cloud on the horizon of nearly every conversation.

The religious authorities fear any loss of status, influence, and control. From the beginning of Jesus's ministry, the priests and Levites were sent to investigate. Jesus stepped onto their turf and created turmoil (John 2:15), so the Jews began to question His authority. Nicodemus, a Pharisee, found it necessary to do a background check (3:1). Satellite photos revealed shifting baptism counts (4:1), and wiretaps revealed that Jesus was planning to destroy the temple (2:19). In one conversation, He even referred to God as His own Father (5:18). If this were not enough, He violated the Sabbath in a brazen way, with no regard for religious protocol, announcing freedom for the captives and doing things like healing people, for God's sake! So they watch closely, hoping to anticipate His every move (Luke 14:1).

R. Alan Culpepper notes that "just as the other Johannine characters carry representative value, so do" the religious leaders.[5] Paradoxically, they symbolize unbelief. They epitomize John 1:11: "He came to His own, and His own people did not receive Him." In his chapter on "Characters," Culpepper's description explains why their conversation with Jesus becomes increasingly acrimonious. They may have the appearance of righteousness, but in reality they

- love darkness rather than light (3:19);
- have never really heard or seen the Father (5:37);
- do not have the love of God in them (5:42);
- are hardened by their own choices and God's judgment (6:65);
- search the Scriptures, but they cannot understand them (5:39–40);
- have no consciousness of an open heaven, for they are from below (8:23); and
- prefer the glory of men to the glory of God (12:43).[6]

The Pharisees serve to warn us what happens when faith becomes rigid, when a courageous heart becomes impressed with its adherence to rules. These religious men were once the heroes of the faith, preserving the temple and standing for righteousness. Over time, they devolved into a political interest group dedicated to reform, order, and strict devotion to the covenant. They added their own regulations, becoming the enemies of true godliness. They also became very good at shaming. They're an advance warning system of what happens when faith becomes rigid, something fresh sours, and shepherds turn into wardens.

THE MESSIANIC PRESENCE THAT FREES

The rumors are flying that Jesus may be in the city, but where is He? His brothers are here. Will He show His face? Jesus slips into the shadows (7:10). Not until the middle of the feast does Jesus step out and enter the temple complex. He is not so dangerous this time. Instead of cleaning house, He turns to teaching (7:14). There is no identifiable text, no podcast to listen to, but we can imagine. Perhaps it's the same text He turned to in the synagogue at Nazareth (Luke 4:16–19). It is the perfect theme for a festival recalling liberation from Egypt. It is the time to celebrate the presence of God. Jesus has come as the King to announce His kingdom, release the captives, and set free those who are oppressed by earthly kingdoms. The people crowding the streets of Jerusalem are oppressed by an empire that coerces, and they stagger under a religious system that harasses. Many hate their four walls.

Before the Syrian civil war, I occasionally traveled to Damascus and Aleppo. I remember watching men sitting on park benches with vacant stares. This is what police states do—they swallow men's souls. I saw it in many of their faces. They could not get beyond the walls. They had no concept of an open heaven. I'm sure many of them also asked, "Will it be like this for eternity?" I'm guessing that's what we'd have seen in the city parks of Jerusalem.

Jesus comes to announce that however earthly affairs may oppress, heaven has opened. His presence has aired out the musty space.

Messengers from heaven are at work. The Spirit of God is moving with dramatic and unpredictable force. He offers life in all of its abundance (John 10:10). It is possible to have a foretaste of eternity's freedom now. This is the core of the message Jesus preaches.

THE MIXED RESPONSE TO A SINGULAR MESSAGE

Some find Jesus's teaching astonishing (7:15). His command of the text is startling. His words are precise and His delivery is spot-on. Like Nicodemus, those with credentials are both surprised and envious, wondering where He completed His degree. Was it University of Rome? Alexandria Seminary? Chicago Divinity School? Others are dismayed and concerned at His departure from the prescribed messages for Jewish services. Isn't He aware of the Book of Common Prayer? Most are simply confused.

Like a church foyer after a controversial guest speaker, there is a lot of chatter. Jesus gets a mixed review, just as He does today. Some are willing to give Jesus a thumbs-up (v. 12). The signs He performs suggest He might even be the prophet. No one will verbalize it beyond a whisper, but He could be the long-awaited Messiah (vv. 40–41). When Jesus later makes His way into Jerusalem for the Passover Feast, these are the ones who will lay down palm branches and shout "Hosanna!" (12:13). At that moment, they will join other Jews, like the disciples of Jesus, who embrace Jesus as the Son of God.

Those who see themselves as religiously together, the Pharisees, view this believing segment of the crowd as vacuous and unsophisticated (7:47–48). They speak in condescending tones: "What do these primitive airheads know? Listen to their drivel as they talk in hushed speech. No doubt they lift most of their opinions from tabloids. They chat online and post the most inane stuff on Facebook. They are easily deceived by charlatans like Jesus." As far as the religious leaders are concerned, most of these in the crowd can go to hell (v. 49).

Others in the throng do not feel the same level of animosity, but they are not so impressed with Jesus either. They may not be pious, but they are in agreement with the religious hierarchy. Jesus is a threat, a misguided man who is either demon-possessed or paranoid (v. 20). At best, He is some brilliant young master of deception, wearing His clergy apparel to impress the hearers. Is He simply another Frank W. Abagnale Jr., seeing if we can catch Him if we can? They have had enough Sunday school to know that Jesus is just another Galilean "messiah" whose roots do not square with their understanding of Scripture.

Like a roving reporter at a major event, John seems to go from one set of people to another. Amidst the favorable and unfavorable are the uncommitted, along for the ride, drawn to the excitement. They listen but are simply confused (7:25, 40). To be sure, He is a crazy mix of abnormal and normal. He seems to be quite decent. He has the look of a prophet and puts on a pretty good show. A nice man, even if He says strange things like, "Where I'm going, you cannot come" (8:21). What does this mean? Where the heck is He going? Off to kill Himself (v. 22)? Perhaps a dysfunctional home explains His odd behavior. Word is out that His own family once attempted an intervention (Mark 3:21).

Maybe He is some sort of alien from beyond—a real whack job. If He has some messianic complex, so be it. If He leads some people astray, it shows their gullibility. Just how dangerous can a homeless man be, one who is unemployed, unmarried, and uneducated? On balance, He brings some entertainment to the stale routines of the festival, so—no harm, no foul. But people with these opinions aren't part of the inner crowd, so they keep a lot of this to themselves (John 7:13). They decline to be interviewed by John.

THE MOOD GROWS DARKER

The plot thickens. Where is this going? John is setting up a conversation that will speak to both the requirements and the benefits of an open heaven. Will the reader stay with the story? A story critic might say John's narrative sprawls: it sags, grinds its gears, and at times almost crashes from frantic multitasking. Protagonists and antagonists go at one another in dramatic dialogue. In theater, it is known as "flyting." The Jews and Jesus continue a long war of words, exchanging curses and insults. It's a show of wits. To the perceptive audience, the irony is that those who are the greatest obstacle to truth are often the most devout. The greater irony is that "Jesus achieves his goals while his fortune apparently changes for the worse."[7] The greatest irony is that by having Jesus crucified one day, they will be lifting Him up (3:14).

As we listen in on the lengthy exchange between Jesus and the Jews, it's like hearing arguments in court between two opponents. They occasionally switch plaintiff and defendant roles, though the Jews have to maintain the position that their learning, their influence, and their political power are superior.[8] Following proper procedures, Jesus testifies that He is the Light of the World (8:12). The Jews shout, "Objection! He is testifying about Himself. There are no witnesses to corroborate His story" (see v. 13). Jesus retorts, "The Father who sent Me testifies about Me" (v. 18). God Himself is the Judge who will settle His case.

Some of the uncommitted begin to shift. Convinced by Jesus's testimony, they believe in Him (v. 30). There emerges at this festival a core of believers. What Jesus testifies about Himself seems to match the evidence. Drawing upon their stories and religious feasts, He connects the dots and draws all the lines to Himself. He is the One from above, the Living Water, the Light of the World.

At the water-pouring rite, a central part of the Feast of Tabernacles in which the people recall God's provision of water in the wilderness, Jesus invites people to come and drink (7:37). When the day draws to a close and light gives way to darkness, Jesus again interposes Himself into the ceremonial tradition and declares, "I am the light of the world" (8:12). His miraculous signs keep pointing this direction; His association with the Father is convincing. He speaks as a prophet, pointing out the real death lines that hover over unrepentant hearts.

He does this with the candor born of anguish and passion, but there is also a soft tone of grace. He is different; He speaks of something otherworldly. He sets the parameters for godliness without being legalistic. He creates real hope that something of heaven has opened, connecting God with humanity. Many are moved to come down the aisle.

A PERFECTLY GOOD MOMENT UP IN SMOKE

But this moment has déjà vu written all over it. Jesus does not immediately embrace those who come forward and fill out the response card. Just like He has in the past, He does not give Himself to an adoring crowd (2:24; 6:26). Jesus is suspicious of initial enthusiasm, of outward professions of faith. Those who claim to follow Jesus must come to terms with the fact that He is looking for disciples, not decisions. Before He's willing to take the adoring crowd into his inner circle, He wants them (and us) to know what life under an open heaven requires. We are called to acknowledge our sin and become His disciples.

Discipleship Explained

What constitutes authentic discipleship? What separates wannabes from actual followers of Jesus? Is a disciple some deluxe, heavy-duty Christian, a luxury-model follower especially padded, textured, streamlined, and empowered for the fast lane on the straight and narrow road? Is Jesus merely adding to the existing rules and regulations, further confining one's life?

To those expressing interest and possible commitment, Jesus answers with simple clarity. A disciple is a person who continues in God's Word. And Jesus makes no assumptions, no matter our pedigree: "If you continue in My word [and it is not certain you will], you really are My disciples [which you may or may not be]" (v. 31). But what does this mean? Why is abiding in His Word the true mark of a disciple, and where does it lead?

The word in verse 31 rendered "continue" or "abide" is a simple verb expressing the closest possible relationship.[9] Jesus unpacks its meaning in John 15. At its core, it means to remain in one place, to make oneself at home.

I live on a street named Harvest. My home is there, and it is a place of rest and security. I continue to explore its boundaries and live out to its edges. It has become a part of my identity. Living in the Word is something like that. It suggests finding a place to settle, becoming deeply familiar with it, and starting to make needed changes there. The Word opens the curtains, slides open the windows, chases out the stale air, and lets in the rays of an open heaven.

"Abide" might sound like a rather harmless requirement to this crowd, but they may not realize it carries the cost of continuing, of persevering. To use Eugene Peterson's language, remaining in the Word is to have "a long obedience in the same direction."[10] A true disciple stays at it, even if it

- requires a disciplined schedule of reading;
- touches a nerve and calls you out;
- may not seem at present to live up to its promises;
- goes contrary to how we would naturally do things;
- does not line up with your values;
- doesn't make sense;
- demands to have ultimate authority over life decisions; or
- costs you your life.

But this is only the half of it. As we abide in His Word, the Word must also abide in us. It must gain permanent occupancy; it cannot be simply an overnight guest. For it to abide in us, the Word must come as an owner—not a renter. If I am a true disciple, the Word has access to every room, every corner, and every closet of my life. It rearranges the furniture, cleans up the mess, and does an occasional refurbish.

Take notice. It doesn't take long to discover that there is something uncongenial about the Word. The prophet Jeremiah found that when the Word gets inside and makes itself at home, it also demands to get out. He likens it to a fire that leads to extreme heartburn (Jer. 20:9). John the apostle had a similar experience. When he encountered the Word, it initially tasted sweet, but as it worked its way deeper into his interior, he got bitterly sick (Rev. 10:10). It woos, then it reprimands; it establishes us, and then it prunes us. It makes claims on the whole life.

So exactly how is it that abiding in the Word authenticates those who follow Jesus? Jesus could have chosen other things (if you sell everything and give to the church, if you pray six hours a day, if you preach the kingdom of God, etc.). The Word, however, has a particular transformative power. J. B. Phillips, a paraphraser of the New Testament, likened the experience of translating Scripture to "an electrician re-wiring an ancient house, without being able to 'turn the mains off.'"[11] The Word brings one into the main-switch presence of God, where one comes to know Him in deeper ways. One also comes to know oneself in more profound ways. Having been exposed to Scripture, we discover things about ourselves we are incapable of knowing on our own:

- How to treat the world (Gen. 2:15)
- What the purpose of our existence is (Acts 20:24)
- How to love people (1 Cor. 13:4–7)
- Who our neighbor is (Luke 10:36–37)
- How to find peace (Phil. 4:6–7)
- How to stay married (Eph. 5:21)
- How to pray (Luke 11:1–4)
- How to invest (Matt. 6:19–20)
- What God requires of us (Mic. 6:8)

There's more. If we're paying attention, the Word will rebuke us when we get out of line. It reprimands me when I begin to move outside of reality (Ps. 127:1) or become enamored with my sense of importance (Ps. 39:6). It admonishes me when I start to be infatuated with things I have no business loving (James 5:1). It calls for change—for true repentance.

This explains our tendency to smooth the rough edges of the Word so that it conforms to our way of thinking. We configure it to suit our personal theology or personal ethics. We try to sand it down, hoping to avoid the sharp splinters of reproof. But God's Word does rebuke—not because it is mean or condemning, but because any sin breaks God's law, breaks the peace, breaks the people who do it, and breaks the heart of God.

To live in the Word, then, is to accept it on its terms, not ours. God's Word must be the first word of the day, since prayer at its best is answering speech—an intimate dialogue in which God first speaks. We must read Scripture as God's revelation, as spiritual writing that requires spiritual reading—reading for transformation, not information. We must read it as if our lives depend on it, for they do.

Discipleship's Benefits Laid Out

Over time, the Word does renovate, transform. We are less inclined to fall for the latest fad. A Word-informed mind discerns the shifting terrain, the traps laid out for us. The heart recognizes truth (John 8:32). This is because the author of the Word is the God of truth, whose words are therefore true. They are the index of reality; they show us things as they really are. Every command is true. Every promise is true, for God keeps them.[12] Abiding in the Word makes us true, real, authentic.

But here is the best part. Abiding in the truth has a way of setting us free. "You will know the truth, and the truth will set you free" (v. 32). The chains start to loosen, old habits begin to release their grip, the chain-link fences surrounding our court are pushed back, and we begin to realize the breadth and depth of an open heaven. One need no longer be confined to

- a life hoping to earn God's favor;
- bondage to a condemning spirit;

- debilitating fear and worry;
- insecurity and tentativeness;
- slavery to our old nature;
- hopelessness and helplessness;
- egoism and autocratic behavior;
- foolishness and general jackassery;
- dullness, boredom, and life without purpose; or
- sin's wages, sin's authority, and sin's power.

We are set free from living in obedience to idols. We are set free of foolish enablement and free to live full-out a full salvation (1 Peter 2:2). It is all part of why Jesus came to this world—to set us free. He will send the Spirit, whose mission is the same ("where the Spirit of the Lord is, there is freedom," 2 Cor. 3:17). Freedom is what new life under an open heaven is about.

Even imprisonment for one's faith cannot change this. John knew incarceration. Banished to a ten-by-six-mile island thirty-seven miles from land, the apostle had a bitter taste of political confinement. Nonetheless, under an open heaven, he could live with a certain abandonment. Christ's freedom transcends any environment ungodly governments might wish to consign godly people to.

Jesus's words are such good news. You would think these respondents are shouting "Amen!" to every word of Jesus. He has given a promise that everyone longs to hear—we do not have to live imprisoned lives. In her wonderful book *Unbroken*, Laura Hillenbrand recounts the scene when prisoners of war in Japan received the message from an American plane flying overhead that the Second World War was over:

> In seconds, masses of naked men were stampeding out of the river and up the hill. As the plane turned loops above, the pilot waving, the POWs swarmed into the compound, out of their minds with relief and rapture. Their fear of the guards, of the massacre they had so long awaited, was gone, dispersed by the roar and muscle

of the bomber. The prisoners jumped up and down, shouted, and sobbed. Some scrambled onto the camp roofs, waving their arms and singing out their joy to the pilot above. Others piled against the camp fence and sent it crashing over. Someone found matches, and soon, the entire length of fence was burning. The Japanese shrank back and withdrew.[13]

All anyone could think was, "I'm free! I'm free! I'm free!"

Discipleship's Benefits Blasted

At this point, one would expect a similar "We're free!" response to Jesus's message. As wonderful as it is to celebrate the Feast of Tabernacles, freedom from Egypt pales in comparison to the freedom Jesus offers. The Word sets our souls free. But instead, His last five words hit a nerve. As in Galilee, the crowd turns on Jesus, only this time it is sudden and deeply antagonistic. They're insulted (John 8:33). By their response, you would think Jesus has just told them they are pig-eating Gentiles who wear tattoos, work a sixteen-hour day on the Sabbath, and hang out with prostitutes.

Is it the call for discipleship? This happens in the church. Some who claim to believe are not inclined to go further. "What? There's more than just saying the sinner's prayer? I give on occasion—isn't this enough? I come at least once a month. Are you expecting me to turn radical? Like some Jesus freak? Can't we just pay our minimal association dues and leave it at that?"

Perhaps they are offended by the insinuation they are not free. "Are you associating us with those who muck out the stalls and wash travelers' feet?" Someone else yells, "How can You say, 'You will become free'? Slaves are the ones without their freedom. They are bought and sold. They have no credentials, no documents, and no rights. Are You suggesting that I am like those who do the menial and mundane: wave ostrich-feather fans over pashas, serve the meals, and pick up one's dry cleaning? Excuse me, Jesus, but I don't serve anyone's wine demands and wipe anyone's disgusting feet. I have never been a slave to anyone!"

Part of the resentment might be based on this misguided notion that they are not abiding in His Word (vv. 31–32). It sounds like Jesus is under the assumption they are Torah deficient. Who wants to be told they don't have the truth? Can't Jesus see the phylacteries they wear during morning prayers? Does He not notice that the leather is practically worn out? Doesn't He realize they have memorized the Decalogue? When it comes to abiding, they are Law abiding. They have a dedicated pew in the synagogue. They do not need anyone suggesting that their faith is less than mature. Who is this aspirant from some backwater town telling them they do not have their act together?

But it's deeper than that. Telling them what they need to do next sounds like Jesus is questioning their very identity. Doesn't He realize they are purebreds? They have their papers. When they go through customs, they stand in the Abrahamic line. Unlike slaves, who have no freedom of movement, no papers, and no permanence, these people have their citizenship. Something of familial permanence is engraved on their souls (vv. 33–35). They are in the household forever.

A GODWARD MOVEMENT THROWN IN REVERSE

The din of the crowd is becoming loud and heated; voices strain in anger as they hurl their insults and demand an explanation. No one likes to be judged, and these "believers" don't want to be told they live in a confined space. They are not willing to admit to the human condition—that all of us are in bondage to our sin (v. 34). This is always sin's aim—to chain us to addictive behaviors, lock us up, and eventually possess our souls.[14] Alvin Plantinga compares sin to "a polluted river that keeps branching and rebranching," "a parasite . . . that keeps tapping its host," and an evil that masquerades as goodness.[15] (As Martin Buber puts it, "Nothing hides the face of God more than religion.")[16] Imagine the howls if Jesus said they needed the saving work of the cross and the generous act of divine forgiveness.

So what is really happening here? Something that is played out every week when religious people congregate. Peterson describes the "tug-of-war" that takes place each Sunday when pastor and parishioner come together.[17] The contest is over conflicting views. Most people see themselves as pretty much together, having a "divine inner core" that needs regular awakening. Sure, they could be more patient. No one is perfect. There is the occasional excess. But God accepts us for who we are, just as we should accept everyone for who they are.

But pastors see people differently. They must. In theological terms, people are sinners. And because sin aims for mastery, people are in bondage to their sin—more than they know. A prophetic voice is needed. Not someone who panders to their wishes. Those who seek to appease are like those who give candy to a diabetic, Big Macs to those with heart disease, and low interest rates to Wall Street.

Instead, there is a terrible need for an intervention. That is what Jesus is doing with this crowd, what Jeremiah was doing in Jerusalem, and what Paul will do before Felix and Agrippa. Even in this crowd of "believers," sin has to be called out, for the consequences are catastrophic. Sin chooses a path that deviates from God's will. It smears relationships, betrays a holy bond. Only when we acknowledge our sinfulness can we begin to experience God's amazing grace, His forgiveness and restoration.

The good news is that under an open heaven there is more than enough grace (Rom. 5:20). There is release and newfound freedom that comes with forgiveness and time spent in God's Word (John 8:36). But the "believers" in John 8 are not free because, for all of their self-righteous posturing, they do not want to acknowledge their heart condition. Jesus and His Word are really not welcome in their hearts (v. 37). Their papers are enough (v. 39).

Sadly, the conversation turns darker. They glare at Jesus. Can you see them? As a cyclist, I am good at glaring. When a motorist with a case of "bike blindness" crosses into my lane, pushes me off the shoulder, or ignores my presence at intersections, I have this defiant stare. If looks could kill, those drivers would be on life support. So here, Jesus has crossed into their lane. The crowds glare and scream insults at Jesus, "You are a bastard!" (see v. 41). "You are such a demon-possessed S@#!@#n!"(v. 48). No doubt this was the Jews' rhetorical flamethrower of choice.

It is hard to imagine, in a shame-based culture, more offensive language. Their hard-heartedness has caused them to become deaf to God's voice (v. 43). Jesus may as well be speaking to a block wall. They think they are bearers of the truth, but in reality they have cast their lives with the father of lies (v. 44). And he is the ultimate taskmaster.

Reversals are a significant part of the story of John.[18] Strangers become followers (4:39), followers become strangers (6:66), and (ironically) believers become unbelievers (8:59). Jesus is received as the Messiah and denounced as a blasphemer. People are blinded by the darkness as well as by the Light. The crowd will shout "Hosanna!" and then choose Barabbas (18:40). Peter will betray Jesus and then be restored (21:19). Jesus will be crucified, and then He will rise from the grave (20:17). People will be offered life under an open heaven of God's making, but they will choose death in a confined prison of their own construction.

IT'S TIME TO LIVE FREE

A few years ago, we purchased a Lakeland terrier. It was really by acci-dent. We were looking at another dog, and in an offhand conversation we heard about Brea. She lived in a kennel for nearly a year. Bred for show, she broke her leg in the first month after birth. Any hopes of making it to Westminster were dashed. She was practically given to us with the assurance that we could bring her back to the breeder if we weren't satisfied. All we wanted was a great pet. At first Brea was tentative. She too had lived in a world surrounded by fences to keep her from running loose. Today, she romps on our two-acre property with the fury of a racehorse. It's as if she is making up for lost time, for she never quits running.

This is what Jesus came to bring us: the freedom to run free, get outside the walls of shame and defeat, and make up for lost time. This is what truth enables us to do. This is life under an open heaven, a precursor to an eternity without materials used to build walls and court fences. And this, I believe, is what an Andre Agassi or a Vincent van Gogh, and everyone else, is ultimately searching for, but not so many find. For to find true freedom is to experience grace, which begins with acknowledging the sin that holds us in.

QUESTIONS

1. *Is it possible believers can become unbelievers? Why or why not?*

2. *Why did the words "the truth will set you free" so offend?*

3. *How has the Word set you free?*

9

LIFE IS ABOUT SEEING THE LIGHT

A Conversation with the Man Born Blind

JOHN 9:1–41

> *After He said these things He spit on the ground, made some mud from the saliva, and spread the mud on his eyes. "Go," He told him, "wash in the pool of Siloam" (which means "Sent"). So he left, washed, and came back seeing.*
>
> —JOHN 9:6–7

PERHAPS YOU REMEMBER AN EXPERIMENT INVOLVING THE FAMOUS violinist Joshua Bell. As *The Washington Post* reported, "He emerged from the metro at the L'Enfant Plaza station [in Washington, DC,] and positioned himself against a wall beside a trash basket."[1] He was nondescript, wearing jeans, a long-sleeved T-shirt, and a Washington Nationals baseball cap. And then he began to play the violin, performing six classical pieces, "masterpieces that have endured for centuries." It was soaring music befitting cathedrals.

Meanwhile, 1,097 people, mostly bureaucrats, passed by during the next forty-three minutes. Some were on cell phones; others listened to their own music. Most assumed this was some mere wannabe artist whose stage will never go beyond the street. But this was one of the finest classical musicians in the world, an internationally acclaimed virtuoso, using a violin worth more than $3.5 million.

Some tossed in a few quarters, some dimes and nickels, even some pennies. It all amounted to just under thirty-two dollars. A few stopped momentarily, but the vast majority walked past without ever noticing that here was someone whose music commands over a thousand dollars a minute.

The experiment was conducted to ask this one question: "In a banal setting at an inconvenient time, would beauty transcend?"

OUR BLINDNESS TO DIVINE PRESENCE

Jesus steps into the ordinary of this world and reveals something of His splendor, expressing His wisdom, His power, His goodness, and His light. If people stop to truly listen, they will witness His brilliance. They will catch a glimpse of an open heaven, gaining a taste of eternity. But few really notice. Even the believing. Because of a deep blindness, most miss seeing the greater things Jesus promised.

Again we should ask, "Do we?"

It's not that God is conducting His own experiment to see if people will notice His appearance. Jesus comes, not to play His music, but to give life. He comes to remove the things that blind us. He comes to the festival and announces He is the Light and makes this promise that those who follow Him will not walk in darkness (John 8:12). It follows that He then goes to a blind man.

As with the other stories, John sets the context for the conversation. This one is to the point: "As He was passing by, He saw a man" (John 9:1). Given what precedes, we expect to read that Jesus is actually running by, for the Jews in Jerusalem are full of mounting rage. Even the "believing" are determined to splatter His blood. But Jesus's ways are not dictated by the plans and passions of humanity. There is never any panic. He moves with certain deliberateness. His perfect will requires that He be with this man. And this chapter, for me, serves as a breath of fresh air. Alienation is replaced with reception.

The darkness attempts to diminish the Light, but Jesus diminishes the darkness. Wherever He goes, He sheds light. In this story, Jesus encounters a man whose whole life has been darkness. He and the paralytic of chapter 5 are like two lines of synonymous poetry, one paralleling the other:

- Both men are nameless.
- Both men are in a desperate condition, consigned to begging.
- Both men have known suffering for most of their lives.
- Both men are approached by Jesus.
- Both healings happen apart from faith.
- Both healings occur on the Sabbath.
- Both men look to the pool for healing.
- Both men suffer at the hands of the religious.
- Both men are unsure where Jesus has disappeared to and who He is.
- Both men again meet Jesus.
- Both men are given the opportunity to address deeper issues.[2]

The blind man cannot connect voices with faces, sounds with images. I have a son diagnosed with Asperger's syndrome. It has its own blindness. His visual center has been active since birth, but he cannot easily read faces. His world is largely black and white. The blind man in this chapter can read nothing. The only color he knows is black; the only day he experiences is night; the only place he lives is on the streets. He has no career, no marriage, and no income. He knows nothing of governmental assistance, food stamps, and health-care. There is no hope until Jesus passes by. The One who declares, "As long as I am in the world, I am the light of the world," steps in with divine intentionality and changes everything (9:5).

OUR BLINDNESS TO SUFFERING'S REASONS

Like other conversations, John 9 unfolds as a drama, this one presented in seven scenes. Discourse goes back and forth. The disciples suddenly appear on the way out of Jerusalem (John 9:2). Maybe they have been there all along, but John often leaves them out when Jesus is interacting with others. It's like watching for a cameo appearance by Alfred Hitchcock. Maybe they were there when Nicodemus arrived, when Jesus spent time with His brothers, or when He went to the festival. Maybe they laid low as things became tense. Did they form a barrier around Jesus when people picked up their rocks? Or were they off for food as was the case in Samaria?

Misunderstanding is part of the disciples' pattern.[3] They confuse metaphors and the literal (2:21; 11:12). They do not understand what sustains Jesus (4:32–33). In this case, they do not get the connection between sin and suffering. When they see the blind man, their interest is less personal and more theological. They want to know, "Who sinned?"

It's an odd question. Did they ask this every time Jesus approached a suffering soul? What does it matter? Why is this the only part they play in the John 9 story? Are they simply foils who potentially thwart the plot?[4]

Was it his father's former life of sexual addiction or a mother's previous struggles with drugs that led to this judgment? Can this blindness be traced to something prenatal? Like Esau, did this man do something sinful in the womb? Was it asbestos or lead in the paint? Can some method of divination get to the root? They are looking for reasons to assign blame. They press Jesus—whose fault is this?

Most cultures make these same assumptions. I have seen this, particularly in places like India where the link between sin and suffering is taken to its logical extreme. In the doctrine of karma, everyone is in a long process of working out the consequences of sin. Visiting a leprosy hospital one day, I found it remarkable that the surrounding community seemed to have little to no empathy. People walked by unaware and unmoved by the hospital's existence. In their worldview, these patients were getting what they deserved. Any help would actually interfere.

In our own culture, we are pretty good at mimicking the disciples' curiosity. We want to know what causes suffering. We want to pin down the sin. Was it her obesity and her lack of control that caused the heart attack? Was it the need to rely on nicotine that caused the cancer? Was it some secret sin or some divine displeasure that led to this untimely death? Was it the long bitterness that led to the colitis? Was it his selfish insistence that Tabasco sauce be poured on everything that led to early dementia? All things have a cause.

It's not that the question raised before Jesus has no basis. Suffering is the natural consequence of life in a fallen world. The Bible often connects these dots, assigning affliction to wrongdoing. Miriam, Uzziah, Gehazi, and Jeroboam were all judged with leprosy for their sin. The psalmist often lamented over the illness caused by his own indiscretions (see Ps. 38:3). Ananias and Sapphira died for their deceit and greed (Acts 5:1–10). Some members of the Corinthian congregation went to their early grave for their version of fencing the table (1 Cor. 11:27–32). Even John writes that there is sin that leads to death (1 John 5:16).

The disciples have been trained to think this way. Their own blindness is ingrained in them. They were raised under rabbinic teaching that stated, *"There is no death without sin, and there is no suffering without iniquity"* (Talmud, Shabbat 55a, emphasis added). Even Jesus warned the paralytic that his decision to maintain his sinful ways would lead to a worse condition (John 5:14). So, like Job's friends, the disciples want to know the explanation for this man's affliction. Maybe there is a lesson to be learned. Maybe Peter will tone down his domineering ways and Judas will quit pilfering the funds if they realize there are consequences.

I wonder if the blind man overhears them. If so, it is probably nothing new. People, especially of the spiritual kind, often assume they know the reasons and have the remedies. During my doctoral work at Dallas Theological Seminary, I rented a room from a saintly family on the northeast edge of town. He was a retired dentist and she handled the landlord responsibilities. In my initial days, Mrs. K. would knock on the door in the early morning and bring me fresh oatmeal. She became a second mom, checking in on me, praying for me, and stopping in on occasion to see if the professors were merciful (some were). Unfortunately, midway through that year, Mrs. K. came down with cancer. There were countless prayers, but her condition only worsened.

One day, she called me to come by and pray. She had been crying. On the table was a letter from a well-meaning, though terribly blind, religious sister who had come to the conclusion that all of this could change if Mrs. K. demonstrated more faith. The concern of these disciples reminds me of this sister.

D. A. Carson in his book *How Long, O Lord?* writes that "it is almost always wrong, not to say pastorally insensitive and theologically stupid, to add to the distress of those who are suffering illness, impending death, or bereavement, by charging them with either: (a) some secret sin they have not confessed, or (b) inadequate faith, for otherwise they would certainly have been healed. The first charge wrongly assumes that there is always a link between a specific ailment and a specific sin; the second wrongly assumes that it is always God's will to heal any ailment, instantly, and that he is blocked from doing so only by inadequate or insufficient faith."[5]

Jesus's response sheds some light into their (and our) dark assumptions. He resists the popular urge to blame victims of misfortune. And so must we. He wants them to see that this man is not judged; he is loved.[6] God gave the same message to Job's friends, but they didn't get it. Sometimes sin has nothing to do with our desperate condition. Sometimes our pain is simply the result of our mortality (2 Cor. 5:4). Sometimes there is some thorn in the flesh to keep us humble (2 Cor. 12:7). In some cases, our malady has nothing to do with us and everything to do with the malicious work of Satan (Luke 13:16).

In the case of the blind man, it has everything to do with God, His mission, His glory, and His further description of life under an open heaven (John 9:3; see also 11:4). As long as we live under an open heaven, we must give our best energies to serving rather than explaining (9:4). This is how Jesus reframes the issue. We must give our core efforts to restoring sight, not explaining blindness—advancing the kingdom, not exegeting it.

OUR BLINDNESS TO GOD'S WAYS

Jesus goes to work (vv. 6–7). Like John 1:1, this passage takes us back to Genesis. This is the way of God. He takes dust and breathes in life (Gen. 2:7). Jesus takes of the clay, mixes it with the life of His saliva, and smears the mud on this man's eyes. One wonders, "Can't He simply speak into the man's condition as He did with Bartimaeus?" But God works with all of us in different ways. There is no set miracle template. Maybe if this man had approached Jesus, coming with a faith that he could be healed, his healing would have been immediate like with Bartimaeus (Mark 10:47–52). But he doesn't. Jesus approaches this man and invites him to be part of the action. He needs to receive this "anointing" and wash out the mud before he can see.

So he is sent to the Pool of Siloam and comes back seeing (John 9:7). We quickly move on, but wait. Slow down. The pool is on the south side of the old city next to Hezekiah's tunnel. It took some care-ful navigation. Still does. The hills are steep and the terrain is diffi-cult. How did he get there? The Pool of Siloam was one of Herod's city projects. Those of means would come to be refreshed. Picture businessmen at midday discussing deals, wives of affluence enjoying the ambience, and those kids not obsessed with their iPhones playing in the pool. And suddenly, a homeless type comes stumbling in with mud-caked eyes. It would have been unnerving. Watching him wash his eyes in the pristine fountains would have been a bit digusting. How did he get in?

We must also slow down and imagine what it would be like to immediately gain sight for the first time. We can't. In her chapter "Seeing," Annie Dillard writes about cases where people born with cataracts see colors and images for the first time.[7] "Form, distance, and size were so many meaningless syllables," and much of seeing is "tormentlingly difficult." We might assume everything was suddenly wonderful for this man who was healed, when actually he might have found the road back home far more challenging.

As long as we are reflecting, we might also consider another irony in John's gospel. In this same spot, one thousand years earlier, King David came to the edge of the city and was taunted by residents of Jerusalem: "You will never get in here. Even the blind and lame can repel you" (2 Sam. 5:6). Jesus, the Son of David, now enters the city and asserts His authority and power over the lame and the blind (John 5:8; 9:7).

As one would expect, the miracle of sight leaves the people won-dering. "Isn't this the man who sat begging?" (9:8). They too are in the dark. This is also part of the irony in John. They have passed by this man nearly every day. He is a regular fixture at the off-ramp, but they have their own blindness. But now, as he stands conversing with others, they are confused. Some are sure it is the same person; others are not so sure. They have never really looked closely at the man. But then, many of us tend to avert our eyes from things we don't want to see.

On my very first journey abroad, I taught at a seminary in Manila. I can still remember my first day of class. I was riding in the back seat of a beat-up taxi, barreling down the road toward school. I was thrilled at the opportunity. Here I was, so many miles from home, hearing different sounds, smelling distinctive scents, and seeing . . . seeing what I did not want to see. We were waiting at a stop, and a small boy, with a look of desperation, suddenly plunged his hands through the open window and asked for help. This was all rather new. I looked into his eyes, and in an unexplainable way, I saw my own son's eyes. We were soon on our way, but each day we took that route, I wanted to avert my eyes from seeing.

The blind man's neighbors are now looking. If this is the same man, then what just happened? How did this happen? Some new miracle drug marketed on late-night TV? Are there side effects—raised blood sugar, cognitive impairment, muscle damage, sexual impotence? Has he consulted his physician or healthcare specialist for advice? Or is there some divine activity at work?

Word spreads, and people continue to badger him. They are perplexed. They want to know how (v. 10). Who wouldn't have the same questions? There was no salve, no medication, and no special surgery for people born blind. There still is not. How is it a person blind since birth can now navigate his way around? The visual center in his brain has been dormant. He has never learned to see until this moment. Was his brain rewired? How can it comprehend the sudden flood of new information? How is there any resolution in the sight? It's all beyond anyone's ability to grasp. Still is!

Meanwhile, Jesus, as He is prone to do, disappears and is absent for the longest period recorded in the book of John. Just like His Father, there are times Jesus is elusive. Why does He do this? Who is this masked man?

This is who He is—He is God who does not force His presence on us. He moves in and out of the shadows. He is always at work, but we often do not see His ways or discern His works.

OUR BLINDNESS TO WHAT IS HAPPENING

We're beginning to get the routine down. Like the paralytic's healing, we know there should be a party. Something has just happened! Heaven has intersected with earth. It's time to give glory to God, and it should begin with friends and family. Spiritual shepherds should be calling for praise. But we know this won't happen. This is Pharisaic country, and there is a neighborhood watch. Religious protocol takes precedence.

No wonder Jesus likened them to children sitting in the marketplace, calling out to each other, "We played the flute for you, but you didn't dance" (Luke 7:32). Jesus played the music, but these party poopers are much more interested in legal procedures. So the neighbors take him to the authorities to be interrogated (John 9:13). The healed man will need to be stamped as legal.

It is here in the story that John adds the same suspense as in the healing in John 5. Those same ominous words found in 5:9 appear here: "The day . . . was a Sabbath" (9:14). Busted. Jesus has again violated the law. He has become a repeat offender. When arrested, His picture will be in the paper under the words "Serial Sabbath Breaker." He might be able to plead insanity, but most religious courts of law will convict Him.

The interrogation with the man leads to bewilderment. Was this man really blind (v. 18)? Obviously, the religious, on their way to work, have a history of averting their eyes as well. It leads to the next scene, the fourth scene. They hope he will show the same gutlessness as the paralytic, but he holds his own under the bright lighting. The Pharisees move on to speak with the man's parents (vv. 18–23). Mother and father are as mystified as the others.

One anticipates that the parents would be overcome with joy at the news of their son's healing. Maybe he can finally get a job, be productive, and find a wife. But the only emotion expressed is fear. Unfortunately, these invertebrates are just as intimidated as the community. They have their privileges to protect. All of their friends go to the synagogue. They are regulars at Wednesday night bingo, and they occasionally have the priest over for cocktails after the Sabbath. They have to be careful.

Sadly, they suffer their own visual impairment. They are sightless when it comes to parental responsibility. They cannot see their son's need for them to stand with him. Like everyone else, they prefer to keep low, avoid eye contact, and deflect the hard questions. They know about Jesus, but they recognize that anything they say about Him could be used against them. *All they can see are themselves and their self-preservation.* They will leave and defer the questions for someone else to answer (v. 21).

It all sets up the fifth scene, the most ironic scene of all. Again, the Pharisees interrogate the man born blind. Those perceived by the community as the seers, the most enlightened—the men in the know—are in the dark. These professional visionaries bump into walls and fall into ditches. Their heavy brows obscure their sight. These men who market illumination are the blind leading the blind. They keep asking the same questions, hoping for different answers (v. 26). They order the man to give glory to God. In classic Johannine irony, they "invoke the name of God to deny the work of God"![8]

They remind me of evening grosbeaks. My *Field Guide to Birds* says they are a stocky finch with a large, pale yellow bill.[9] They are found in conifer forests in the Northwest and forage mostly in trees for seeds and berries. They are also fond of sunflower seeds. This is why they have recently taken over our bird feeder at our cabin. They are attractive, interesting to observe, and stupid! In the past two weeks, eighteen (and counting) have flown into our windows. Every once in a while, as I type away, I hear this loud *bam!* Another victim. They keep flying in the wrong direction. Can't they see? Apparently not. And neither can these religious leaders (who are not so attractive and not at all fun to watch).

Their legalistic regulations get in the way. They cannot see the hand of God. They cannot see what is happening. They are blind to the words of Isaiah that announce a messiah will come to set the captives free and recover sight to the blind. Like the wedding guests at Cana, they are oblivious to the wine that has just been poured, the miracle that has just been performed. Like the Galilean crowd, they are clueless that the King of Kings is in their midst. They miss the fact that the Lord of the Sabbath is at work, and the best day to do works of mercy and grace and bring people into a more perfect rest is on the Sabbath!

OUR BLINDNESS TO BELIEF

But John 9 is less about the blind religious leaders and more about a man who now can see. Everything else in the story is background. The scene shifts to Jesus and the healed man (vv. 35–38). Just as with the paralytic who was healed, there is unfinished work to be done. *Until eternity, there is always unfinished work to be done.* Until we get to heaven, Jesus will occasionally seek us out. He may search for us and exhort us to stop sinning (5:14). He may warn us of the consequences when people choose to ignore Him. He will come into our present condition from time to time and comfort and challenge us. He will speak timely words of forgiveness and mercy. And, as in the case of the healed blind man, He will sometimes ask penetrating questions (9:35).

At the top of the list is this question: "Do you believe?" Belief and unbelief are "at the heart of the great Johannine divide that separates humanity."[10] It goes to the stated purpose of the book of John, "that you may believe Jesus is the Messiah" (20:31). Jesus wants to know if this man is convinced. Does he have faith? Some will claim to believe, but they really don't (8:31–59). Some will never really put their trust in Jesus (3:1–12). Many will vacillate (12:12; 19:15). So Jesus asks him—asks us—"Do you believe? Is it for the long haul?"

In this question, Jesus is telling this man that to be healed of physical blindness does not mean he can really see. Real sight is about moving from unbelief to belief (9:39). The healed man might have assumed a world where everyone but him could see. In reality, the whole world has a certain blindness. Jesus came and used many signs, but most refused to believe, for their eyes were blinded (12:37–40).

So it comes down to this question of whether one believes. "This is the work of God," Jesus told the crowd, "that you believe in the One He has sent" (6:29). This is what enables one to live the optimal life under an open heaven: "The one who believes in Me will also do the works that I do" (14:12).

In this question, we can hear God asking this man, "Do you believe I am not some mere shaman using homeopathic magic—that I am indeed the Son of Man? Do you believe I can heal more than your eyes? Do you believe that I can also touch your mind and heart and soul to see? Do you believe that, because heaven is open, you can now see the greater things? Do you believe I have this thing for you, such that I am willing to not only live for you but die for you? Will you entrust your life to Me? Will you abide in My Word? Will you be My disciple?"

It is reasonable to assume that every day, throughout the day, Jesus is asking the same question of us: "Do you believe in the Son of Man?" (see 6:35). Do I believe He has a word for me today if only I will hear? Do I believe my day will be different if I have prayed as He has taught us to pray? Am I convinced that those long unanswered requests—that easily lead to heartsickness—are always answered in the best possible way? Will I continue to believe, even if He leads me into the wilderness where things are feral? Do I believe that He is perfectly wise and good and powerful in everything He does? Do I really believe heaven is open? Can I truly see?

Unlike the paralytic, the man wants to believe, but he is not quite sure. He recognizes the familiar voice that told him to wash his eyes, but who is this "Son of Man"? Jesus could have made it easier. "Do you believe I am from God?" Or, "Are you convinced I am a prophet?" Jesus knows this man is already convinced of this (9:17, 33). What Jesus wants to know is if he believes Jesus is the Son of Man.

There is something obscure in the title. In John 12, the crowd will respond as the blind man, "Who is this Son of Man?" (v. 34). Could it be Jesus hides just enough of Himself to require faith, test our willingness to believe, and give space for us to articulate our commitment? Looking at the whole of John, it is obvious that "Son of Man" is Jesus's favorite self-designation. He introduces Himself in this way to skeptics (1:51), seekers (3:13), the crowd (6:27), and His disciples (13:31). And perhaps it is His name of preference because it best expresses the central mission of Jesus: God becoming a man to identify with humanity, redeem lives, feed the hungry, raise the dead, and give sight to the blind.

Somehow, this man associates the title with Jesus. And he believes (9:37).

In reflecting on the similarities of John 5 and 9—of the paralytic and the blind man—the closing words also underscore the dissimilarities. They are two lines of antithetical poetry, one contrasting the other: one gives no indication of belief, and the other believes; one throws Jesus under the bus, while the other gets on the bus; one is repelled by the light, and the other is drawn to it; the paralytic irritates, and the blind man inspires.

John 9 is one of the high points of the book. From a literary standpoint, "the author's art is at its consummate best."[11] It is well crafted from scene to scene. From a spiritual perspective, it raises significant questions: Will I step out in faith if Jesus does something counterintuitive in my life? Am I living in light of God's anointing work, now that He has smeared (anointed) my eyes to see? Do I have the humility to give the credit to Jesus for any work that has changed my life? Will I stand my ground in the face of intimidation? Do I ask the same question of others, "Do you want to be His disciples?" Am I willing to be tossed out and excommunicated from the only community I have known for choosing Jesus?

I am forced to ask, "How well do I see?" So much of life under an open heaven is about seeing. It is seeing the greater things (1:50). It is finding clarity where there has been confusion. It is also seeing mystery where I once thought I had things figured out. It is discerning the land mines that I once had a propensity to trip. We can now see the streaks of sinful attitudes that the dimness once obscured—the darker crevices of the heart where idols have been manufactured.

We are able to reassess. What looked like healthy self-esteem is actually pride; what appeared to be self-improvement is really vanity; what we once explained as "following the heart" was really about self-centeredness; and what we imagined to be following the American dream has been exposed as greed.

We can also see more clearly into the lives of others. The carefree life of the party is often a person using personality to cover deep shame. Gaining spiritual sight, we are better able to see the true size of people. We can identify the empty suits while discerning those who truly have weight, gravitas. Concerns we thought to be huge and important (another's opinion or one's portfolio) are seen in their truer dimensions. What we perceived to be minimal and insignificant is suddenly much greater and more central.

In the light, we can see that we are human and not God. We can now see beyond creation to the Creator. We are no longer inclined to worship rocks or trees or self. There is someone far more worthy. There is a wider presence. We now see more than moon and stars and amazing sunsets. We see the glory of God (Ps. 19:1). In our banal setting and inconvenient times, beauty has transcended and we have beheld it. We can now recognize the music.

QUESTIONS

1. *All of us experience a certain blindness to spiritual things. Talk about yours.*

2. *How has God opened your eyes? What can you now see that you had not been able to before?*

3. *Imagine how this man's life played out after Jesus's intervention. What did it look like?*

10

LIFE IS ABOUT LIVING BY GOD'S TIMING AND GOD'S PURPOSES

A Conversation with Martha

JOHN 11:1–3, 17–44

> *Then Martha said to Jesus, "Lord, if You had been here, my brother wouldn't have died. Yet even now I know that whatever You ask from God, God will give You."*
>
> *"Your brother will rise again," Jesus told her.*
>
> *Martha said, "I know that he will rise again in the resurrection at the last day."*
>
> *Jesus said to her, "I am the resurrection and the life. The one who believes in Me, even if he dies, will live."*
>
> —JOHN 11:21–25

"WHERE WERE YOU, GOD?" MARTHA'S LAMENT ECHOES THROUGH the ages. "Where were You, God, when I prayed all these years for Dad?" "What were You doing when we hoped for healing, but nothing changed and death won out?" "Did You not care when the job I prayed for was offered to someone else?" "Couldn't this storm have been diverted?" "If You move the hearts of kings like You turn the course of a river, couldn't you have simply moved the heart of this professor?" "Really, if heaven is open, where are the signs of God's activity?"

All of us come to God from time to time with questions. Philip Yancey notes in his book *Disappointment with God* that disappointment "does not come only in dramatic circumstances. . . . It also edges unexpectedly into the mundaneness of everyday life."[1] "God, why did the car have to break down on this bridge?" "You surely could have moved the heart of the loan officer at the bank (or the judge at the hearing)." "How could You allow this special moment with the family to become so un-special?" "Why did the sermon I worked so hard on end up having all of the impact of the FBI warning on a DVD?"

Behind all of these questions are failed expectations. *And failed expectations lie at the heart of every disappointment.* John 11 is a story about disappointment. We are confronted with the reality that our days under an open heaven are by no means trouble free. In this tension of already and not yet, we face a certain amount of confusion, ambiguity, grief, anger, reversal, hopelessness, criticism, and tension.

Like other conversations in John, this one has two main characters. Jesus and Martha are center stage, while other characters enter and go off. But the setting is more fully developed, and this creates tension and complications.

THE TIMING OF GOD'S ABSENCE

The adventure continues. Jesus and His disciples have moved east of the Jordan, away from Jerusalem, which continues to be a danger zone. Jerusalem is even more of a hotbed after Jesus's latest miracle, when He again dared to heal on the Sabbath. Jesus's subsequent discourse in John 9:40–10:39 makes matters even worse. The Pharisees might have seen themselves as Israel's shepherds, but Jesus likens them to strangers, thieves, robbers, and hired men. Jesus's claim to be one with the Father pushes them over the edge (10:30). They want to grab Him by the throat, but Jesus again eludes their grasp and now heads some twenty miles east across the Jordan (vv. 39–40). It is not yet time.

This eastern region isn't some wilderness wasteland but a destination of choice for city dwellers. Weekenders flee to escape the noise, pollution, and madness of the metropolis. East of the Jordan has become something of a royal estate ever since the days of Alexander the Great. The Hasmonean rulers built palaces over here. Cleopatra owned a luxury condo and rented it to Herod for his occasional getaways. The Romans contributed to the building of aqueducts, plantations, fortresses, and pools.[2] It's an ideal place to rest. And we, the readers, hope for a bit of rest. John's account of Jesus begins with a stunning promise, but what follows has been a series of tense conversations.

So why did Jesus head here? It's doubtful He came for the pools, theme parks, or bike trails. Why go east? He could have retreated to the coast, but there might have been too much military traffic, given the large fortress in Caesarea. There wasn't much to the south, unless you wanted to float on the Dead Sea, visit the gift store, and purchase some pricey mineral-laden skin products. He's already been north to Galilee. John 10:40 hints they may have come here to the Jordan because this was where people came to hear John the Baptist, the voice telling people to prepare the way for the Messiah (1:23).

John tells us Jesus remained here for some time. Days? Weeks? We are not sure. What we do know is that, unlike in Jerusalem, the way has been prepared and people here are responsive (v. 41). They are seeing the signs, they are witnessing the evidence of an open heaven, and they want a taste of freedom. We do not have the numbers, but John tells us many believed (v. 42). Amidst dates and palms, orange-juice vendors, and camel rides, ministry appears to be thriving. The Jordan area is a nice respite from the chaos in Jerusalem. At least here, Jesus's picture is not posted in the office where the mail is delivered.

But life's realities have a way of interrupting our halcyon days. The connective "now" of verse 1 of the next chapter indicates that John wants to prepare the reader for the fact that things shift. The good news of the gospel's reception is confronted by the bad news that life is fragile. Jesus's friend is dying (11:3). In a broken world, sickness and death are never far from the story.

Often when I take time out and head east to the desert or north to the wilderness, sad news of someone's loss follows me. An email or call informs me that a parishioner has died. (It just happened this morning while I was writing!) Nearly every week, someone in our church has lost his or her job, has been evicted, has been diagnosed with cancer, or has lost a loved one. D. A. Carson puts it succinctly: "All we have to do is live long enough, and we will suffer."[3]

Now into the desert comes word that Jesus's friend Lazarus is deathly ill in Bethany, a bedroom community of Jerusalem. In what appears to be unfortunate timing, Jesus and His disciples, who had just passed through, are now somewhere else. Why isn't He here? Why couldn't events leading to this tragedy have happened a few days earlier? We sometimes ask these same questions.

THE TIMING OF GOD'S RESPONSE

We expect Jesus will drop everything. This is an important family after all. John does not want us to mistake identities, so he clarifies (v. 2). This is the man whose sister is Mary. You know, the one who will soon anoint Jesus with perfume (wiping out a large portion of her inheritance) and then take her hair and do the unimaginable—wipe

His feet. This is the man whose other sister is Martha. Remember her? She attends to Jesus whenever He comes to town. She provides for His food and makes sure the sheets are clean and does the laundry for all of the disciples (Luke 10:38). She works tirelessly for them.

This is the family that Jesus has been loving and loving and loving as His own (John 11:5). John is setting up an expectation. Jesus will surely drop everything and take a nonstop to Bethany. Instead Jesus tells His disciples the fever will pass and Lazarus will be good as new (v. 4). At least it sounds this way. But then He adds something both heartening and troubling: "This sickness . . . is for the glory of God." What on earth does this mean?

The theme of divine glory keeps coming up. Reading the gospel of John, one finds that the subject is more prominent here than in any other book.[4] You could preface every moment with these words. This sickness, this wedding in Cana, this encounter with Nicodemus, this stop in Samaria, this rejection by the crowd, this conversation with His brothers, this livid response by the Jews, this arrest, this death—it is all for God's fame.

Whether we can recognize—or accept—it, everything can be prefaced with the same words, "for the glory of God." This sickness, this delay, this opportunity, this dismissal, this waiting, this rejection, this heartache, this victory—everything—is for the glory of God. But we're not always sure. Where is the glory? From our earthly perspective, sickness and death often appear invincible. They charge into the present, taking no note of justice, snatching babies and children at school, causing incalculable misery.[5] But death, like the Devil, will ultimately submit to the purposes of God. Everything is all about showcasing God's fame and marking God's presence among us. Timing has everything to do with His reputation. Everything else is secondary.

I am up here in the Washington wilderness, and the fire conditions posted at a nearby fire station read "very high." Every now and then, I stop to sniff. Is that smoke? Is that evidence of a fire or just a cloud over the hills? In Martha's story, I am also sniffing for evidence, for some assurance. John seems to be going somewhere with this, but where? Something is lurking around the bend. We're curious but cautious. When someone says to me, "You know, this is for God's glory, and I want you to know I love you very much," I get nervous. There's something behind the words, but what is he setting me up for?

THE TIMING OF GOD'S PRESENCE

It is incredibly agonizing for Martha when Jesus remains where He is—for two days (v. 6)! This is beginning to sound like a lesson about disappointment or patience. Maybe Jesus will heal from a distance like He did with the royal official's son (4:46–53). Given the seething conditions in Judea, it makes perfect sense. And then, inexplicably, Jesus says, "Let's go" (11:7). This makes no sense. This is suicidal! That's how the disciples feel (vv. 8, 16). Thomas, ever the positive one, sees the writing on the wall. "Let's get our affairs in order, identify an executor for the wills, and send one last text to loved ones."

Jesus's next comments only add to the confusion. First, He informs them there are only twelve hours of daylight in a twenty-four-hour cycle. The words seem condescending. What does this have to do with Lazarus's sickness? Jesus creates even more consternation when He remarks that Lazarus is sleeping, and He must go and wake him up (vv. 9–11). No! Wait. What? I'm confused. Wasn't Jesus listening? Did He miss the words "deathly ill"? If Lazarus was only sleeping, a simple rooster could wake him up. Or maybe he could figure it out on his own.

So far, there is little that is making sense in this story. The disciples are hopelessly bewildered by Jesus (v. 12). And so are we.

But look closer. Here's what Jesus is saying to His disciples: "I am heading back to a very dangerous place, and it is necessary I go. There is only so much time left to accomplish My Father's will" (v. 9). Pay attention to the clock. As in His conversation with His brothers (7:6), Jesus is in effect saying to His disciples, "My timing and My will determine everything, so there is no need to fear. To fear is to stray into the darkness. The only way to avoid stumbling through life, of finding yourself in the dark, is to journey with Me. So align yourselves with My movements (11:10). There is a need that requires My presence (v. 11). There is something I am doing that goes beyond your imagination. And yes, I am using all of this to bring God glory and strengthen your faith (v. 14). Any questions?"

Mary and Martha have their questions. They are missing His glory and His love. They are mystified and maddened by Jesus's absence. Did Jesus lose track of time again? Is He—is God—too consumed with other matters, too distracted to notice our pain? Maybe He is simply booked with other ministry engagements, preoccupied with another world beyond the Jordan, beyond Bethany? This is all fine, but Lazarus has been His friend. This is a family that has always had an open-door policy that says, "Stay with us."

Jesus seems to be an equal opportunity disappointer.[6] And disappointment creates its own sickness (Prov. 13:12). Hopes are deferred and dreams are pushed back. Are they lost forever? This is what Langston Hughes, the poet, wonders:

> What happens to a dream deferred?
>
> Does it dry up
> like a raisin in the sun?
> Or fester like a sore—
> And then run?
> Does it stink like rotten meat?
> Or crust and sugar over—
> like a syrupy sweet?
>
> Maybe it just sags
> like a heavy load,
>
> *Or does it explode?*[7]

Mary and Martha want to know, now that their hope seems to have shattered. Mary remains home in mourning, but Martha finds out Jesus is on His way and comes to meet Him (John 11:20). It's an uneasy conversation. "To meet" is language often used in an adversarial context (see Matt. 8:28; Mark 5:2; Luke 14:31). She has lost her brother and likely their means of support. Lazarus's passing creates its own loneliness, as well as potential poverty and destitution. As the older sister, Martha feels the weight of this. There is a mix of lament and reproach, grief and anger, worry and fear driving this conversation. Martha is trying to resolve this. In effect, she says to Jesus: "Lord, if You had been here (which You weren't), my brother would not have died (which he did)."

We do the same thing. We tell God how the story could have ended if He had simply been on time. In some of my valleys of disillusionment, I have acted out just like Martha. I contend and scream. I try to square things and reconcile my faith with life's realities. I too present my case, informing God as if He was unaware of what is going on.

One of the hardest things to understand is God's timing. Everything has its expiration date—pears, potatoes, pills, passports, and people. Martha gets this. She does not spend her time reading sensational articles about a coming robozombie apocalypse. She is not holding on to some fantasy that we can be ageless. Death is inevitable. Decline creeps in like a vine. Bones and teeth will soften and everything else will harden. "We wear down until we can't wear down anymore."[8] But Lazarus's terminus point is premature. He is not supposed to die yet, at least as far as Martha and Mary are concerned. This could have been prevented if someone were more attentive!

Scripture tells us Martha is a woman of order. Everything has its time and its place. She needs a God who follows protocol. She assumes God thinks like her and will side with her. We've seen this before (Luke 10:40). What she needs are answers to questions she never anticipated she would ask: "Lord, don't You care? Don't You get it? It has been four days" (see John 11:17). According to rabbinic law, on the fourth day of death the lingering soul leaves (Talmud, Sanhedrin, 90b–91a). It is a graphic way of saying that the opportunity has come and gone. *It is the fourth day, and it is too late.*

Like some of our dialogues, the conversation is less *with* Jesus and more *at* Jesus. People let us down, but God shouldn't! Especially if we have decided to give our lives to Him. A certain entitlement kicks in. We *are* the ones Jesus loves. So when life has not gone as planned, when things do not conform to our schedules, we can begin to sound like the writer of Ecclesiastes—it is all a chasing after the wind (Eccl. 2:26). We are pretty good at talking at God rather than to God. We remind Him of what could have been. We point out the things that He may have missed, especially if we are into the details like Martha. We remind the One who created and controls time of the time.

More difficult than resolving God's timing, Martha is trying to reconcile life's tragedies with divine sovereignty. She wants Jesus to know that things could have been different because she knows, *and has always known*, that Jesus can do whatever He sets His mind to doing (John 11:22). He can meet our highest expectations. He and His Father are not confined to the four-day rule. His Father is the one

- who is immeasurable and incalculable;
- whose center is everywhere and circumference is nowhere;
- who can put all the oceans in a thimble;
- who can never be informed and is never surprised;
- who knows every truth we have yet to discover; and
- who views the rulers of this world as seedlings and their power as chaff.

She also knows the Father is the sovereign one who will respond to whatever His Son asks. We know this too. So we wonder why Jesus does not intercede when our loved ones are failing or our dreams are dying. These heartfelt, difficult questions swirl around in Martha's mind: "So why didn't You come when You heard? And if You couldn't come, couldn't you have simply asked the Father to heal my brother? Why didn't You use Your influence, pull the right heavenly strings? What is this open heaven stuff? Are we not to believe that You live to make intercession?" (Heb. 7:25).

Martha isn't wrestling with Christ's "ableness" but His "willingness."

Times spent together have convinced her He is God in the flesh. But she is having a hard time squaring all of this with life events. Who exactly is Jesus? Wait, maybe His power is limited? Is His will triggered off and on by some celestial timer? Like John the Baptist, you can almost hear her faith wavering and her need to ask, "Are You the one who is to come, or should we expect someone else?"

The two statements of verses 21–22 ("Lord, if You had been here. . . . Yet even now I know") are a mix of depression and hope, lost confidence and core conviction. And often, we experience the same mix. We're trying to reconcile circumstances with our theology—our heartbreak with His sovereignty—and they don't always fit together.

As I read over the weekly prayer requests of our congregants, I imagine that behind many of the stated requests are really unstated perplexities. There is the same struggle of reconciling the character of God with life's circumstances.

STATED: Our unmarried daughter is about to give birth to a second child.

UNSTATED: *If You are sovereign, why are we going through this again, knowing we will have to do the lion's share of parenting?*

STATED: Jim lost his job of twenty-eight years this week.

UNSTATED: *Lord, if You know everything, why now? We were so hopeful for a good retirement from the place he so faithfully served. Doesn't faithfulness to a job for twenty-eight years matter?*

STATED: Cyndi is so lost. She is nowhere near God anymore.

UNSTATED: *If You protect Your sheep, why did You allow her to drift?*

STATED: Pray for employment, money, and a place to live.

UNSTATED: *If You own the cattle on a thousand hills, why are we in such a desperate condition, especially since we are in this mess because we went out in faith and trained for ministry?*

Reviewing these requests weekly removes any superficial assessment that I am a shepherd to complacent consumers looking for the best pew. It reminds me, as Eugene Peterson puts it, that I minister "to people who [are] in the lion's den, to men and women facing wild beasts in the Colosseum"—the coliseum called life.[9]

THE TIMING OF GOD'S WORDS

We find that keeping our heart in this journey is the most important mission of our lives—and the hardest. What does the living, incarnate God say in these situations? How does He respond to the one who clings to the assumed promise in Proverbs that no harm befalls the righteous (12:21)? What will He say to a grieving sister who is trying to resolve core convictions of her faith with a dead brother?

What does God say to us in our disappointment?

Words of Hope

The first thing Jesus does is *reassure future hope.* In the right moment, Jesus makes one simple statement: "Your brother will rise" (John 11:23). A time is coming (is it distant or imminent?) when Lazarus will no longer be supine. He will get up and stand, full of life. This underscores what Jesus said earlier to the disciples: "I'm on My way to wake him up" (v. 11).

In this response, we see the nature of God. Over and over He initiates conversations with words intended to dispel distress. To us He says, "Fear not!" To Abraham and Sarah, whose patience is nearly exhausted, God promises His will *will* be done (Gen. 21:1). To those disappointed that dreams have not materialized, He speaks through the sage, declaring, "For then you will have a future, and your hope will never fade" (Prov. 23:18).

He does not intend for us to remain in our despair. Jesus knows the lies of the Evil One. He knows the Devil's principal mission is to drain life from us and bury us in hopelessness. He understands what despondency can do. To lose heart is to lose everything, starting with our health (Prov. 13:12). In the midst of death and loss, resurrection is our profound promise. We have a confidence that transcends a mere scientific-materialist worldview where death wins.

We should—we must—look for this hope. But divine assurance at the right moment does not mean everything is resolved. For Martha, and maybe for us, reassuring words go only so far. Our problem is that we are time bound. We tell ourselves things work out in the end. But when is the end, and how can we cope in the present? I think of a young father who lost his wife to cancer, and while we rejoiced together in future hope, we couldn't help but feel the weight of sadness and disappointment that a five-year-old and a nine-year-old will have to go forward without their mom.

Martha tells Jesus that she knows, and has known, that Lazarus will rise again (John 11:24). She gets it. The hope of immortality is embedded in Jewish teaching. She knows her Old Testament, which refers to existence beyond the grave, beginning with Enoch and Job and moving through the psalmists and the prophets (Gen. 5:24; Job 19:26; Ps. 73:23; Dan. 12:2). She recalls Jesus's earlier words, asserting that an hour is coming when the dead will rise, and the righteous will enter a resurrection of life (John 5:29). Life under an open heaven anticipates this future eternal life. We will see our loved ones once again.

Perhaps Jesus sounds a bit like a pastor giving solace, assuring people of God's ultimate goodness and calling people to the kind of faith that "believe[s] in advance what will only make sense in reverse."[10] We will see our loved ones once again. Martha knows this and has probably been hearing these words again and again in the house of mourning. But coming from Jesus, this future hope is cold comfort. It does not help so much with present grief, especially since this death could have been prevented. This loss is so unnecessary! There has to be some explanation.

Yet divine reassurance does not necessarily include explanations. Jesus will not satisfy her need for explanation. Martha is finding, as we do, that though God reassures, He does not necessarily explain

His ways. Even though we live under an open heaven, things are still inaccessible. We will have to wait for some answers to the difficult questions. Jesus offers no excuse and no apology for His delay.

We've seen this before. Jesus owes no one an account except to say that He is driven alone by the will of the Father, a will that is perfectly good and wise and aimed to bring glory. He does not operate His schedule or His plans by people's expectations. Unlike us, He is not trapped in time. He operates by a divine clock that operates on "God's will" time. But He does give us hope—real hope.

Words of Trust

Here's the second thing God says in our disappointment: *trust Me*. In the statement "I am the resurrection and the life" (11:25), we can imagine Jesus saying, "Martha, look beyond your memorized Bible verses, your Sunday school instruction, and your affirmations. Look beyond your expectations. Look at Me. Do you see who I am? Can you see that *I am* the resurrection? Can you see that Lazarus is not beyond the range of My power?"[11]

I like it that Jesus calls Martha back to Himself. So much of faith seems third person when God intends that it be first person. Ultimately, all theology must become personal. The cognitive must reach to the heart; insight must tie itself to experience. Left to promises made and verses quoted, theology can leave us cold.

It's not the first time Jesus personalizes faith. He also does this with His other "I am" statements: "I am the Bread. Come and eat My flesh and you will never hunger." "I am the Living Water. Drink from Me and you will never thirst." "I am the Light of the World. Come into My light and gain the sight that will replace your blindness." "I am the Resurrection. Come enter into My abundant life." In none of these is Jesus trying to impress or "flaunt His credentials; he doesn't bully or intimidate with a show of authority."[12] He is widening our view, drawing us into a deeper, more intimate relationship with Himself. And this, alongside reassurance, is what really matters.

Sometimes we can get so immersed in studying the Word that we miss the person behind the Word. It happens in seminary. I see it in my students. I saw it begin to happen to me when I began theological studies. My love affair with God began to fade rather than deepen. The Word of God began to turn into a textbook. My devotional life diminished into preparation time for exams. I no longer met God on the mountaintop. I observed Him in the laboratory through the lens of courses like Critical Problems. I began to study theology proper with all of my mind but with less and less of my heart.

Thankfully, wise mentors guarded me from going much deeper into the wilderness. If this is not corrected, we will take such habits out into the ministry. We will become professional caregivers, competent expositors, and effective leaders, all at the loss of our souls.

In her revealing book *Leaving Church*, Barbara Brown Taylor describes how it began to happen to her:

> The demands of parish ministry routinely cut me off from the resources that enabled me to do parish ministry. I knew where God's fire was burning, but I could not get to it. I knew how to pray, how to bank the coals and call the Spirit, but by the time I got home each night it was all I could do to pay the bills and go to bed. I pecked God on the cheek the same way I did [my husband,] Ed, drying up inside for want of making love.[13]

Jesus can see that Martha is missing the fact that the Author of Life is right in front of her. In His declaration that He is the resurrection *and the life*, Jesus gives Martha a radical reformulation of her expressed eschatological expectation. To put it more simply, He brings her out of the small space she has been working, closed in by walls that have no windows, and takes her to the top of the summit. He is bringing her to Himself, as He does with us, to show us life, show us His heart.

But He will not leave it at this. In this conversation with Martha (and with us), He wants to know if she gets it. "Do you believe this?"

(John 11:26). "Do you trust me?" He is driving her to the same questions Jesus asked the man born blind: "Do you believe in Me? Is there personal faith to be found?"

Is your trust in Me bigger than your disappointment? Will you be driven by expectation or expectancy?

Martha needs this shift in perspective, for disappointment has morphed into personal unbelief. It often does. Death has become the running headline. It is Martha's preoccupation. In our loss, it can be ours.

Death and the Devil need to be moved to the back page. Though loss and grief are a real part of life, physical death (when contrasted with the life we have in Christ) is really an inconsequential matter, a "sting," no matter when it happens (1 Cor. 15:55). It does not deserve the emphasis it gets. It is not the last word. Death is simply a transition, the backdrop to life that never ends.

THE TIMING OF GOD'S FUTURE

Jesus is inviting Martha into a resurrection that is both personal and present. In Greek it's *egō eimi*, "I am" the resurrection. The resurrection is not merely some future rebirth at the end of time. In some mysterious way, we experience something of a raised life now. Jesus is getting to the heart of what life is under an open heaven. This is what Paul writes to the church at Ephesus: "Together with Christ Jesus He also raised us up and seated us in the heavens" (Eph. 2:6). This is what he declares to the church at Colossae: "So if you have been raised with the Messiah, seek what is above" (Col. 3:1). Resurrection is now!

Jesus is telling Martha what He told Nathanael—the future has burst into the present (John 1:51). "The final resurrection expected at the end of the age . . . is burgeoning in the spiritual life Jesus imparts to his followers" in the present.[14] The life we look forward to, the power and joy we will experience in eternity, are ours to experience now.

As Eugene Peterson puts it: "Resurrection country is no longer an extravagant landscape before which we stand in reverential awe. It is the land we live in."[15] We are invited to live eternity in time, experience eschatological life in the present, where one has no need for worry, despair, and hopelessness.

Jesus is framing Lazarus's death for Martha, just as He is framing death, loss, and disappointment for all of us. My father recently came to the end of his years here on earth. What got me through the loss was trusting that Jesus is the resurrection. In all of resurrection's power to raise one from death and all of its glory to transform—in the center of all of it is Jesus. The losing of a loved one is a temporary loss, but it is not a tragedy. It is the beginning of life in eternity with Jesus.

I hear Jesus saying to Martha, "*Life wins!* Lazarus is alive, really alive, more alive than he ever was alive."

Could it be that sometimes we set ourselves up for profound disappointment because we are too "pro-life"—pro *this* life? We can be so focused on this world, chasing after every technology to extend our stay, that we ironically avoid what we want most—life! We have too weak a resurrection theology, too thin a view of what it means to be with Jesus. We miss this—*that what is lost is nothing compared to what is found.* As Larry Crabb puts it, "We dream lower dreams and think there are none higher."[16]

The truth is, Lazarus is presently living the dream. He is in the presence of the Father. Jesus wants to know if Martha believes this (11:26). Does she see the bigger picture of what resurrection means? Do we? At some point, "one has to decide whether one's fears or one's hopes are what should matter most."[17]

Martha wants Jesus to know that she not only knows (v. 24); she believes (v. 27). But it's a stock answer. Martha believes Jesus is the Messiah, but this is not enough to invalidate her disappointment. Jesus is the incarnate Son of God. She is not looking for someone who is yet to come. She is not looking for someone who has the power over disease and death. But she is looking for someone who will exercise messianic power in the way she expects.

THE TIMING OF GOD'S POWER

Martha exits and Mary comes onstage. It has the feel of a cameo appearance. She is given the same lines as Martha (compare v. 21 with v. 32). She too is wrestling with a sense of letdown. With everyone else, she grieves. Death has won, and Jesus was not there to prevent the tragic loss. She also misses the fact that when God seems most absent He is most present.

In this moment, Mary's grief, as well as the grief of others, triggers something powerful inside the heart of Jesus (v. 33). Up until now, "His emotions tend to run on a rather flat plane."[18] John's description of Jesus does not reveal any mood swings. But we are reading with a lens that can see only so far. Like the ridge in front of our cabin that blocks my view of the other side, the reader is kept from seeing many of the emotional valleys Jesus experiences. But here, we are invited to the other side and into His feelings.

Most translations tell us Jesus "groaned" or was "deeply moved" in His spirit (v. 33), but this does not capture what is going on inside. There is something gut-wrenching, a mixture of sadness and anger in His spirit. Jesus is provoked. He bristles. What He witnesses around Him is disturbing. What is it? We're not told.

The crowd misreads Jesus's tears. They see someone overcome by the grief that death brings to His world. He mourns over a world that suffers the consequence of sin. Death is like a playground bully. Evil, death, and Satan are always interfering with the world as it should be. And Jesus feels the weight of the loss of a friend. Hence, they see His weeping and remark, "See how He loved him!" (v. 36).

But it is not the spectacle of death that arouses Jesus's emotions. Look into the story, into the hearts of these who have come to pay their respects. What provokes Jesus to both grieve and feel indignant is a culture of unbelief. The same emotion comes out when Jesus laments over Jerusalem (Luke 13:34). The same grief must go on in heaven continually.

Jesus is looking into benevolent faces that cover unbenevolent hearts. They feel sorry for Jesus because they don't take Him for who He is. They view Him as a helpless and harmless soul, a wandering peasant sage to be pitied. They feel sorry for a family that has signed on with a messiah wannabe from Nazareth who stands as helpless as every other mourner.

Jesus is also aware of the critics who whisper, "If Jesus can heal the unbelieving paralytic and still the storms and open the eyes of the blind, couldn't He have prevented this death? If He cared for strangers, why wouldn't He care for His friends?" (see John 11:37). They too are disappointed in Jesus for His failure to come through.

The real tragedy in this story, and in most stories, is that "Jesus [is] an unrecognized power in their midst."[19] People choose to either ignore or dismiss the one who has changed everything with His coming. They are like the unbelieving people at a funeral who much prefer hanging on to despair rather than turning to hope.

Adding to all of this must be Jesus's agony of knowing what He is about to endure for the sin of this world. Knowing that Lazarus's burial and resurrection prefigure His own death, burial, and resurrection must bring its own emotion. And knowing that Lazarus's emergence from the grave will serve as a tipping point, intensifying efforts to arrest Jesus, must also explain His passion at Lazarus's tomb (v. 38).

But perhaps—perhaps—Martha's unbelief, as well as Mary's, as well as His disciples', trouble Him most. Despite her claims to the contrary, Martha is still lacking faith. Disappointment like a deep fog has disabled her ability to see the lines. We see this at the tomb. Jesus commands someone to remove the stone, but Martha objects. She is back to informing Jesus: "Lord, he's already decaying. It's been four days" (v. 39). She sounds like the disciples, who earlier saw the need to inform Jesus that people who sleep can awaken on their own (v. 12).

Here again is Johannine irony. Through Jesus, all things are made (1:3), but those closest to Him speak as if He needs to learn how life works.

Jesus knows how life works, and He knows what is possible under an open heaven. In the perfect moment, Jesus displays His power and wakes Lazarus up and calls him from the tomb. And in this moment, the ways of God make perfect sense. Lazarus's death has served to showcase God's love and power and ultimately bring glory to God in ways that other story lines could not. Lazarus's rising provides the moment for Jesus to ask Martha, "Didn't I tell you that if you believed you would see the glory of God?" (11:40). The pronoun is singular, but it may as well be addressed to everyone in the story—including us.

THE GLORY THAT IS OURS TO SEE

Annie Dillard, in her book *Pilgrim at Tinker Creek*, writes a chapter on seeing. It's not merely seeing the hemlocks across the way, but the air in front of them. Nature is a sort of now-you-see-it-and-now-you-don't affair. One catches a glimpse of a deer, and then it seems to ascend into heaven.

Seeing the glory of God under an open heaven is like that. Those who gain the greater glimpse are those who believe in God's perfect timing and purpose. It is there every day, but it will require the kind of faith Martha and Mary and the disciples lacked. It will require a steadiness of commitment, even if God does not meet our expectations and operate in our time frame. Even if our suffering is not always minimized. It will demand faith, even if things come apart.

It is true Martha did not have the full story. Jesus did not explain up front, as He did to His disciples, that His glory trumps everything else (v. 4). He did not convey to her in advance that Lazarus would sleep, but take heart: he will be awakened. He did not alert her and Mary that Lazarus would emerge in good health with stories to tell his grandchildren.

Neither did He share that Lazarus will come with news that they would have to pay for two funerals instead of one, and with occasional complaints that he was recalled from a place far better than any earthly paradise. It's hard to get excited about rice cakes when you have had a taste of filet mignon.

I imagine that if anyone in the story was truly disappointed, it was Lazarus.

We don't have the full story either. God's ways will sometimes appear to be just as mystifying. On this side of heaven, there is "hiddenness, reversal, and surprise, [and] those who follow Jesus find themselves repeatedly failing to understand the will of God."[20]

The only thing we can rely on, and must rely on, is that God is wise and good and powerful in all that He does. This is what I will tell the parents of a dying son this weekend, whose battle with cancer is all but lost, and he leaves a world at the young age of twenty-one. God's love for us is never distracted. His timing is always perfect. His sovereignty is fully intact. He acts when His ways will bear the greatest fruit.[21] He does what will ultimately make the most sense. He does what will bring Him the greatest glory—what allows for an overflow of His essence—in His own time. Disappointment really has no place. This is how it is under an open heaven.

QUESTIONS

1. *Describe a time you wrestled with hope that was deferred. How did it (or might it still) turn out for God's glory?*

2. *Do you think Martha ever fully understood Jesus's delay? Do you?*

3. *Is it really possible to be too "pro-life"? How so?*

11
LIFE IS ABOUT PURSUING YOUR DIVINE RACE

A Conversation with His Followers
JOHN 13–17

*Believe Me that I am in the Father and the Father is in Me.
Otherwise, believe because of the works themselves.*

*I assure you: The one who believes in Me will also do the
works that I do. And he will do even greater works than these,
because I am going to the Father.*

—JOHN 14:11–12

In LONG-DISTANCE RELAY RACING, HANDING OFF THE BATON SUC-
cessfully is a surprisingly delicate and difficult part of the sport:

> It is the sound no relay runner wants to hear, a sound so soft and
> unassuming it might barely be noticed in the stands but nonethe-
> less reverberates, over and over, down on the track.
>
> *Ping. Ping. Ping.*
>
> Four years ago at the Beijing Olympics, the United States
> men's and women's 4×100-meter relay teams dropped batons—
> and heard the pings of them hitting the track. . . .
>
> Four years earlier in Athens, shoddy baton passing by the
> American men had allowed a British relay team to pull off an
> upset, while the United States women were disqualified after a
> botched exchange.[1]

It doesn't matter if you have blazing feet but sloppy hands.

TIME TO RUN THE RACE

In John 13, Jesus is about to pass the baton, and the handoff is critical. The future of the church—the future of the world—rests upon its
success! As William Vanderbloemen and Warren Bird stress in their
book, "There is no success without successors."[2] When the baton is not
passed, the results can be devastating. Joshua's failure to mentor future
leadership led to a period of unpredictable and ungodly behavior
(Judges 1–21). When Rehoboam dropped the baton from his father,
the wisdom of a golden era quickly devolved into folly (1 Kings 12:8).

Scripture records numerous farewell discourses: Jacob (Gen.
49), Moses (Deut. 1–33), Joshua (Josh. 24), Elijah (2 Kings 2), David
(1 Chron. 28), Paul (Acts 20), and us (2 Tim. 2:2). In almost every

case, news of one's imminent departure is accompanied by a tone of loss. Wisdom is imparted and recipients are admonished to continue the work, press forward, run the race, and fulfill the mission.

In this story, Jesus is transitioning, passing His leadership to the Twelve. Up to this point, the disciples have been little more than benchwarmers. They are part of the team, but rarely are they seen on the field. To use other metaphors, they are the window dressing behind most of John's stories. They are in the credits but are not given many lines. But now the disciples take center stage with Jesus. The longest conversation of the book, John 13–17, is devoted to them.

Tumultuous might be one way to describe the past few days leading up to this night. Unnerving, shocking, thrilling, heart-stopping, breathtaking. All apply. There has been the long trek back up to Jerusalem, dinner with Lazarus, his tales of what life is like on the other side, Mary showing unrestrained and extravagant devotion to Jesus, and Judas simply pontificating. This day began with a donkey ride through the Golden Gate. This was unusual in itself, for the common entrance was on the south side. But the screaming crowds were there to meet Him anyway, shouting, "Hosanna!" Some among them were simply curiosity seekers, wanting to get a selfie with Jesus (12:18–21). Oh, and there was this audible voice from heaven (or was it thunder?). Most in the crowd were preoccupied, as if some divine fog had obscured their vision. This is because it did (vv. 39–40).

Amidst the chaos, Jesus gave His final public address, summing up His life purpose. He declared what He had said so often—that the will of the Father is what matters (5:19, 36; 6:38; 12:50). Jesus made it clear that it has always been His mission to be indifferent to anything but His Father's wishes. And submission now required a faithful handoff.

WHERE IS ALL OF THIS GOING?

The time to which all of eternity has pointed is finally here (12:23). Jesus will be betrayed, arrested, brutally beaten, sentenced to death, and executed. For all the impressions of chance encounters and stalled moments, Jesus has always known where He is going and what He wants. With perfect clarity, He has pursued His course with unswerving conviction. The time has come, and it is nonnegotiable and unmovable.

But first there is the handoff. It begins with supper and a conversation with His disciples, where everything shifts from the public to the private. This section of the gospel is often referred to as the Upper Room Discourse. But if a discourse typically refers to a formal and orderly presentation on a subject, this is something different. This is not a lecture with a whiteboard and captive students, writing notes easily deciphered. It's not a coach's impassioned speech before the race starts. It's more like memos jotted on scraps of paper and passed on to semidistracted participants.

What Jesus says is much more wrinkled than starched. There is a casualness, an ongoing movement of washing and eating and reclining and talking and listening and stopping and starting. Anyone who attempts to outline this section (let alone preach it as a sermon series) will find the journey difficult. *One could wake up with vertigo!*

Much of this conversation is prompted by questions from the floor, first by Peter and then by others, including Thomas and Philip and Judas (not Iscariot). They are "surrogates for the church . . . and often ask questions that may naturally occur to the reader."[3] In the process, the discourse goes in one direction, takes a quick turn, veers to the left, and then goes in reverse. Jesus seems to be instructing, then departs from His notes to talk about His feelings. He then moves to talk about their feelings; then midway, He suggests everyone get up and leave.

Maybe this happened in the course of an evening, or it could be a compilation of conversations that took place over a series of days during Passover week.[4] This may explain some of the repetition and odd shifts.

Regardless, Jesus has gathered His team to prepare them for His departure, instructing them regarding their mission. It is now their race! It is imperative they grasp the magnitude of God's purpose for them. They must know their objectives. It is critical they are aware of their support. It is absolutely essential they stay connected; otherwise, they may stray off course. They may lose sight of their capabilities. They may lose heart and capitulate.

There is some familiarity with the material Jesus is about to share. The Twelve have been party to most of Jesus's previous conversations; students following their rabbi run His race, quietly taking notes. As they have leaned against this divine ladder linking heaven and earth, they have beheld divine activity ascending and descending, angelic forces that blow apart one's manufactured assumptions. They have had a front-row seat to divine attributes working through flesh. They have seen power they could have never imagined on their own. They have encountered goodness that transcends any earthly kindness. They have seen at least seven miraculous signs, all of which constitute a divine opening.[5]

Still, where is all of this going, and what does it have to do with them? Jesus is still a mystery, an elusive Messiah, impenetrable and incomprehensible.[6] His leadership is demonstrated in ways foreign to their upbringing. He is doing things unexpected, things that don't fit the code of behavior. If heaven has opened, why would the Davidic Messiah, the Mosaic prophet—all of Israel's hope bound up in one person—hold back? Why does He enter His capital riding on a borrowed donkey, and why is He now getting up and grabbing a basin and a towel? Later they will ask why it is necessary to wait (Acts 1:6).

ARE WE GOING IT ALONE?

What is it with this talk of their leader leaving them? Jesus has told the world His hour has come (John 12:23). Things are beginning to shift. Like a store announcing that it is closing, Jesus has announced that the lights are turning off (v. 35). The owner is preparing to leave for home, but the customers have assumed things are open 24/7 and the owner is on for the night shift. Doesn't an open heaven stay open?

None of this should have really come as a shock to the disciples, but it does. As the "preaching genius" Fred Craddock puts it, "The disciples had been as children playing on the floor, only to look up and see the parents putting on coats and hats."[7] Jesus has told them numerous times, and He will tell them again in an upper room that He is leaving:

- "I am only with you for a short time. Then I'm going to the One who sent Me. You will look for Me, but you will not find Me" (7:33–34).
- "I'm going away; you will look for Me, and you will die in your sin. Where I'm going, you cannot come" (8:21).
- "Children, I am with you a little while longer. You will look for Me, and just as I told the Jews, 'Where I am going you cannot come,' so now I tell you" (13:33).
- "I am going away to prepare a place for you" (14:2).
- "In a little while the world will see Me no longer" (14:19).
- "You have heard Me tell you, 'I am going away and I am coming to you'" (14:28).
- "I am going away" (14:31).
- "But now I am going away to Him who sent Me" (16:5).
- "A little while and you will no longer see Me; again a little while and you will see Me" (16:16).

To us, Jesus sounds like one of those departure announcements that repeat over and over at an airport. Are the disciples not hearing? Have these words just become background noise? Why are they not getting it? As Carolyn Weese and J. Russell Crabtree put it, "It is difficult to imagine a man more insistent and articulate regarding His own leadership transition than Jesus of Nazareth."[8]

Maybe none of this is registering because the disciples find His leaving irreconcilable with life as they understand it. It makes no sense that life under this open heaven does not include His visible, *permanent*, kingly presence on earth. The announcement of His departure raises troubling questions: Will heaven remain open? Will there still be divine activity? How will angels ascend and descend if there is no ladder? Will absence replace presence? Have these three years really mattered? How does one reorient to a non-future?

Or perhaps this "disciple disconnect" has more to do with denial than denseness. These desultory Twelve do not want to face the fact that Jesus is leaving. It's like going to a wake when the coroner has yet to confirm a death. It's all happening too fast. We do the same, avoiding and ignoring when we hear upsetting news. Even at a minor level, we have learned how to tune out lots of things in life we don't want to hear: "Since you're going to the garage, can you take out the trash?" "The dog just threw up." "There's a noise downstairs. I think it's mice." "There's a telemarketer on the phone for you."

Then again, could it be they are actually coming to grips with the fact that Jesus is passing the baton? What uncertainties and changes would that mean for them? They've already experienced plans going terribly wrong. So many in the religious establishment are filled with rising hate. The occasional brush fires ignited after healings on the Sabbath have gusted into a firestorm since Jesus raised Lazarus. Could Jesus be telling them that His departure might include betrayal, arrest, sentencing, and execution? If the religious are now determined to destroy Jesus once and for all, this will likely mean personal suffering for those who follow Jesus.

Let's not overlook the fact that the disciples are also wrestling with their own issues. John doesn't tell us, but the other gospels reveal a bickering group of men posturing for control and power on this final night. It's human nature. It starts on the playground. Sizing up happens in nearly every profession. It occurs at parties, class reunions, family reunions, company dinners, as well as on Facebook.

In this case, even family members are involved (Matt. 20:20). If the hour has come and the kingdom is at hand, there are positions to grab. Each one is hoping the emerging King has been impressed with his performance. As yet, they have no clue Jesus is about to die, rise, and come back three days later. They are unaware He will leave and replace Himself with Himself, but they are sure someone needs to take charge.

ARE WE COMPREHENDING THE MAGNITUDE?

Sometimes the disciples are clueless, caught up in their own self-importance. At other times, they are oblivious to just how important they really are. They are the key to God's continuing plans. Jesus did not invite them to simply be part of a traveling Bible study, assist in setup and teardown, and collect response cards. He did not enlist them to send first-time letters, count offerings, and direct traffic. All along, He has been preparing them to pursue a most strategic mission. This has mega-implications.

All too many settle for something less. Coming to the wilderness for an occasional retreat, I hear about these pockets of people in the deeper parts away from towns and roads. On the back side of a mountain or down in a deep canyon, people live. When I inquire as to what they do, most are unsure. Do they simply exist? Some are on welfare. Others are off the grid. It might sound romantic at first. Maybe they sit by ponds and read Thoreau and write their own *Life in the Woods*. Maybe they scrutinize nature with a monastic patience like Annie Dillard or Wendell Berry. It might seem to be an idealistic life, but "meaningless" seems a more fitting term. What is life if you live without a cause greater than survival, a purpose no higher than yourself and your contemplative thoughts?

Walter Isaacson recounts a conversation Steve Jobs, cofounder of Apple, had with John Sculley, then CEO of PepsiCo. Jobs on numerous occasions attempted to lure Sculley over to Apple. It eventually happened. One day, Jobs asked Sculley this simple question: "Do you want to spend the rest of your life selling sugared water, or do you want a chance to change the world?" For the first time in four months, Sculley could not say no.[9]

What Jesus is talking about is far greater. He does not come onstage to announce the latest technology or the latest performance shoe that will transform the way people live. He is calling them and us to continue what He began—preaching the kingdom, reaching the lost, building the saints. He is calling us to continue the revolution for the hearts and souls of men and women. Comparatively, everything else is sugared water and passing fads, sustained only by hype.

ARE WE LAUNCHING SOMETHING NEW?

Jesus does not leave His disciples with the challenge to devise something novel and audacious. There's nothing to be invented. He did not come to create so much as to continue what the Father began. He said this often:

- "Anyone who does not honor the Son does not honor the Father *who sent Him*" (John 5:23).
- "These very works I am doing testify about Me that the Father *has sent Me*" (5:36).
- "No one can come to Me unless the Father *who sent Me* draws him" (6:44).
- "I and the Father *who sent Me* judge together" (8:16).
- "I didn't come on My own, but *He sent Me*" (8:42).
- "The one who sees Me sees *Him who sent Me*" (12:45).

Now He is sending the disciples on the same mission: "As the Father has sent Me, *I also send you*" (20:21).

All of this underscores that God is a sending God, who for the joy set before His Son called Him to run His race (Heb. 12:1–3). Jesus now sends us, calling us to throw off everything and run with perseverance the race set before us. There is a mission to fulfill. Mission is part of God's nature (John 4:4). Hence, mission is more than the church's function, with a missions department to carry it out. It is the nature of the church to cross barriers with the gospel. Everyone who views themselves as a disciple must also see themselves as apostles, sent ones. Under an open heaven, there has been a shift—centripetal to centrifugal, attractional to incarnational, motion outward rather than merely inward.

WHAT EXACTLY IS JESUS PASSING OFF?

Listen carefully to what is going on in this conversation. In the back and forth, one discovers that Jesus is passing on the leadership necessary to guide the future church. What does this look like?

Servant Leadership

Jesus is looking at this ragtag group of men, knowing they will have to step up and lead. Most leadership books will tell you that leaders are about three things: First, leaders attract followers. Without followers, you are simply taking a walk. Second, leaders are influencers. They have a transformative effect. Finally, leaders are those who give direction. They catalyze movement. They sustain what has begun. The disciples will have to do this.

But Jesus does not begin here. He could have. He could have laid out those characteristics in a leader that cause people to follow. He could have talked about the kind of force that energizes a crowd, a Douglas MacArthur–type presence that fills a room. He might have shared the importance of having a vision, of acquiring an ability to foresee the trend lines, see around the curves to where history is going.

Instead, without a word, Jesus begins to act out the true nature of leadership. He takes a towel and a basin and does something both radical and unnerving: He washes the feet of His disciples. Washing feet was an act reserved for the lowest slave. "To touch another person's feet was an act of profound subjugation," the antipode of power.[10] Jesus took the same hands that held and hold all power and authority in the universe and washed the dirtiest parts of one's body—where dust and dirt and filth and dung and waste collect. He asks: "Do you know what I have done for you?" (John 13:12).

They don't. As far as they're concerned, He has gone against all protocol. This is irrational behavior. But in this one moment, Jesus has shown them what leadership under an open heaven looks like. *One leads by serving.* In this one act, Jesus reverses all human assumptions of importance and rank. He has turned upside down all Greek and Roman codes of conduct, all good Jewish ways of moving ahead, and the best secular approaches to leadership. He's acted contrary to all rabbinic assumptions that religious leaders should be served rather than serve. He has leveled the sort of posturing that curves in on itself, and silenced that inner voice that so often asks, "What will they think of me?" God's kingdom works on inverted principles: "Whoever wants to become great among you must be your servant" (Matt. 20:26).

This is unsettling for Jesus's followers, as revealed by their silence. To do something so demeaning and degrading is threatening, especially to anyone who is insecure. But Jesus can do this, for He accepts Himself perfectly and knows His place (John 13:3). This is not someone losing power; this is someone who has been given all authority "restoring [power] to its original purpose."[11] In contrast, the disciples are threatened. They know that for any one of them to do a particular menial and mundane task might establish an expectation. *It may become a permanent assignment.*

Peter breaks the silence. He will have none of this (v. 6). His question is actually a challenge: "Lord, You? You wash my feet?" Jesus surely knows that servants typically serve masters. It is an incomprehensible contradiction for the teacher to wash the feet of His students. Leaders worth their weight give the aura of someone in charge. They can't be bothered with the trivial! CEOs do not refill the paper towel dispensers, up-and-coming kings do not unplug toilets, church leaders do not park cars, and worshippers with important roles do not assist a single mother who needs to pick up her children in the nursery.

They don't—unless they are intentionally carrying out the mission to manifest Jesus. Jesus did not have a need to hang on to His credentials, showcase His authority, or make a display of His importance by manipulating and exploiting those around Him (Phil. 2:5–11). He was fine with hanging out with the lowlifes. He did not live for people to make Him a king. He did not come to be served but to serve. And in this, He exhibited the kind of leadership God expects of everyone who self-identifies as a leader.

Barbara Brown Taylor recalls her days in seminary. She would often meet with God on a fire escape that hung from the side of a deserted Victorian mansion next to the divinity school. Like other students she longed for a word from God that would tell her what to do with her gifts and passions. Out of these long sessions with God, she came to this discovery: "It was not *what* I did but *how* I did it that mattered."[12]

Yes, in an upper room Jesus is calling these men to be missional leaders. But making sure they know *how* it is to be executed is what matters. Two thousand years after this first foot washing, the church is still working on this. The church, especially since Constantine, has had this tendency to get in bed with power and politics. There is a strong attraction to the kind of decisive, strong leadership that controls the levers and establishes policies. Pastors tend to gravitate to models that look more like CEOs with autocratic power than servants who wash feet. Getting a seat at the table of rank becomes a single-minded pursuit.

Sociologist Michael Lindsay has tracked this rise of what he calls "a new power elite" in American evangelism.[13] Today they wield power from the White House to Wall Street, from Harvard to Hollywood. But in all too many cases, those with this thirst for power and influence have been forced to renegotiate their relationships. Their faith has met American culture, and culture has triumphed. Celebrity leadership is preferred over servant leadership, and in the process the church fails to carry out its mission to be the presence of Jesus. It drops the baton and loses the race.

Godlike Love

After washing their feet and sitting down, Jesus issues a "new" decree. Under an open heaven, old ways of relating are to be replaced (John

13:34). To fulfill its mission, the church must not only "love your neighbor as yourself" (Lev. 19:18). We must love others as *He* loves others.

But what does having a godlike love mean? We have to admit, Jesus's behavior doesn't correspond with our notion of loving. There are certain moments He appears to have an almost granitelike disposition. Love as He loves? Tenderness and compassion are not one's immediate impressions of Jesus at Cana. He is rather cold to Nicodemus, matter-of-fact to the woman at the well, straightforward with the paralytic, brusque with the crowd, cool toward His brothers, aloof to the Pharisees, theological with the blind man, and painfully unresponsive to Martha and Mary and Mary Magdalene. On top of this, He is occasionally impatient and confrontational with His own disciples.

If the gospel of John is music, the brass and wind and percussion sections seem to overpower the strings. But maybe we're not listening very well. Maybe "we've become deaf to the richer parts of the symphony of love."[14] Let's replay the music:

- Out of His love and obedience to the Father, He responds to the needs in Cana when the Father says yes. And when He does, Jesus acts with compassionate urgency (John 2:7).
- Out of His love for Nicodemus, He invites him to begin fresh and get in step with the Spirit (3:8).
- Out of His love for the woman at the well, He reaches out to her while everyone else shuns her (4:7).
- Out of His love for the paralytic, He directs His focus only to him in the crowd, reaches out to liberate him, and speaks to the deeper issues that have entrapped his life (5:6).
- Out of His love for the crowd, He invites them to a better feast (6:35).
- Out of His love for His brothers, He challenges them to live a life that matters (7:6).
- Out of His love for the Jews, He offers faith over religion (8:31).

- Out of His love for the blind man, He gives more than sight—
  He reveals Himself (9:35).
- Out of His love for Martha and Mary, He replaces their grief
  with joy (11:43).
- Out of His love for the disciples, He gives them the dignity
  of purpose (14:12).
- Out of His love for the world, He goes to the cross to lay down
  His life for the sheep and pay for our failures (19:18).

We witness a love that is not empty words or sentimental platitudes; it is sacrificial action. To love as God loves is to love in a spontaneous way; it does not wait for deserved moments. It is "rugged covenantal commitment"; it does not love conditionally.[15] Divine love is generous. Jesus loved His disciples to the end (*telos*) with a full, robust, and perfect love (John 13:1). Pastor and evangelist F. B. Meyer once described God's love as being like "the Amazon river flowing down to water a single daisy."[16] He loves us with a depth that reflects another world. This is how Jesus loved and we are to love.

When we seize this Christlike love and pass it on, this is what it looks like in today's church:

- walking in to worship prepared to expend my spiritual gifts where needed—in order that others might find life
- welcoming someone I have never met
- embracing others who are different
- forgetting about oneself to attend to others' needs
- accepting others in all their achingly frail reality
- reaching out to the single dad—the barren woman—the person dealing with a medical complication or mental deficiency
- listening when I would rather be on my way
- giving no ear to gossip
- singing songs that are not always my preference
- showing the utmost grace in the greatest disagreement
- mentoring the next generation and putting up with their mistakes

- getting up earlier to pray for the needs of one another
- expecting the best—rather than assuming the worst of someone
- giving my resources to the whole—rather than dictating where God's money should go
- being committed to one's success
- always saying thank you

Christlike love matters. It authenticates our faith (13:35). Jesus is saying, "The world will know you are My disciples, not because you do amazing miracles or put on impressive concerts or create slick videos or travel the world doing conferences, but because you are a community radically devoted to showing the love of God to one another." This is what makes God visible. It is what brings an awareness of God, a revealing of His reality. It tells the world the heavens have opened and He remains in our midst.

Sometimes we drop the baton. We bicker and divide, and in the process we lose the energy and drive necessary for mission. John's subsequent writings addressed a community in Ephesus that had a torturous time loving one another. In the small space of his first epistle, he referred to love forty-six times. For John, "love formed the center of [his] moral vision," the foundational substratum, and the relational act par excellence.[17] Little wonder the Devil tries so hard to create a wedge between believers, rip apart families, and stir up hate in the church. This is a sure way to slow the race.

Empowered Life

It would not be enough if Jesus merely passed on a model of leadership and a definition of love that will radically change the world. To run this race, we will need a new capacity. We will need His supernatural power. But things slow up for a moment.

Remember, this dialogue is a bit messy. Things don't flow easily. The discourse gets hijacked by interruptions and time-outs. In this moment, the disciples are having a difficult time staying focused. Jesus is taking them forward, but they are still looking back. They can't stop thinking about Jesus's departure. If only Jesus hadn't prefaced His love command with the announcement that He is leaving. This is a bit like a pastor prefacing his sermon with an announcement that this is his last Sunday. It's hard to transition back to the text printed in the bulletin.

The disciples realize they need to know what authenticates their faith, but they are feeling exposed and vulnerable. With a rising desperation in his voice, Peter wants to know where Jesus is going and if he can skip the race and come with Him (13:36–37). Thomas wants a course map. Jesus tells him, "You know the way. I am the way" (see 14:5–6).

They remind me of certain parishioners who come up after I have preached. On the heels of the benediction, they ask, "Will childcare be provided for Wednesday night's event?" "Did you notice on your last Korean trip that they package their bananas in cellophane?" "Have you heard my son made JV?" "Will you be here for the wedding?" "Did you get that tie at Nordstrom?"

Was anyone listening?

Jesus has much more to say about this new command (and He will say it in 15:12–17), but the disciples are preoccupied at the moment. They are feeling unsupported and abandoned. They have no desire to be the cast of characters in a novel entitled *Left Behind*. If there is an ascension, they want to join the ride.

The discourse evolves into a full-out Q&A. Philip breaks in: "Lord, show us the Father, and that's enough for us" (see 14:7). He wants what many want—some epiphany, some vision, some tangible experience to mark the way and assure us of God's presence. Jesus answers with His own question, one that surely comes with the exasperation of a parent with an obtuse child: "Have I been among you all this time without your knowing Me, Philip? The one who has seen Me has seen the Father" (v. 9). There has been more to the presence of God than they realize.

Suddenly, in this moment of growing despair and confusion, Jesus makes the most astonishing statement of the whole discourse.

"I assure you: The one who believes in Me will also do the works that I do. And he will do *even* greater works than these, because I am going to the Father" (v. 12). He will run an even more incredible race!

What the disciples perceive to be a disadvantage is actually to their advantage. They fear Jesus's departure means they will be left alone and they will have to run by themselves. They fear they will not make it to the tape. They are envisioning scarcity and stagnation upon His departure, but it's just the opposite. In His leaving, God's presence will be *more* available than ever. And this means they will transcend the works Jesus has done.

Jesus has just taken them (and us) to another level, to the "no imagination has ever conceived" level (see 1 Cor. 2:9; Eph. 3:20). This is what good leaders do—take people "to places where they have never dared to go."[18] But how can these words be true? It's one thing to extend the mission, but how is it possible to expand the work? Is Jesus speaking about something merely quantitative? Will it be "more works" because there are wider fields and more of us? Or is this something more profound? Will it be more spectacular?

It is hard to imagine feats more impressive than turning water into wine, restoring the sick to health, feeding five thousand people, quieting storms, giving sight to the blind, and raising the dead. Is belief all that is required? He is beginning to sound like Zig Ziglar or some other motivational speaker telling us He will see us at the top.

Yes, in part. Jesus is speaking of something quite different and even more astonishing. In His leaving, our works will be greater because our divine support will be more expansive. His transition means a more—not less—empowered life for us. The whole weight of the Trinity will be involved in our lives, now that heaven has opened.

As John Jefferson Davis writes, "The ascension does not mean the absence of Christ so much as it means the presence of Christ in a new way."[19] Having disarmed the rulers of darkness, He will soon sit on high at the right hand of the Father with judicial power, ruling invisibly over empires and nations. All things will be under His feet (Eph. 1:22–23), and He will fill all things (4:10). He will adorn His church with gifts and empower them for radical impact. His kingdom will be "more extensive in its global reach and more intensive in its redemptive power than any earthly empire in history."[20]

His ascension will set in motion the Spirit's descension (John 14:16). The second person of the Trinity is handing off to the third person. Through the Spirit, the disciples will experience the presence of Christ and shalom of God in a new way. With the fullness of the Spirit in the lives of His followers, God's presence is no longer limited by Jesus's physical body. He is now with us in a more transformative and interior way.

It's not that the Spirit has been absent up to this point, but His presence has been more seemingly random, rushing upon certain people, clothing unassuming people like Gideon and questionable characters like Samson with power. But after the ascension this will change. The Spirit is coming to take up residence (v. 17). He is no longer like some hotel guest abruptly coming for the night. He now is coming to settle in, moving in all the "nooks and crannies of daily details" with the aim of taking over, claiming us for God's purposes.[21] The Spirit will no longer be *with* but *in* the disciples. And this will give Jesus's followers a more profound and ongoing sense of His presence, as well as the potential to reveal His radical power (v. 19).

The presence of the Spirit will press God's truth more deeply within our souls. He will take what Jesus has already said about service and enable us to serve. He will take what Jesus has modeled in love and empower us to love; He will take what Jesus has taught about prayer and move us to pray; He will take what Scripture has already declared about God's will and move us to follow it; He will take what God has taught us about faith and open the eyes of our imaginations. And He will take what Jesus has said about the indwelling Spirit and fill our lives.

With Jesus's departure, the disciples will also have a new relationship with the Father. Entering heaven, Jesus will bring us before God in ways He has not previously. He will live to make intercession for us as the perfect mediator. He will continually pray for the accomplishment of His mission, plead our cause, and secure for us the benefits of His death (Rom. 8:26–27; Heb. 7:25).

Because of this work of divine intercession, our personal prayer life will take on greater power. Prayers prompted by the Spirit and teamed with Jesus's ongoing petitions will release the Father's willingness and ability to act (John 14:13–14). Great prayers will have the potential for great answers. Jesus underscores this several times in the upper room:

- "Whatever you ask in My name, I will do it" (14:13).
- "If you remain in Me and My words remain in you, ask whatever you want and it will be done for you" (15:7).
- "Whatever you ask the Father in My name, He will give you" (15:16).
- "Anything you ask the Father in My name, He will give you" (16:23).

To a nervous, insecure, and tiny band of followers (so like us), Jesus is declaring that He will not change the world with armies, swords, legions of angels, and lightning bolts. It will be through full-of-faith men and women. The ministry of the Trinity will soon enable them to step out and do the greater things, speaking the same words and demonstrating the same passion for God's holiness (the kind that goes in and cleanses irreligious temples). We are enabled to live out the same righteousness, call for the same justice, confront the same darkness, and boldly speak the same prophetic word. We can have the same indifference to anything but the will of the Father; we can cross the same barriers to reach the marginalized and love on people; we can be the same instrument of healing, carrying out the same work of spiritual renewal. We too can awaken people to true spirituality and authentic faith and do the same work of reconciliation, building community, removing alienation, extending grace, and ministering forgiveness.

One can imagine Jesus's excitement in the room. Did they get it? Do we?

The disciples might be a bit tentative. Like little boys trying on their dad's shoes, the disciples have attempted some of these works already, such as walking on water and casting out demons. It has not gone so well. At times they were impotent to change anything, but this had nothing to do with God's power and everything to do with the smallness of their faith (Matt. 17:19–21). To experience divine empowerment, they had to—will have to—believe (John 14:11). So far, His track shoes don't seem to fit.

Do we believe? Jesus's words in 14:12 force us to ask hard questions: Could it be that behind our failure to experience divine support and do the greater works is a skepticism squeezing out belief? Do I believe it is possible to have the kind of faith that moves mountains? Do I really believe prayer matters? Am I certain the Son is interceding, the indwelling Spirit is empowering, and the Father is responding? Do I have the conviction He is able to do above and beyond all that we ask or think? It all may go back to this question: Do I really believe heaven is open?

Suddenly, Jesus tells them it's time to "wake up" and leave (v. 31). Maybe it is time for a break. Perhaps it is overload. It is getting late. Maybe the disciples are afraid to ask another question. The conversation, however, continues. Time is running out and there is much more to be said (v. 30; 16:12). There is something else He wants to pass on, and now He does so as they leave and make their way to the Kidron Valley, possibly passing through a vineyard.

Vital Connection

Jesus wants to see them take the baton and run as servant leaders, racing with His love and competing in the power of the Trinity. But this will require that they stay closely connected, just as He and the Father are connected (14:10). They cannot afford to run this race as if they are on their own. In some mysterious and profound way, Jesus is passing on the baton and then running with them.

But what does this look like? Literal language falls short. Technical language cannot keep up. Jesus shifts to pictures to make more concrete what might seem abstract. Jesus does this often: if you want nourishment, think of Jesus as the Bread of Life; if you want to see, think of Jesus as the Light of the World; if you need direction, think of Jesus as the Way. If you are looking for vital connection with God, think of Jesus as the Vine.

The shift to metaphor in John 15 is risky. As Eugene Peterson notes, "metaphor requires participation."[22] Jesus is enlisting their imagination, so the disciples cannot afford to be passive. But they have tripped over figurative language in the past ("Lord, if he has fallen asleep, he will get well," 11:12; see also 2:21–22; 4:32–33). They are still trying to work through Jesus's symbolic washing of their feet. They again will need to focus in order to capture the implications of the vine and branch. *So will we.*

If we are to experience this abundant life under an open heaven, if we are to run this race well, we must, like a branch, remain in vital connection to the vine. This is the overarching imperative of the passage (15:4). This is the test of discipleship and the demand of discipleship. Jesus has already made this clear (8:31). No branch is a self-contained entity.

Jesus commands us to remain in him because it is not inevitable. One does not assume it nor stumble into it. Remaining in union with Christ, who now resides in another realm, is not an automatic pattern of life.[23] So what does it look like, and how does one remain connected?

Remaining attached to Jesus implies a total union, a connection that is tight and able to endure the forces that would seek to break it apart. In relational terms, it is slowing down and entering into the solitude, the silence, and the deep to find God. It involves receiving the life-giving sap of His Word. It includes prayer, where we now shift from listening to responding. This requires the same focus, the same determination to leave the distractions. It amounts to give-and-take, inhale and exhale in an ongoing way.

To ensure the greatest success in all of this, the husbandry of the Father is required. Think of Him as the Vinedresser who oversees the whole process. The vineyard is His to plant, His to tend to, and His to protect and care for. Every branch will feel the pruning knife of the Vinedresser. Those branches that are unproductive, diseased, or dead are taken out so as to not inhibit those who are abiding. The Gardener does not tolerate branches that fail to yield, that pretend to be part of the vine—that diminish the witness and impede another's union.

The essential purpose of any vineyard is to bear fruit. This is part of our mission. As we abide, the Father looks for ways to make us more fruitful. Even branches that produce are also under His knife. If a vinedresser fails to prune branches that produce, there is a good deal of unproductive growth over time. There can be superfluous shoots, and branches can become straggly and tangled, growing in all the wrong directions—inward when they should be growing outward. All of this saps the fruit-bearing process, interfering with the bottom line.

The Gardener uses multiple instruments, beginning with the Word (15:3). This is the nature of the Word, sharper than a two-edged sword (Heb. 4:12). Spend any serious time in the Word and one may be cut to the core. There are passages intended to lop off the self-life, rebuke pride, and redirect desires.

Sometimes God uses other instruments, such as setbacks, closed doors, and lost dreams. Life's difficult people are sometimes God's particular tool to lop off things that have become too important, activities that have become too distracting, and trivial pursuits that have begun to amount to nothing. This process can be quite painful, but it is all to ensure greater fruit in the future. Hopefully we can begin to see that some of our losses in life are nothing less than the divine Pruner at work (e.g., Mary and Martha in John 11). There are some things that are not ours to recover, things God has intentionally cut off so we can be His ongoing presence in our world.

In sum, remaining in the vine amounts to practicing the presence of Christ, entering into an intimacy that takes on His power, His energy, and His love. In the process, His will, His affections, His wisdom, and His ways can become ours. We can love as He loves. Abiding leads to profound works (14:10).

This is how Jesus reveals Himself to the world: through a community serving and loving and doing the work of God in the power of God, living in such a powerful union that people will see God. This is how Jesus will close His prayer: "I am in them and You are in Me . . . so the world may know You have sent Me" (17:23).

Undaunted Courage

As Jesus comes to the end, He warns His disciples that this race will have its dangers. Being in union with Him will come with a price. If you intend to fulfill His mission and run His course, prepare for a mixed response. Some will cheer us on (Heb. 12:1). Others will hate us (John 15:18–25). Continuing the presence of Christ will provoke the same response Jesus received. While some will be drawn to us by our lives and our convictions, others will become hostile—we become a fragrance of life to some, a scent of death to others (2 Cor. 2:15–16). The world will continue to hate those whose way of life passes implicit judgment on society. It will despise those who declare that the gods of this world are false gods, and it will certainly take offense when the church declares that there is only one way.

Many will do all they can to silence God's judgment. History bears this out. Tradition says Matthew was killed by a sword, Peter was crucified upside down, Andrew and Nathanael were crucified, James was beheaded, John was exiled, Philip was stoned, Thomas was stabbed with a spear, and Judas was clubbed to death. Paul the apostle was roughly treated, reviled "like the world's garbage, like the dirt everyone scrapes off their sandals" (1 Cor. 4:13). And still today, Christians—those who continue the work of being Christ's ongoing presence—are statistically the most persecuted group in the world.[24]

The Spirit will come and prosecute the world through us (John 16:7–11). He is putting the world on notice that it is not Jesus who is on trial—it is the world! He will convict, penetrate the self-deceptions and defensive ploys, confront, expose, cross-examine, and prosecute. He will open the world to things it does not want to see. He will come to bring forth the most damning charge, the charge of unbelief. This is the most characteristic sin, the classic sin, the deepest sin. It is the unpardonable sin.

This can be unnerving, but Christ never promised that following Him would be a cakewalk. It is a grueling race, an enlistment into a dangerous mission. Everywhere the kingdom of God advances, there is a violent engagement against a dark kingdom. The world doesn't have a place for truth, divine righteousness, and grace.

Up until now, in America, we haven't had much threat of losing our lives. More often, we are simply dismissed as fanatics or buffoons or hypocrites, shamed if we choose to be biblically rather than politically correct. Encouraged to be nice. The same cultural forces determined to turn Jesus into a therapeutic counselor work to turn Christian leaders into gentle religious figures who smile reassurance.

I recently read about a controversial MTV VJ who has struggled in the past with addiction and his own rising fame, but now he is using his platform to "change the world." But I fear his choice of words may add to the general impression one has of Jesus and the church in our culture: "I think that Jesus is really brilliant. All those things He did: the miracles—that was kind. The sacrifice of His own life that we may be free from sin: I think that was a really, really nice thing to do."[25]

What Jesus did had little to do with niceness and kindness. Jesus came to serve notice to evil. His own words liken His coming to someone entering a strong man's house, tying him up, carrying off his possessions, and declaring, "Now the ruler of this world will be cast out" (John 12:31). As John wrote, "The Son of God was revealed for this purpose: to destroy the Devil's works" (1 John 3:8). What He did, and continues to do, is so provocative it leads to alienation and attack.

So it follows that life will be a mix of victory and defeat, struggle and rest, bad news and good news:

- *BAD* NEWS—In a little while, Jesus's earthly ministry is ending.
- *GOOD* NEWS—In a little while, the Spirit is coming to replace and continue Jesus's ministry.

- *BAD* NEWS—Jesus has been sold out, betrayed by the world into the hands of the Evil One.
- *GOOD* NEWS—The ruler of this world has been judged, having no power over Jesus.

- *BAD* NEWS—Jesus will soon be on trial.
- *GOOD* NEWS—It is really the world that is on trial.

- *BAD* NEWS—In this life, we will face intense pain, like a woman in childbirth.
- *GOOD* NEWS—The joy of new birth will transcend any pain of the past.

- *BAD* NEWS—This all raises a lot of questions.
- *GOOD* NEWS—One day, things will make much more sense.

What Jesus gave to the disciples in this upper room was courage. He assured them, and us, that we can be fearless. We will have suffering in this life, but He has overcome: "I have conquered the world" (John 16:33). The tense describes past action with ongoing results. No matter the attacks, we have nothing to fear as we "bear witness to the sovereign rule of Jesus, holding the world to account."[26] Though Satan has not conceded defeat, he has been overthrown. He has not yet been eliminated. We still live in a fierce war zone. When we ignore this, there are unnecessary casualties. We must fight the good fight, resist the Devil, and take on Christ's armor (Eph. 6:10–19).

To reinforce their courage, Jesus prayed at the close of their time in the upper room. He brought these men and His future church to the Father (John 17:1–26). His mission was near completion. Jesus didn't ask God to send rescue planes to evacuate His disciples. He didn't ask that we be excused from the race. That would nullify the purpose of a disciple, which is to continue the work of Jesus. He didn't pray that we be wrapped in "some plastic, danger-free safety casing."[27] Those who wish to hide in a Christian ghetto, living like the sectarian Qumran community, miss the point.

IT IS NOW OUR RACE

Jesus knows we are vulnerable, exposed, and at risk in a world that does not embrace His mission. His prayer is that the Father will protect His church (John 17:11). Under an open heaven, one lives in no-man's-land. We come to Christ and suddenly find ourselves living between two worlds, two kingdoms. We find ourselves somewhere between the physical world we have been born into and the spiritual world we have been reborn into. We live at the crossroads between good and evil, standing between victory and final victory. We are caught in the cross fire in a cosmic struggle between the kingdom of light and the kingdom of darkness. This triad of world, flesh, and Devil continue to resist the rulership of God. It is all-out spiritual war!

But we have the Trinity with us in this pursuit of serving His purpose, we have this open heaven under which we race, and we have these "witnesses," men and women who have paid the price (Heb. 12:1). They include Chrysostom, Tyndale, Bonhoeffer, Elliott, disciples throughout the ages. These are runners who have gone before us, members of the same relay team who have now passed the baton to us. This is now our leg, our divine mission, and these witnesses cheer us on, for we are part of completing the race. And soon, it will be our turn to pass this mission on to others:

- servant leadership—as Jesus served us
- godlike love—as Jesus loved
- empowered life—as Jesus laid hold of the Father's power
- vital connection—as Jesus abided in the Father
- undaunted courage—as Jesus demonstrated

In the process may we not hear "Ping. Ping. Ping."

QUESTIONS

1. How have these words of Jesus impacted your life: "I assure you: The one who believes in Me will also do the works that I do. And he will do even greater works than these, because I am going to the Father" (John 14:12)? What do they do to your imagination?

2. Jesus's mission includes servant leadership, godlike love, empowered life, vital connection, and undaunted courage. Which of these is the most difficult for you? Why?

3. How would you describe the race God has called you to run?

12

LIFE IS ABOUT FLOURISHING UNDER GOD'S AUTHORITY

A Conversation with Pilate

JOHN 18:28–19:11

> *So Pilate said to Him, "You're not talking to me? Don't You know that I have the authority to release You and the authority to crucify You?"*
>
> *"You would have no authority over Me at all," Jesus answered him, "if it hadn't been given you from above."*
>
> —JOHN 19:10–11

IN AN ARTICLE IN *THE NEW YORK TIMES*, "HAVE WE MET?," MARK Herrmann comes out of the closet to admit a condition he has suffered all of his life. It is called *prosopagnosia*, the inability to identify faces. He's not alone; some 5 million people in the United States suffer from this affliction. It means that, outside of a person's own face and a few close loved ones, it is impossible to recognize people. Parties with lots of people, movies with a large cast, or services at large churches are often confusing and embarrassing experiences.[1]

Pilate suffers from a similar malady. But his is more than confusing or embarrassing—it's terribly tragic. He cannot recognize the face of God before him. John 18 introduces him as a man who prides himself as a man in the know; he views himself as perceptive, but he does not get how life operates under an open heaven. Nor does he care. He, like the rest of the powers of Rome, is too distracted and disinterested to notice that heaven has opened, that a far more powerful force is now in play.

THE ASSUMED AUTHORITY OF EARTHLY POWERS

So who is Pilate? John 18:28 tells us he is a man of rank, a Roman governor whose official title other sources identify as prefect. He is an appointee of Tiberius, and his office and tenure suggest he is an important person, a man of weight on the world stage. His authority is nearly absolute. Like other governors, he is charged with maintaining order and carrying out the will of the Roman emperor. He possesses "the full imperium," meaning he has "criminal, jurisdictional, and military authority."[2]

Pilate's jurisdiction includes Judea, but he has little sympathy for his Jewish constituents. Though his position must command some respect, many of the Jews know he is there as a political favor. Maybe he made a generous contribution to the emperor's recent campaign. Pilate is not much better than the worthless sons of Herod, the ones he has replaced. He likes to flaunt his newfound authority, making him a ruthless thug. Philo, a Jewish philosopher and contemporary of Pilate, found Pilate's crimes to include briberies, robberies, wanton injuries, executions without trial, and "ceaseless and supremely grievous cruelty."[3] In a letter written to his friend, callous Herod Agrippa described Pilate as "naturally inflexible, a blend of self-will and relentlessness."[4]

Pilate is protective of his authority, putting down any and all demonstrations with blunt force. Luke records that on one occasion, likely at a feast requiring his presence, he massacred a group of Galileans (terrorists in his mind) and mixed their blood with the blood of animal sacrifices (Luke 13:1). He views the Jews the same way they view their sacrifices—as objects to be slit and placed on an altar. He has nothing but contempt for Jewish religion and sanctity. Their gatherings interrupt his vacations at Club Med in nearby Caesarea, a Roman port and holiday town with magnificent palaces and lavish public buildings.

There will be other occasions where he unleashes violence on his subjects.[5] It does not seem to matter to the upper tier. Rome is generally unconcerned with how governors carry out their duties "so long as the taxes were collected and allegiance to Rome remained firm."[6] But Pilate's behavior will eventually exceed even Rome's harsh ways, requiring the empire's intervention and decision to dismiss him.

THE LIMITED AUTHORITY OF EARTHLY POWERS

At this moment in John's gospel, Pilate is facing a growing hostile crowd, Jewish leaders, and a Galilean named Jesus. Things are discomforting. Pilate is sensing some limitations. He is unable to read this person who has been arrested by the temple police (John 18:12).

Is He another terrorist to be thrown on the altar and His blood mixed with lambs?

The encounter gets off to a bad start. Despite his governing authority, Pilate will have to come out to meet the Jews. The Jews have their standards; they cannot risk sullying themselves by entering into a pagan's quarters. This would defile and disqualify them from participating in the Passover. Passover is holy, and these are holy men. They have their righteousness to protect.

The Jews have their own blindness. Over the past few months, they have become obsessed with killing Jesus. In one of John's ironies, they see no incongruity in preserving their sanctity for the lamb while crucifying the Lamb. But they know that their religious concerns will cut no ice with Pilate. As he has constantly revealed, he couldn't care less about Sabbath laws and religious codes. They must convince Pilate just how dangerous Jesus is, for only Rome has the authority to put men to death.

So the Jewish authorities refashion their case in political terms: Jesus is an "evildoer." Malevolence is His profession; it's what He *does* for a living. He is a terrorist leader down there with ISIS and al-Qaeda. They want Pilate to know that He is a threat to the community, and to Rome itself. He is a self-proclaimed Messiah with intentions to incite a rebellion against the empire. He claims to be the King. This is a capital crime. This is treason!

From Pilate's perspective, this is more than an intrusion into his schedule. This is a bad dream that he knows will not end anytime soon and will have far-reaching consequences. There are certain conflicts you want to avoid. American President Dwight Eisenhower was determined to not tangle with Joe McCarthy, a US senator, a demagogue, and a man on a witch hunt for communists. "Never get into a pissing match with a skunk," Eisenhower liked to say.[7] He could leave the fight to others. But Pilate cannot escape the witch hunt of the religious leaders. He has no one else to face these agitators. Will he be characteristically obstinate, or will he cave in to their demands?

We must remember that Pilate is a politician. He watches the polls back home. He checks his approval rating. He knows that any disturbance that gets out of control does not play well in Rome. But Pilate must also appease a crowd he despises.

This again is high drama. John captures the dilemma. He takes us outside to inside, front stage to back stage. There are seven Pilate episodes in all, giving us a picture of a dithering politician:

- He is outside, discerning the charges (18:29).
- He is inside, questioning Jesus (18:33).
- He is outside, declaring Jesus is innocent (18:38).
- He is inside, where Jesus is scourged (19:1).
- He is outside, presenting Jesus (19:4).
- He is inside, pushing around his weight (19:9–10).
- He is outside, hoping to release Jesus (19:12–13).

Pilate shuttles back and forth like a mad diplomat, a Henry Kissinger flying from one set of demands to the next. Like so many others in the book of John, Pilate is faced with a crucial decision. It is the most important one everyone faces at some point in life—what will I do with Jesus? You can't live in the middle, playing one role against the other, having it both ways. At some point, a person must decide where he or she will stand. And indecision is ultimately to choose the world.

As the conversation begins, its tone is markedly different from the last one in the upper room (John 13–17). This is less a conversation and more a confrontation. With Jesus's arrival on earth, God's kingdom has come. Sooner or later, it will collide with the world's kingdoms. It is now reaching its height. Behind the scenes, it is a battle with an unseen spiritual force "working through the treachery of Judas and the callous power of Rome."[8]

Like other conversations in John, this one tells us what life is like under an open heaven. It lays out the way things work. It puts kings and kingdoms and their assumed authority into perspective. It serves to prepare us for our own confrontations, when the fear of God and the fear of man vie for our attention and submission.

John breaks the conversation into two main acts (18:28–38a and 18:38b–19:11). On the surface, it appears Pilate initiates the conversation. As the prefect, he summons Jesus; he does the talking. But it is really Pilate who will be interrogated. It is Pilate who is on trial. This is another one of John's ironies. The apparent judge, along with his accusers, are in fact judged and condemned by the one assumed to be on trial.[9]

Pilate confronts Jesus with a question: "Are You the King of the Jews?" (18:33). "You" is the first word in the Greek sentence, suggesting that it could also be translated, "You are King of the Jews?" As if to say, "Wh–wh–what? You . . . *You* are King of the Jews! Really?" In other words, "You, a pretender, a no-name misfit from some backwater town in the north, whose followers have all but abandoned you? You claim to be the sovereign of some vast realm? Where are the trappings of authority, the special vehicle tags for Your aides? Why are they not wearing seersucker suits with pastel bow ties?"

But Jesus poses His own question: "Are you asking this on your own, or have others told you about Me?" (v. 34). One hears the depth of God's love in these words. Jesus is prompting Pilate to consider his question more deeply. Has he done his own investigation or simply accepted rumors he has heard? Or . . . or could his own heart be prompting him to seek the truth about the gospel and eternal life?

Pilate is riled. You would think Jesus had asked him if he wants to meet at Starbucks and work through Rachel Zahl's *Converting to Judaism: How to Become a Jew*. He's thinking, *Do I look like a Jew? Do You think I have one speck of interest in becoming one of these—these Torah-toting circumcised schmoes? Wait, are You, You, suggesting I would want You, You, to be my king?*

Jesus's question goes over about as well as the blind man's encounter in John 9 when he asked his Jewish inquisitors, "You don't want to become His disciples too, do you?" (9:27).

How dare Jesus even ask questions! Pilate represents the empire.

He is not used to being put on the stand and examined. So Pilate maneuvers to keep Jesus in His place. He will ask the questions (18:35). Pilate wants to get to the bottom of what Jesus has done. What is behind the animosity of this crowd—*what is this crisis and why is it messing up his Friday afternoon?*

Pilate's aides have been gathering evidence. Jesus has had several altercations with the law, though most amount to no more than misdemeanors. Rumor has it He was a big-time contributor to a wedding party in Cana that got out of hand when He provided free wine. He threatened to take down the temple, but the NSA is on it. It appears He tried to pick up a whore in Samaria, but it turned out to be a misunderstanding. He caused a pretty big commotion up in Galilee, nearly playing into the hands of the Zealots, those terrorists forever attempting political insurrection. He has had numerous incidents with the Jewish religious police, breaking laws on the Sabbath. Jesus appears to be an equal opportunity offender.

One could go on with reported incidents, but so far there doesn't seem to be enough to hold Him in custody. True, He has attracted large crowds, which like the "Occupy Jerusalem" herd never bothered to secure permits. This unfortunately has led to additional security and clean up, which will directly impact Pilate with cost overruns and threaten next year's budget. It is also reported that Jesus actually called Antipas a "fox" (Luke 13:32). (But then, Pilate wishes he had the guts to say that publicly, for everybody knows Herod likes to think of himself as a lion.) Finally, it is true that Jesus does claim to be a king of God knows what (John 18:37). So He could be a loon, another deluded messianic quack whose dots are not all on the dice. But is He really as dangerous as the Jews claim?

Pilate is mystified. If His kingship amounted to a revolutionary mission to threaten and destroy Rome, Jesus would not have run the other way when a crowd wanted to make Him their royal king. He would not have ridden triumphantly into Jerusalem on a donkey only to take off to join a ragtag army in an ordinary home in the suburbs. If He sought power, He would not have worked on the margins of society or hung out with prostitutes and people with serious moral, mental, and medical deficiencies.

Instead, He would have positioned Himself alongside power people, schmoozing with the likes of Nicodemus. He would have attended palace parties and hobnobbed with the rich and famous, looking for all the right levers to pull. He would have sought interviews in the press, kissed babies, criticized foreign policy, and funneled arms to the Galileans.

So is He a king or not? Pilate is obsessed with protecting his turf. He still is not certain Jesus represents a threat. Like many, he does not know what to do with Jesus, but he has to do something. At this point, Pilate unwittingly affirms in a statement what the Jews will not, "So then, You are a king" (see v. 37), though it could also be framed as a question: "You are a king then?" In other words, "Am I dealing with royalty?"

In this moment, Jesus makes one of His most penetrating statements: "I was born for this, and I have come into the world for this: to testify to the truth. Everyone who is of the truth listens to My voice." It's as if Jesus says to Pilate, "Let's get past the charade, can we? This is a world of lies. Your superiors are full of fabrications and falsehoods, and you have bought into many of them yourself. You think gaining power and privilege fulfills one's life, but you know, and I know, that you are hollow and shallow inside. You and your high-flying über-class wear your Brioni suits to impress one another, but behind closed doors, you stare in the mirror and realize that you and your tribe are little more than empty suits. You stuff yourself at parties and banquets and state dinners and leave with a dull hunger that won't go away. But I have come to bring food that will satisfy that hunger. I am real food, real truth, Pilate. I am what you have searched for your whole life. I can give you life, life in abundance. I can show you life as it is meant to be lived under an open heaven."

Such truth talk pushes Pilate to the edge. Jesus is getting too close. His eyes pierce through and into Pilate's soul, and they are beginning to hit a nerve.

In my second year of college, I took a required course in philosophy. I wish I could recount something I learned. Anything. There is no notebook hidden in some box of memories in an attic. My only recollection is of a young professor, with long hair and beard, sitting on a barstool. Every class began with him staring up at the ceiling (as if something was about to descend), asking this question, "What is truth?" No, actually I have to try to write it as I heard it, for his words are entrenched in my memory: "What . . . [*sigh*] . . . is . . . [*sigh*] . . . truth . . . [*really deep sigh*]?" Silence. We all waited in anticipation. But he had no answers, certainly nothing memorable. He strikes me as someone who, if he is still alive, is still asking this question.

Pilate might have been an ancestor of his. In one of John's greater ironies, Pilate asks, "What is truth?" (v. 38), missing that the answer is right in front of his face. Did he sigh between each word? What was the tone? We can only guess. Was he looking for a way out of this conversation?

The words give us a glimpse into Pilate's soul. Into every soul. At the deepest levels of our lives we hunger for truth, for something beyond ourselves. As Peterson puts it, "The taste for eternity can never be bred out of us by a secularizing genetics. Our existence is derived from God and destined for God."[10] Did Pilate suddenly get a glimpse of life under an open heaven and become completely unnerved? Did his question reflect the beginnings of interest, or was it the despair of a man who saw life with a blank incomprehension?[11] Was he remarking that the discovery of truth is beyond the grasp of any man? Or was Pilate being cynical?

It is not certain, but what is clear is that Pilate is suffering prosopagnosia: he cannot recognize Truth's face. In the confusion of the tumultuous crowd, it is hard for him to see anything. Jesus has created a dilemma, and he cannot find his way out. Pilate has no idea what to do with Him, let alone himself. Jesus has ruined a perfectly good day.

End of Act I. The drama takes a pause, as if to encourage the reader to reflect on the same questions: What am I to do with Jesus? Do I know what truth is? Have I been set free?

Pilate would like to be anywhere else. He could use some serious downtime. He is beginning to receive text messages asking when he can catch a flight and join the fam for shish kebabs and hummus by the sea, as well as catch a little surf action. One cannot waste a time-share at one of Herod's palaces, where tiled floors and opulent baths await. There are also these nasty calls beginning to come in from Rome. These bureaucrats always have a meltdown when crowds in the kingdom get testy. They demand to know if Pilate has things under control. Should they contact the Pentagon?

This crowd is exactly the sort of situation Pilate has been hired to control. Rome insists on well-behaved gatherings. Anything else threatens the absolute rule of Rome. Pilate must be wondering, *Why me? Why can't this be like other Passovers?*

But Pilate cannot walk away. This bad dream will not end. The conversation with Jesus is not over.

Act II. Perhaps a token beating and some mocking will appease the crowd. Anything to satisfy their bloodlust. But nothing less than the cross will do (19:6). These chief priests, who give such nice invocations in the legislature, quoting from their psalms and blessing the pols, are suddenly rabid. For reasons Pilate cannot discern, Jesus has them frothing at the mouth.

Pilate is desperate to wash his hands of all of this, and he will—literally (Matt. 27:24)! But there are questions still circulating in his brain. Back inside headquarters he demands to know, "Where are You from?" (John 19:9). This strikes me as a really odd question. Does it matter at this point? Does this have any relevance? Will it change anything? With the fate of Jesus seemingly in his hands, could Pilate really be asking things like, "I've heard that You are from Nazareth. What was it like growing up in that part of the world? I hear they grow really good peaches. Do You get back often? Did You play tennis in high school? Did You and Your father incorporate any new technology in Your carpentry business? Were You part of the workforce that rebuilt nearby Sepphoris after Varus overreacted and burned it to the ground?"

Perhaps I am being unfair. After all, this background check has been a point of concern throughout the gospel of John (see 1:46; 7:27–29; 8:14; 9:29). Maybe Pilate really is trying to sort out where this kingdom is, if there really is one.

Short answer, for those who will hear—it is not of this world.

For some reason, Jesus goes silent. He will not answer Pilate, and this silence increases the level of Pilate's anger. Doesn't Jesus get it? There are no attorneys here to advocate (which, BTW, is saving Jesus a ton of money). Only Jesus can exonerate Himself. But He won't. To Pilate, "Jesus's silence [is] at best stupidity, at worse a baiting sullenness."[12]

Pilate will have to further assert himself. Obviously Jesus does not understand the influence Pilate commands. He is a representative of the world's only superpower. He controls the destinies of men, sitting on the bema seat where he alone pronounces judgments. So Pilate erupts: "You're not talking to me? Don't You know that I have the authority to release You and the authority to crucify You?" (19:10). Translation: "Work with me, man. I can get you off. No jail, no bail. I control the levers."

This is exactly what worldly power does. It presents itself as a "totalizing system."[13] Its leaders must assert their control, letting everyone know they dominate!

I wonder if in this moment Jesus has to restrain Himself from laughing. Surely, this is what God does when the kings of the earth take their stand and rulers conspire against His Anointed: "The One enthroned in heaven laughs; the Lord ridicules them" (Ps. 2:4). One imagines Jesus saying, "Stop it, Pilate. You are making Me split a gut. I'm getting this drink all over My face. This idea that you have sovereign authority, that you (a man among millions I have created), you (like a seed barely planted that the wind carries away) call the shots when it comes to ultimate decisions is downright hilarious. Have you not read Isaiah 40:23: 'He reduces princes to nothing and makes judges of the earth irrational'? Do you really think you can hold God in custody and determine His outcome? Really?" One can hear the whole throne of heaven falling over one another in laughter. Pilate is a real scream.

THE IMPLICATIONS OF LIVING UNDER GOD'S AUTHORITY

With one statement, Jesus now puts worldly claims in their place. He exposes Pilate's myopic self-knowledge, showing him that the world's claim to power and authority is fraudulent. Jesus, who can read every face perfectly, looks into Pilate's eyes, and with the gravitas of His being declares, "You would have no authority over Me at all . . . if it hadn't been given you from above" (John 19:11).

Pilate, like all of us, owns nothing, has nothing, and rules nothing. Eugene Peterson puts it this way:

> Everything that goes on is under God's rule, is penetrated by God's rule, is judged by God's rule, is included in God's rule—every one of my personal thoughts and feelings and actions, yes; but also the stock market in New York, the famine in the Sudan, your first grandchild born last night in Atlanta, the poverty in Calcutta, the suicide bombings in Tel Aviv and New York and Baghdad, the abortions in Dallas, the Wednesday-night prayer meetings in Syracuse, the bank mergers being negotiated in Chicago, Mexican migrants picking avocados in California—everything, absolutely everything, large and small.[14]

Under an open heaven, any authority possessed by mayors, governors, presidents, rulers, and kings is derived. Authority does not come from a ballot, human appointment, or notable accomplishments. Any civil authority like Pilate's is derived authority.

Picture Dorothy's little dog Toto in Oz, pulling away the curtain to expose a pathetic and feeble wizard. It is God, not Rome, who has established the ends of the earth. Only He has gathered the wind in His hands and bound up the waters in a cloak (Prov. 30:4). The world is His realm; He is no helpless bystander. He rules over emperors and kings and governors and prefects. Their hearts are like water channels in the Lord's hand; He directs them wherever He chooses (Prov. 21:1).

The conversation between Pilate and Jesus is such assurance! Under an open heaven, we are freed from the need to position ourselves. We do not have to fear earthly powers or get tied in knots over who will win the next election. Kings and presidents only further kingdom purposes. We see with greater clarity the contrast between powers that dehumanize and those that make one more fully human. We experience a King who is not coercive but is compassionate; He rules by love and not by oppression. We live under a sovereignty that forgives rather than condemns, whose weapons are not sword and chariot but Word and prayer. He has transferred us from the kingdom of darkness to the kingdom of light. We can live with profound confidence. We can fearlessly speak truth. We can laugh at pontificating powers that make absurd claims. We can pray audacious prayers.

The emerging church of the New Testament got this. Saints began to literally shake foundations. Confronted by "the authorities," Peter and John and the community of faith stood together and fearlessly prayed, "Master, You are the One who made the heaven, the earth, and the sea, and everything in them" (Acts 4:24). They affirmed what life under an open heaven reveals: the kings of the earth are simply instruments of His power. The likes of Herod, Pontius Pilate, the Gentiles, and the people of Israel, assembled together against the anointed Jesus to do whatever God's hand and God's plan had predestined to take place. And in affirming this, God empowered them with holy boldness (vv. 28–31).

What about us? Kings and queens and prime ministers and presidents still strut and swagger and make outrageous claims. On occasion, they threaten the church. Will we be intimidated and turn silent? Or will we fearlessly stand and make our arguments?

At other times, they promise to share their authority with the church. Will we rest our hope in political elections, getting all lathered up over men and women who make their promises? Will we look to them to legislate our beliefs? Will we compromise to align? Or will we see through the noise and empty suits?

There was a period of time in the Netherlands when a core of us met on Tuesday nights to pray. It was a mix of nationalities, but most were Nigerian. We prayed against a tyrant who used his power to bleed the country of Nigeria dry. I saw it firsthand on my first trip to Africa. People in an oil-rich nation stood in line for days to find fuel, while corrupt leaders sold it abroad and lined their pockets. Eventually, we saw God remove him, and others like him. We believed—and still believe—that God took serious those who take serious His reign.

Obviously, evil still sullies our world. Modern-day Pilates still attempt to get their way. They do not see (because they cannot read the face of God, discern the will of God, or hear the voice of God) that under an open heaven, there is only one true kingdom, and it is now present in Jesus. He alone is our hope. In Him alone we fear. Only His authority matters. It is ours to claim!

QUESTIONS

1. *Who do you think Jesus had more compassion for—Nicodemus or Pilate? Who do you believe was a greater adversary? Why?*

2. *If Jesus wanted to avoid His death, what would He have said to Pilate? How is that similar to how you might react in the face of persecution?*

3. *How does this conversation impact how we should approach politics and earthly power?*

13
LIFE IS ABOUT RESTORATION REPLACING FAILURE

A Conversation with Peter
JOHN 21:1–19

When they had eaten breakfast, Jesus asked Simon Peter,
"Simon, son of John, do you love Me more than these?"
"Yes, Lord," he said to Him, "You know that I love You."
"Feed My Lambs," He told him.
A second time He asked him, "Simon,
son of John, do you love Me?"
"Yes, Lord," he said to Him, "You
know that I love You."
"Shepherd My sheep," He told him.
He asked him the third time,
"Simon, son of John,
do you love Me?"
Peter was grieved that He
asked him the third time, "Do
you love Me?" He said, "Lord,
You know everything! You
know that I love You."
"Feed My sheep," Jesus said.

—JOHN 21:15–17

LIFE IS FULL OF SETBACKS: A PROMOTION THAT DOES NOT COME through, an injury that puts everything on hold, a financial decision that goes south, a poor choice that has painful consequences, or an election that goes all wrong. Under an open heaven, life still has its bumps. As the conversation with Martha underscores, even in the midst of God's kingdom presence on earth, there remains a sense of incompleteness. Aches still occur; "all wrongs do not become right."[1]

In his third bid to be president, Theodore Roosevelt experienced his own pain. He lost. For eight years he was at the apex of power and prestige. But it all changed after his terms were up. No longer was he in the headlines; he wasn't even on the back page. In the cruel world of politics, he was no longer in the inner circle. His party treated him as an outcast, a pariah. Roosevelt could have given up. He could have dropped out of sight, drifting down a path called irrelevancy. But he chose a different one.

In typical fashion, Roosevelt sought out a greater test, losing himself in punishing physical hardships and danger. It was the only therapy he knew when dealing with defeat. After his 1912 loss, Roosevelt gathered a small band and headed for the River of Doubt, an unexplored tributary of the Amazon, throwing himself against the cruelest trials nature could throw at him. It is here that he nearly lost his life.[2]

Simon Peter, a disciple of Jesus, also experienced a stunning setback. Enjoying a certain prestige among his peers, he suddenly came crashing down to earth. For a while, he dropped out of sight. He no longer made the news. He too had to cope with failure. It is through his collapse that John tells us something more about life under an open heaven. There is grace and mercy under this opened heaven. There is a new chapter. One can live again.

Simon is introduced in John 1, and he turns out to be one of the more complicated characters in the book. John's portrayal of him is mixed. It's an understandable combination: Simon is a complex man, there's a clear rivalry between the two men, and John has a penchant for setting up contrasts and irony. John gives Simon less press than the other gospels. It is not assumed that Simon is the leader of the band. But it is clear Peter has failed.

Yes, Simon is the disciple whom Jesus chooses to affectionately call "*Petros*" (John 1:42). But for what reason? John does not attach the statement to any profound act of faith on Peter's part, as Matthew does (Matt. 16:17). It's simply a passing reference to what Jesus chose to nickname him. Maybe it was a device to inspire Peter to become someone he wasn't—a man with rocklike stability, a follower who is stable, solid, unwavering, and steady.

To be fair, John leaves out some of Peter's less glorious moments, like the time he stepped out of the boat and flopped big-time. John does not recount the time Jesus blasted Peter, referring to him as Satan. And John does paint a picture of a man who at times was fearless, self-confident, and heroic. It was Peter who affirmed loyalty to Jesus while most everyone else chose to walk out (John 6:68–69). When Jesus bent down and wiped the grime off the feet of His disciples, it was Peter who verbalized what others were too afraid to say (13:6).

But in his portrait, John does not leave out all of the flaws. There are these black smudges. Peter could be brash, impetuous, impulsive, and vacillating. His passion often got ahead of his head. There were times Peter was a windbag, a blowhard. He made these unnecessary— as well as empty—boasts. In the upper room, Peter bragged to Jesus that he would lay down his life for Jesus (v. 37). In the garden, it was Peter who pulled out his sword, madly swinging like a crazy man (18:10). What a hot dog!

After his braggadocious ways, Peter totally collapsed (vv. 17, 25, 27). The irony of the big man failing crashes through the story. John (assuming he is the unnamed "other disciple" in verse 16) had his connections in high places and was able to get Peter past the gate. To Peter's credit, he was willing to continue to put his life in jeopardy. Peter clearly wanted to still show Jesus and others he was undaunted.

But alone and in close proximity to Caiaphas, who was wealthy and powerful and cozy with Rome—and had the power to incarcerate—Peter blinked. The sword-slinger melted under the heat of a female slave's questions.[3] Three times he denied any association with this political prisoner named Jesus, each denial more profane than the previous.

Was John jealous of Peter? Who knows, but it's interesting that he informs the reader that it was he—not Peter—who reclined next to Jesus (13:23). While John followed Jesus to the cross, Peter was nowhere to be found after the cock crowed (19:26). And, oh, don't forget, it was John who won the footrace to the tomb (20:4); it was John who first recognized Jesus on the shore and pointed Him out to Peter (21:7); and it was John, and only John, who was referred to as the one Jesus loved (according to John).

The two seem to have spent a fair amount of time positioning themselves and comparing themselves. At the end of this conversation, Peter will want to know how his future compares to John's (v. 20). He will discover that their journeys will be very different: Peter will shepherd Jesus's flock and die a martyr; John will remain and be a witness. The road will be difficult for both, for what both have in common—equally—is a mission to follow Jesus. And this is not a path to privilege and higher standards. Nonetheless, in the end, they are to "follow in Jesus's footsteps, not in each other's."[4]

The same goes with us.

LIFE HAS ITS MISSTEPS

Like so many, Peter was a man victimized by his words. Having boasted of his faithfulness to follow Jesus, he came to the stark reality that he wasn't up to the task. The "complete" disciple, having it all together, ended up as an incomplete disciple.[5]

Peter disappears. In his own mind, he is now a loser, an outcast. So much for life under an open heaven. Whatever promises Jesus made to Nathanael no longer apply. Peter had seen the greater things, but all he could now see was a self-built wall of failure. He was unworthy of the benefits that come with life in a messianic age.

Life is a series of choices, and some of them are wise and some of them are foolish. Behind folly is wrongheadedness and potential capitulation. Ultimately, they are the work of the Enemy, who tempts us to succumb, smashes us under the weight of his work of condemnation, and finally consigns us to the garbage heap of irrelevancy. This was true of Peter, a man the Devil delighted in sifting like wheat (Luke 22:31).

Several years ago, the mayor of Inglis, Florida, a woman by the name of Carolyn Risher, became fed up with this work of the Evil One to tempt, condemn, and consign people to failure. In her official position, she witnessed an endless number of drunken drivers processed through the court system, numerous fathers arrested for molesting their daughters, and lots of people caught stealing from their neighbors. She began to feel deep within a "creeping presence" coming over the city.[6]

So she sat down at her kitchen table and started writing. Not that it mattered, but it was Halloween. Maybe it was a fitting moment to take on evil. As she wrote, the words she crafted were fierce and determined. She wrote out a proclamation, complete with an official seal:

> Be it known from this day forward that Satan, ruler of darkness, giver of evil, destroyer of what is good and just, is not now, nor ever again will be, a part of this town of Inglis. Satan is hereby declared powerless, no longer ruling over, nor influencing, our citizens.

Risher was convinced Satan is only present where we let him be present, so she banned Satan from the city limits. She made five copies. One was kept for her office wall, which is covered with pictures of Elvis, framed letters of thanks, and a painting of the Last Supper. The rest were rolled and stuffed into hollowed-out fence posts placed at the four entrances to the town.

Unfortunately, the Devil does not respect human decrees. There are no safe city limits. There were none for Peter; there are none for us. As a result, there tend to be casualties. Things fall apart. The Devil loves to raise hell with our lives. Peter is now a broken-world man who bought into the myth, "It can't happen to me."[7]

Roosevelt's therapy was to attempt something more audacious. Peter's therapy for failure was to go back to what he once did. The other disciples followed suit. The briefing in chapters 13–17 of John's gospel seems to have had all of the impact of an annual stewardship sermon. So much for the race. They have returned to a more placid setting up north, away from the craziness of Jerusalem. Away from the horrific act of crucifixion, intended to instill fear and terror in anyone who would even think to challenge the empire. They have gone back to what they were doing before Jesus invited them to leave their professions, follow Him, and take the baton. You can practically hear the "ping, ping, ping" of the baton falling on the race course. The disciples have come home to loved ones who declare, "Welcome back from the deep end." And now they fish, but either they have lost their touch or the fish are not biting. It is a fruitless night of fishing (John 21:3). It is all a bad dream.

For Peter, this fruitless effort symbolizes his whole, empty life. He too has bottomed out. Like Moses who disappeared into the wilderness, David who ran to the other side, Elijah who escaped to the desert, and Jonah who jumped into the sea, Peter runs back to a place where he can get lost. But things only seem to get worse. They've lost hope and are slipping into despair. Maybe this life under an open heaven has been one grand illusion. Where is the kingdom that has come? Where is the evidence of doing "even greater works" (14:12)?

GOD DOES NOT WRITE US OFF BUT RESTORES US

Given Peter's offense, one would not be surprised if a resurrected Christ condemned him. Or simply wrote Peter off, something churches are really good at doing with people who disappoint them. But severe as Jesus is in certain conversations, He does none of this here. He sends word to the disciples, with emphasis on Peter, that He will meet them in Galilee (Mark 16:7). He stands on the beach and calls out to these men offshore, but there is no mistaking that His eyes are focused on Peter. Little wonder Peter jumps ship and heads straight to Jesus. Jesus has this way of drawing people to Himself (John 12:32). All of this sets the context for the last conversation in John.

The first thing we notice is that Jesus uses Peter's full name. This is how things start. Why? Is it a tone of rebuke? Growing up, there were times my folks used my full name when addressing me, "John Edwin Johnson" (middle name—not good!). In almost—no—in *every* case, there was something I fell short of doing right. Here, however, there is no way of knowing the tone of voice.

The larger question is what Jesus means when He says, "Do you love Me more than these?" More than these what? It's hard to know what Jesus is asking. The objects are not specified. We are left to imagine. More than these men? Is Jesus wanting to know if Peter has put more weight on his relationship with others than with God? Is his life driven by their acceptance and applause and approval?

Do "these" refer to the things in front of Peter? Does Peter love these fish, these nets, this boat, these oars (i.e., career, material things) more than Jesus? Is his affection for the things of the world more than for the things of God? Or is Jesus asking if Peter loves Jesus more than these . . . these others who claim to love Jesus?[8] Does Peter still think that he stands above everyone else when it comes to loyalty to God? Is he still ready to say, "Even if everyone runs away because of You, I will never run" (Matt. 26:33)? Jesus asks such penetrating questions. Can you hear them?

Perhaps all are true, just as they are for us. When we are confronted with our love for Jesus, it is a centering question that puts everything else in needful perspective. To live life to its maximum under an open heaven will require complete devotion to Jesus. We're back to abiding, back to mission, back to getting in the race.

Peter's response is measured. No longer is Peter using comparative language. His swagger has been reduced to a simple affirmation of affection. And even here, he is cautious to use the highest word for love.[9] He is realizing that one's words do not impress Jesus. Jesus can see through him—has always seen through him. This is the one who knows all things, knows what side of the boat the fish are on, what side Nicodemus, the paralytic, the brothers, the crowd are taking. He knows what side the heart is on.

Jesus is not finished with the conversation. He is doing heart surgery, and this requires time. One imagines Jesus stopping and looking more deeply into Peter's face. No longer is Jesus asking Peter if his love trumps others. He wants to know if Peter *really* does love Him. Again, Peter responds with the same exact words. Once more Jesus asks, and once again Peter affirms his love. But this time, Peter is offended. And inside, Peter might be asking: "Are You not listening? Are You not taking me seriously? Don't You believe me? Don't my words mean anything?"

What is Jesus doing here? He could be reflecting the Near Eastern etiquette of reiterating something three times to express a solid obligation.[10] Maybe. For certain, He is "sifting Peter to the core" to make sure his actions will back up his words.[11] He could also be helping Peter to hear, in the repetition, the hollowness of affirmation without action.

Looking deeper, Jesus is doing the same thing He does with us when we fail—He is taking Peter through a process of healing. Jesus is putting something back together that has been torn and broken. God doesn't intend to leave people wallowing in their failures, sitting on the sidelines. Jesus is putting Peter's broken world back together, and this is not always pleasant. Jesus's questions "offer gentle and excruciating reproach."[12]

There is a sense of déjà vu: charcoal fire and three questions. Only they are not asked by a servant girl but by Jesus. And maybe with each question of love He is erasing each statement of denial. With every question there is a corresponding charge. Jesus wants Peter to hear three times, "I have a future for you," rather than, "You are no longer salvageable."

This is how Frederick Bruner puts it: "Perhaps Jesus wanted Peter's last memory of his last main meeting with Jesus to be Peter's threefold

'*I do love You, Lord,*' '*I do love You, Lord,*' and '*I do love You, Lord*' rather than his shameful threefold, 'I don't know the man,' 'I don't know the man,' 'I don't know the man.'"[13]

More than putting back together, Jesus is reinstating Peter. Rather than consigning Peter to the "of no further use" pile, simply forgiven but no longer functional, Jesus is putting Peter back into the action. Under an open heaven, He does more than untie the knots and repair the holes and put things back together—He restores and reinstates. His restorative work can take a broken life and make it "somehow more magnificent *because* it has been ruined."[14] Like an athlete who has stumbled and recovered, Peter can now approach the race with a different intensity.

On the southwest side of Jerusalem, near the house of Caiaphas, stands the church of St. Peter in Gallicantu (Latin for "cock's crow"). It is a monument to Peter's failure. It is a reminder to every contemporary pilgrim that it is here Peter crashed. But in this conversation, Jesus chooses to forget Peter's failure (just as He chooses to forget ours). He is recalling Peter back to shepherding, back to mission, back to fruitfulness, back to life in all of its abundance under an open heaven. Fishing will have to take a back seat. The mission will require rocklike grace and humility and gratitude—and courage. Restoration is also a summons to dangerous and difficult tasks.[15] Jesus begins to hint at Peter's own death.

Discipleship has its own path for each of us. This prompts comparison, and for Peter, he wants to know how his course will differ from the disciple John (John 21:21). Like all of us, Peter has his rough edges. He is still concerned with standing and status. This underscores that restoration takes longer than a conversation. God will continue to confront Peter, as He does us. He will continue His repairs, for old habits do not die easily. They will need to be replaced by new habits, disciplines that form character. He will use people like Paul, who severely rebukes Peter for caving in to people's expectations (Gal. 2:11–14). Jesus will continue to say, "Follow Me" (John 21:22). But the conditions for success are in motion, and by the time he writes his epistles, Peter is a rock. He has embraced how life is to be lived under an open heaven. This complex man, full of shadows, is also "full of a light that causes them."[16] Martin Luther described Peter's first letter as "one of the noblest books in the New Testament."[17] There is no doubt his letters in the New Testament are filled with courage.

Open heaven or closed, God has been in the restoration business since Genesis 3, offering restorative hope to sinful humanity. From Adam to Jacob to Moses to David to Jonah to Matthew to Mary Magdalene to Paul—to everyone who has ever lived—we will stand together in heaven as trophies of God's grace. But under an open heaven, we stand on the other side of the cross, where Jesus's death and resurrection allow no uncertainty of forgiveness. A personal life breaks in pieces, a marriage falls apart, a career crashes to the ground, or a hope collapses. It is no matter.

This is Jesus's letter to the church, calling saints to get back up when they fall. When we stray outside of His will and screw up, and join this worldwide fraternity of those who know what it is like to feel useless and hopeless, there is repairing and restoring and reinstating to be found.[18] We will face the same searching questions, as well as a fresh commissioning. There is a resurrection power under an open heaven that enables us to be whole. There is no place to skulk in defeat. Christ has made you free indeed.

As N. T. Wright puts it, "Those who find the risen Jesus going to the roots of their rebellion, denial, and sin and offering them love and forgiveness may well also find themselves sent off to be shepherds instead. Let those with ears listen."[19]

QUESTIONS

1. *Why are the hard questions sometimes the most loving?*

2. *Have you experienced the same piercing, restorative questions in your relationship with Jesus? How are you different now?*

3. *How does Jesus's encounter with Peter shape your view of God?*

CONCLUSION

This is the disciple who testifies to these things and who
wrote them down. We know that his testimony is true.
And there are also many other things that Jesus did,
which, if they were written one by one, I suppose not even the
world itself could contain the books that would be written.

—JOHN 21:24–25

I BEGAN THIS BOOK WITH THE STORY OF GEORGE BELL, AND PEOPLE like him, who exist in confined spaces of their making until they die. Recently, I read about Johnny Perez, another man who lived an imprisoned life. For thirteen years, Perez did time—not in an apartment but in a prison cell at Rikers Island penitentiary in upstate New York. Three of those years were spent handcuffed and shackled in solitary confinement.

Isolation in a small cell is a dangerous place. Over time, one can suffer spatial and cognitive distortions, as well as suicidal tendencies. Many go insane. And for those who survive the walls, the world outside can "regularly collapse in on itself."[1]

The argument of this book is that there is hope for those who find themselves in confined spaces. All too many live in worlds that regularly collapse in on themselves. Most are bound by walls of ignorance, oblivious to what Jesus has announced and God has opened up for us. Low ceilings of unbelief keep many from seeing that heaven has opened and everything has changed. Something of eternity is here. Jesus and His kingdom have broken in.

This is what Jesus was announcing to Nathanael (John 1:50–51).

There is a new order; previous concepts of reality have been revised.[2] The God who spoke to Abraham, who revealed His glory to Moses, who poured His anointing on David, and who touched the tongue of Isaiah, has now come in the flesh. The seeds of a new era were sown at His baptism (Luke 3:21–22). In this moment, the heavens were ripped open, declaring that something extraordinary was taking place. The Spirit descended and anointed Jesus for His task, and the Father gave His affirmation. Hence, Jesus tells Nathanael that the very presence and power of God are now evident wherever He goes and in whatever He speaks. Nathanael is on the front end of this.

For three years, God's overpowering otherness walks this earth in the person of Jesus. The seeds of this new era germinate. Everywhere He goes, Jesus smashes fixed conclusions. He confronts myopic thinking and pint-size living. He bucks expectations and mystifies people's assumptions. He announces His kingdom and inaugurates a messianic age. *Any assumption of divine absence is shattered.*

The announcement to Nathanael (John 1:50–51) not only speaks of the past and the present but also of the future—of His death, resurrection, ascension, and sending of the Spirit. There is an immediacy and an intimacy with God to enjoy. There are greater things to see. The ensuing conversations—to those who serve as types in the church—unpack what this means. They serve as "field reports" telling us what we should expect under an open heaven. Here is what we have discovered.

In His conversation with His mother (2:2–4), and in the changing of water into wine (vv. 5–11), Jesus revealed that the powers of the age to come are already present (Heb. 6:5).

To Nicodemus (John 3:1–21), Jesus announced to a man constricted by law and tradition that there is freedom when one is reborn, enters the kingdom of God, and is filled with the Spirit. Speaking with the woman at the well (4:7–26), He demonstrates that there are no barriers that should divide us. Under an open heaven, the walls of hostility have come down.

With the paralytic (5:5–15), we realize we do not have to live in a confined space, either physically or spiritually. There is no place for mere existence, becoming like blank slabs of black asphalt. He tells us that under an open heaven He is able to do whatever we ask, whatever we have dreamed about and imagined in the night (Eph. 3:20–21). Neither the boldest prayer nor the wildest thought can overwhelm God's ability to act. And He does this through the power presently at work within us.

Addressing the crowd (John 6:25–65), Jesus invites them to a better table. Under an open heaven, you no longer have to be driven by your earthly appetites. There is better food offered. The Truth is the only one who really satisfies.

Conversing with His brothers (7:2–8), Jesus challenges them and us to live for something—live for Someone. Under an open heaven, life is no longer reduced to simple existence. We can live the abundant life, where our choices matter and God's timing leads to a satisfaction in our purposeful lives.

To the unbelieving believers (8:31–58), Jesus announces a freedom made possible through His Word. When the Word finds its way in and makes its home in us, affecting our life choices, we are freed from everything from impurity to fear to guilt. Its truths re-center and reorient.

In His conversation with the blind man (9:6–39), Jesus declares that there is a blindness that can now be treated. An open heaven can open our eyes to recognize things we were once blind to.[3] What was confusing now becomes clear. Where we once just looked, now we see. The indwelling Spirit illuminates our minds, putting us in contact with unseen spiritual realities.

Through His encounter with Martha and Mary (11:21–40), Jesus assures us that everything He does is prompted by His love and determined by what will bring God the greatest glory. This gives us the courage to face life's disappointments at every level. God is never too late, but always on time. And death never wins.

With His disciples (13:6–16:33), Jesus dispels any fear that we are left alone without his physical presence. God is more present now than ever; we're grafted into the vine and He's passed us the baton. Under an open heaven, we live daily with the possibility that we can extend the ministry of Jesus. When we abide in Him as the Father abides in the Son, we can run the race with a supernatural power (14:10–12).

In His conversation with Pilate (18:29–19:11), Jesus declares that no authority rules apart from His authority. Under an open heaven, our God reigns . . . now! We who believe have been transferred to His domain (Col. 1:13). By His authority, we can command another earthly power, the Devil, to flee, and he must (James 4:7). We can live without intimidation. The rulers of this world wield only the power God permits. We have no one to fear but God, and fearing Him represents our best wisdom (Prov. 1:7).

Finally, to Peter, Jesus declares that He is a God who loves to restore (John 21:1–19). Under an open heaven, it is not three strikes and you're out. God is in the business of rebuilding broken worlds. He specializes in this, as Moses and David and Elijah and Jonah and Mark and Peter—and you and I—can affirm. As He surely did for the nets of fishermen, Jesus is busy untying knots and repairing holes so we can be His fishermen and fulfill His mission.

Heaven is not only open; heaven has come down to earth and exists in unseen dimensions. In words that seem to almost go off the page, the writer of Hebrews tells us we have come to Mount Zion, to the city of the living God, to the angels ascending and descending, to the God who is the judge of all, and to Jesus (Heb. 12:22–24). These are words that are not future tense—they are present tense.

So let's dare to believe that ripped-apart heaven remains wide open. Let's step into the day believing God is more active than ever, enabling a rigorous process of inner transformation and an outer work of supernatural living. Let's not settle for a faith that is routine and predictable. There is no place to be "remorselessly parochial . . . peering out at life from [our] single point of view and trying to stuff everything [we] see into [our] prefabricated categories."[4] Let's open our eyes to see the evidence of angels who continue to ascend and descend. Let's live with the conviction that the earth is so thick with divine possibilities that it's a wonder we can go anywhere "without cracking our shins on altars."[5]

If we do, prayers may again shake walls, messages will be spoken with a holy boldness, and a divine presence through His church will change the world.

NOTES

Acknowledgments

1. William Faulkner, quoted in Peterson, *Pastor*, 6.

Before We Begin . . .

1. N. R. Kleinfield, "The Lonely Death of George Bell," *The New York Times*, October 17, 2015, http://www.nytimes.com/2015/10/18/nyregion/dying-alone -in-new-york-city.html?_r=0.
2. Plantinga, *Reading for Preaching*, 45. Plantinga is responding to Walter Brueggemann's discussion of the power of preaching God's Word in *Finally Comes the Poet*.
3. Franz Kafka, quoted in Peterson, *Pastor*, 90.
4. Duke, *Irony in the Fourth Gospel*, 111.
5. Munro, *Lives of Girls and Women*, 484.
6. Craddock, *John*, 6.
7. Booth, *Rhetoric of Irony*, ix.
8. Plantinga, *Reading for Preaching*, 35.
9. Douglas Colin Muecke, quoted in Duke, *Irony in the Fourth Gospel*, 7.
10. Parker, "The Passion of Flannery O'Connor," 38. Parker uses these words to describe O'Connor's irony, but they could just as rightly be applied to her Lord.
11. Luther, quoted in Smalley, *John*, 7.
12. Purves, *Pastoral Theology in the Classical Tradition*, 10.
13. I adapted my imagined review of John's gospel from a recent review in *The Economist*, "On the Cocaine Trail," 73.
14. Hoskyns, *Fourth Gospel*, 20.

CHAPTER 1: Life Is About Expanding One's Vision

1. Gawande, *Being Mortal*, Kindle ed., loc. 374.
2. Taylor, *When God Is Silent*, 55.
3. Capernaum and the region of Upper Galilee, where Nathanael lived, were breeding grounds for insurgents who periodically rebelled against Roman occupation. They longed for a militant messiah who would ride to battle on a white stallion, take on the wolves, break the yoke of slavery, and end oppression.

4. Ortberg, "Slaying Spiritual Skepticism," 25.
5. Nof, "'Walking on Water' and the Geoscientists' Fear of Social Controversy," 406, 409.
6. Smedes, *My God and I*, 175.
7. Suk, *Not Sure*, Kindle ed., loc. 800.
8. Bruner, *Gospel of John*, 112.
9. Smalley, *John*, 94.
10. Bauckhman, *Gospel of Glory*, 168.
11. Witherington, *John's Wisdom*, 72.
12. Beale and Kim, *God Dwells Among Us*, 83–84.
13. Hays, *Moral Vision of the New Testament*, 133.
14. Hays, *Moral Vision of the New Testament*, 88.
15. Hengstenberg, *Commentary on the Gospel of St. John*, 114.
16. Morris, *Gospel According to John*, 171. Another helpful source is Christopher Rowland's *The Open Heaven*. He looks at early apocalyptic assumptions in Judaism and early Christianity and the occasional uses of "open heaven."
17. Noll, *Angels of Light, Powers of Darkness*, 76.
18. Strachan, *Fourth Gospel*, 11.
19. Peterson, *Subversive Spirituality*, 42.
20. McKnight, *Kingdom Conspiracy*, 35.
21. Köstenberger, *John*, 86.
22. Purves, *Crucifixion of Ministry*, 12.
23. Koester, *Word of Life*, 12.
24. Köstenberger, *Theology of John's Gospel and Letters*, 342. Some of the clusters of references to life are 1:4; 3:15–16, 36; 4:10, 14; 5:21, 24–26; 6:27; 8:12; 10:10; 11:25; 14:6.
25. Lewis, *The Lion, the Witch and the Wardrobe*, 168–69.
26. McKnight, *Kingdom Conspiracy*, 41.
27. Wright, *Simply Good News*, Kindle ed., loc. 1658.
28. Rolheiser, *Shattered Lantern*, chap. 3.

CHAPTER 2: Life Is About Experiencing God's Sudden Shifts

1. Associated Press, "Woman Gets Beer from Her Kitchen Faucet," *USA Today*, March 13, 2006, http://usatoday30.usatoday.com/news/offbeat/2006-03-13 -beer-on-tap_x.htm.
2. Peterson, *Christ Plays in Ten Thousand Places*, 92.
3. Crouch, *Playing God*, 108.
4. Bruner, *Gospel of John*, 129. See also Lane, *Gospel of Mark*, 183.
5. Peterson, *Eat This Book*, 86.
6. Culpepper, *Anatomy of the Fourth Gospel*, 111.
7. Willimon, *Why Jesus?*, Kindle ed., loc. 1054.

8. Oden, *Word of Life*, 295.

9. Lewis, *Miracles*, 163.

10. Wright, *Simply Good News*, Kindle ed., loc. 493.

11. Witherington, *John's Wisdom*, 76.

12. Oden, *Word of Life*, 318.

13. Hays, *Moral Vision of the New Testament*, 89.

14. Peterson, *Christ Plays in Ten Thousand Places*, 87.

15. Bird, *Jesus Is the Christ*, 105.

16. Crouch, *Playing God*, 109.

17. Brown, *Gospel According to John I–XII*, 104.

18. Bird, *Jesus Is the Christ*, 113.

19. Isaacson, *Steve Jobs*, Kindle ed., loc. 540.

20. Newbigin, *Light Has Come*, 27.

21. Crouch, *Playing God*, 109.

CHAPTER 3: Life Is About Moving with the Spirit

1. Burke, *No Perfect People Allowed*, 15.

2. Culpepper, *Anatomy of the Fourth Gospel*, 145.

3. Butler, *Pursuing God*, xiv.

4. Koester, *Word of Life*, 54.

5. Wright, *Simply Jesus*, Kindle ed., loc. 3121.

6. Peterson, *Christ Plays in Ten Thousand Places*, 14.

7. Klink, "Could I Have a Word?"

8. Brant, *Dialogue and Drama*, 2.

9. McKnight, *Kingdom Conspiracy*, 51.

10. Newbigin, *Light Has Come*, 38–39.

11. Wright, *John for Everyone*, 30.

12. Newbigin, *Light Has Come*, 37.

CHAPTER 4: Life Is About Dismantling Barriers

1. King, "Social Justice," 22. King made these remarks during a Q&A session after delivering a speech.

2. Culpepper, *Anatomy of the Fourth Gospel*, 136.

3. Peterson, *Christ Plays in Ten Thousand Places*, 17.

4. Köstenberger, *John*, 147.

5. The Druze faith is one of the major religious groups in Lebanon, Syria, and Israel, looked upon by Muslims as infidels and worse.

6. Witherington, *John's Wisdom*, 118.

7. Boyer and Hall, *Mystery of God*, 127.

8. Duke, *Irony in the Fourth Gospel*, 101.

9. Bruner, *Gospel of John*, 249.

10. Peterson, *Christ Plays in Ten Thousand Places*, 16, emphasis added.
11. Yancey, *Jesus I Never Knew*, 153.
12. Thompson, "How Neuroscience—and the Bible—Explain Shame," 65.
13. Köstenberger, *John*, 154.
14. Scholars question the inclusion of this story in John 8. It is absent in most of the earlier manuscripts. Nonetheless, wherever one would place it, the story is consistent with Jesus and His ministry to outsiders.
15. "Bart of Darkness," *The Simpsons*, season 6, episode 1, FXX Video, 20:09, http://www.simpsonsworld.com/video/300925507538.
16. Frederick Treves, quoted in Sittser, *Love One Another*, 24.

CHAPTER 5: Life Is About Living Expansively

1. Cain, *Quiet*, Kindle ed., loc. 464.
2. Wright, *Simply Good News*, Kindle ed., loc. 786.
3. Gaiser, *Healing in the Bible*, 241.
4. Craddock, *John*, 44.
5. Wright, *Simply Jesus*, Kindle ed., loc. 2554.
6. McKnight, *Kingdom Conspiracy*, 51.
7. Buchanan, *Rest of God*, 107.
8. Peterson, *Christ Plays in Ten Thousand Places*, 111.
9. Yancey, *Jesus I Never Knew*, 166.
10. Gaiser, *Healing in the Bible*, 242.
11. Newbigin, *Light Has Come*, 64.
12. Isaacson, *Steve Jobs*, Kindle ed., loc. 383.
13. Culpepper, *Anatomy of the Fourth Gospel*, 145.
14. Rolheiser, *Shattered Lantern*, 165.
15. Witherington, *John's Wisdom*, 145.
16. Card, *Parable of Joy*, 67.
17. Bernanke, "Economic Prospects for the Long Run."

CHAPTER 6: Life Is About Consuming the Better Food

1. Lukianoff and Haidt, "Coddling of the American Mind."
2. Culpepper, *Anatomy of the Fourth Gospel*, 112.
3. Galli, *Jesus Mean and Wild*, 18.
4. Dawn and Peterson, *Unnecessary Pastor*, 183.
5. Bauckham, *Gospel of Glory*, 181.
6. McKnight, *Kingdom Conspiracy*, 149–50.
7. For the other gospel accounts of Jesus's miraculous feeding of the five thousand, see Matthew 14:13–21, Mark 6:31–44, and Luke 9:10–17.
8. Galli, *Jesus Mean and Wild*, 171.
9. Woodley, *Gospel of Matthew*, 170.

10. Wright, *Simply Jesus*, Kindle ed., loc. 284.
11. Craddock, *John*, 51.
12. Dylan, "When You Gonna Wake Up."
13. McKeown, *Essentialism*, Kindle ed., loc. 246.
14. For a helpful discussion on the role of sanctuary and space, see Bartholomew, *Where Mortals Dwell*.
15. Culpepper, *Anatomy of the Fourth Gospel*, 112.
16. Galli, *Jesus Mean and Wild*, 19.
17. Card, *Parable of Joy*, 85.
18. Oden, *Life in the Spirit*, 130.
19. Köstenberger, *John*, 211.
20. Morris, *Gospel According to John*, 374.
21. Kierkegaard, quoted in Johnston, *God's Wider Presence*, 1.
22. Rainbow, *Johannine Theology*, 323.
23. Brant, *Dialogue and Drama*, 156.
24. Wright, *How God Became King*, Kindle ed., loc. 1397.
25. Wright, *How God Became King*, Kindle ed., loc. 1397.
26. Peterson, *Eat This Book*, 18.
27. Bruner, *Gospel of John*, 440.

CHAPTER 7: Life Is About Something to Live and Die For

1. See MacDonald, *Resilient Life*, 52–58.
2. Peterson, *Pastor*, 25.
3. Bruner, *Gospel of John*, 464.
4. Mariucci, quoted in Webber, "Why Can't We Get Anything Done?"
5. Buchanan, *Rest of God*, 36.
6. Cullmann, *Christ and Time*, 44.
7. Rolheiser, *Sacred Fire*, Kindle ed., loc. 345.
8. Culpepper, *Anatomy of the Fourth Gospel*, 72.
9. Peterson, *Contemplative Pastor*, 122.

CHAPTER 8: Life Is About Being Set Free

1. Agassi, *Open*, Kindle ed., loc. 17.
2. Van Gogh, quoted in Agassi, *Open*, Kindle ed., loc. 4.
3. Peterson, *Jesus Way*, 211.
4. Saldarini, *Pharisees, Scribes and Sadducees in Palestinian Society*, 188.
5. Culpepper, *Anatomy of the Fourth Gospel*, 128.
6. Culpepper, *Anatomy of the Fourth Gospel*, 129–30.
7. Culpepper, *Anatomy of the Fourth Gospel*, 88.
8. Saldarini, *Pharisees, Scribes and Sadducees in Palestinian Society*, 191.
9. Brown, "Remain," in *New International Dictionary of New Testament Theology*, 225.

10. Peterson, *Long Obedience*, 5.
11. Phillips, quoted in Peterson, *Eat This Book*, 174.
12. Packer, *Knowing God*, 103.
13. Hillenbrand, *Unbroken*, Kindle ed., loc. 5299.
14. Plantinga, *Not the Way It's Supposed to Be*, 27.
15. Plantinga, *Not the Way It's Supposed to Be*, 53, 89.
16. Buber, quoted in Plantinga, *Not the Way It's Supposed to Be*, 107.
17. Peterson, *Contemplative Pastor*, 125.
18. Brant, *Dialogue and Drama*, 4.

CHAPTER 9: Life Is About Seeing the Light

1. Gene Weingarten, "Pearls Before Breakfast: Can One of the Nation's Great Musicians Cut Through the Fog of a D.C. Rush Hour? Let's Find Out," *The Washington Post*, April 8, 2007, https://www.washingtonpost.com/lifestyle/magazine/pearls-before-breakfast-can-one-of-the-nations-great-musicians-cut-through-the-fog-of-a-dc-rush-hour-lets-find-out/2014/09/23/8a6d46da-4331-11e4-b47c-f5889e061e5f_story.html.
2. For a more extended list, see Culpepper, *Anatomy of the Fourth Gospel*, 139–40.
3. Culpepper, *Anatomy of the Fourth Gospel*, 117.
4. Duke, *Irony in the Fourth Gospel*, 118.
5. Carson, *How Long, O Lord?*, 101.
6. Yancey, *Jesus I Never Knew*, 170.
7. Dillard, *Pilgrim at Tinker Creek*, Kindle ed., loc. 383.
8. Duke, *Irony in the Fourth Gospel*, 121.
9. Peterson, *Peterson Field Guide to Birds*, 388.
10. Köstenberger, *Theology of John's Gospel and Letters*, 292.
11. Duke, *Irony in the Fourth Gospel*, 117.

CHAPTER 10: Life Is About Living by God's Timing and God's Purposes

1. Yancey, *Disappointment with God*, 22.
2. Rasmussen, *Zondervan Atlas of the Bible*, 213.
3. Carson, *How Long, O Lord?*, 16.
4. Peterson, *Christ Plays in Ten Thousand Places*, 99.
5. Gaiser, *Healing in the Bible*, 15.
6. Koessler, "Jesus Disappoints Everyone."
7. Hughes, "Harlem (2)," in *Collected Poems of Langston Hughes*, 426. Emphasis in original. Used by permission.
8. Gawande, *Being Mortal*, Kindle ed., loc. 29.
9. Peterson, *Pastor*, 20.

10. Yancey, *Disappointment with God*, 224. This book is a helpful read on lost expectations.
11. Borchert, *John 1–11*, 356.
12. Peterson, *Christ Plays in Ten Thousand Places*, 90.
13. Taylor, *Leaving Church*, 98–99.
14. Bird, *Evangelical Theology*, 249.
15. Peterson, *Practice Resurrection*, 89.
16. Crabb, *Shattered Dreams*, 3.
17. Gawande, *Being Mortal*, 232.
18. Culpepper, *Anatomy of the Fourth Gospel*, 111.
19. Borchert, *John 1–11*, 361.
20. Hays, *Moral Vision of the New Testament*, 90.
21. Westcott, *Gospel According to St. John*, 82.

CHAPTER 11: Life Is About Pursuing Your Divine Race

1. Sam Borden, "For U.S. Relayers, Dread of Another Dropped Baton," *The New York Times*, July 23, 2012, http://www.nytimes.com/2012/07/23/sports/olympics/olympics-2012-us-track-relays-hope-to-avoid-another-baton-drop.html.
2. Vanderbloemen and Bird, *Next*, Kindle ed., loc. 410.
3. Culpepper, *Anatomy of the Fourth Gospel*, 115.
4. Witherington, *John's Wisdom*, 231.
5. Bird, *Jesus Is the Christ*, 111.
6. Bird, *Jesus Is the Christ*, 97.
7. Craddock, *John*, 98.
8. Weese and Crabtree, *Elephant in the Boardroom*, Kindle ed., loc. 320.
9. Isaacson, *Steve Jobs*, Kindle ed., loc. 2827.
10. Crouch, *Playing God*, 163.
11. Crouch, *Playing God*, 162.
12. Taylor, *An Altar in the World*, Kindle ed., loc. 1572.
13. Lindsay, *Faith in the Halls of Power*, 229.
14. Galli, *Jesus Mean and Wild*, 19.
15. McKnight, *Kingdom Conspiracy*, 169.
16. Meyer, quoted in Ray Steadman, "Cambridge Encounter," *Men of Integrity*, July 2, 2002, https://www.christianitytoday.com/moi/2002/004/july/cambridge-encounter.html.
17. Köstenberger, *Excellence*, 224.
18. Tichy, *Leadership Engine*, xiv.
19. For an insightful discussion on the age to come, see chapter 3 of Davis, *Meditation and Communion with God*.
20. Horton, *Christian Faith*, 524.
21. Levison, *Inspired*, 69.

22. Peterson, *Jesus Way*, 215.
23. McKnight, *Jesus Creed*, 198.
24. Pew Research Center, "Trends in Global Restrictions on Religion," June 23, 2016, http://www.pewforum.org/2016/06/23/trends-in-global-restrictions-on-religion/.
25. Russel Brand, quoted in "Rebranding," *Relevant*, 16.
26. Wright, *Simply Jesus*, Kindle ed., loc. 4139.
27. Borchert, *John 12–21*, 200.

CHAPTER 12: **Life Is About Flourishing Under God's Authority**

1. Mark Herrmann, "Have We Met?," *The New York Times*, December 11, 2013, http://opinionator.blogs.nytimes.com/2013/12/11/have-we-met/.
2. Witherington, *John's Wisdom*, 280.
3. Philo, *On the Embassy to Gaius*, 301–2, quoted in Jeffers, *Greco-Roman World of the New Testament Era*, 105.
4. Herod Agrippa, quoted in Jeffers, *Greco-Roman World of the New Testament Era*, 131.
5. Edwards, *Gospel According to Luke*, 391.
6. Jeffers, *Greco-Roman World of the New Testament Era*, 115.
7. Eisenhower, quoted in Thomas, *Being Nixon*, Kindle ed., loc. 1636.
8. Wright, *How God Became King*, Kindle ed., loc. 2317.
9. Duke, *Irony in the Fourth Gospel*, 127.
10. Peterson, *Reversed Thunder*, 5.
11. Duke, *Irony in the Fourth Gospel*, 130.
12. Carson, *Gospel According to John*, 600.
13. Brueggemann, *Truth Speaks to Power*, 150.
14. Peterson, *Jesus Way*, 203.

CHAPTER 13: **Life Is About Restoration Replacing Failure**

1. Woodley, *Gospel of Matthew*, 125.
2. Millard, *River of Doubt*, 1.
3. Duke, *Irony in the Fourth Gospel*, 97.
4. Witherington, *John's Wisdom*, 358.
5. Witherington, *John's Wisdom*, 96.
6. Rick Bragg, "Florida Town Finds Satan an Offense unto It," *The New York Times*, March 14, 2002, http://www.nytimes.com/2002/03/14/us/florida-town-finds-satan-an-offense-unto-it.html.
7. Few have described this journey of brokenness better than Gordon MacDonald in *Rebuilding Your Broken World*.
8. Köstenberger, *John*, 597.
9. Westcott, *Gospel According to St. John*, 367.

10. Köstenberger, *John*, 597.
11. Witherington, *John's Wisdom*, 356.
12. Duke, *Irony in the Fourth Gospel*, 98.
13. Bruner, *Gospel of John*, 1230.
14. Willard, *Renovation of the Heart*, 63, emphasis added.
15. Wright, *Surprised by Hope*, 241.
16. Plantinga, *Not the Way It's Supposed to Be*, 117.
17. Luther, quoted in Jobes, *1 Peter*, 1.
18. MacDonald, *Rebuilding Your Broken World*, 222.
19. Wright, *Surprised by Hope*, 241.

Conclusion

1. Neilson, "How to Survive Solitary Confinement."
2. Davis, *Meditation and Communion with God*, 64.
3. Davis, *Meditation and Communion with God*, 77.
4. Plantinga, *Reading for Preaching*, 94.
5. Taylor, *An Altar in the World*, Kindle ed., loc. 325.

BIBLIOGRAPHY

Agassi, Andre. *Open*. Kindle ed. New York: Alfred A. Knopf, 2009.

Bartholomew, Craig G. *Where Mortals Dwell: A Christian View of Place for Today*. Grand Rapids: Baker Academic, 2011.

Bauckham, Richard. *Gospel of Glory: Major Themes in Johannine Theology*. Grand Rapids: Baker Academic, 2015.

Beale, G. K., and Mitchell Kim. *God Dwells Among Us: Expanding Eden to the Ends of the Earth*. Downers Grove, IL: InterVarsity Press, 2014.

Bernanke, Ben S. "Economic Prospects for the Long Run." Commencement speech delivered at Bard College at Simon's Rock, Great Barrington, MA, May 18, 2013. http://www.federalreserve.gov/newsevents/speech /bernanke20130518a.htm.

Bird, Michael F. *Evangelical Theology: A Biblical and Systematic Introduction*. Grand Rapids: Zondervan, 2013.

———. *Jesus Is the Christ: The Messianic Testimony of the Gospels*. Downers Grove, IL: IVP Academic, 2013.

Booth, Wayne C. *A Rhetoric of Irony*. Chicago: University of Chicago Press, 1974.

Borchert, Gerald L. *John 1–11: An Exegetical and Theological Exposition of Holy Scripture*. New American Commentary 25A. Nashville: Broadman and Holman, 1996.

———. *John 12–21: An Exegetical and Theological Exposition of Holy Scripture*. New American Commentary 25B. Nashville: Broadman and Holman, 2002.

Boyer, Steven D., and Christopher A. Hall. *The Mystery of God: Theology for Knowing the Unknowable*. Grand Rapids: Baker Academic, 2012.

Brant, Jo-Ann A. *Dialogue and Drama: Elements of Greek Tragedy in the Fourth Gospel*. Peabody, MA: Hendrickson, 2004.

Brown, Colin, ed. *The New International Dictionary of New Testament Theology*. Vol 3. Grand Rapids: Zondervan, 1986.

Brown, Raymond E. *The Gospel According to John I–XII: Introduction, Translation, and Notes.* The Anchor Bible 29. New Haven: Yale University Press, 2006.

Brueggemann, Walter. *Finally Comes the Poet: Daring Speech for Proclamation.* Lyman Beecher Lectures at Yale, 1988–89. Minneapolis: Fortress Press, 1989.

———. *Truth Speaks to Power: The Countercultural Nature of Scripture.* Louisville: Westminster John Knox, 2013.

Bruner, Frederick Dale. *The Gospel of John: A Commentary.* Grand Rapids: Eerdmans, 2012.

Buchanan, Mark. *The Rest of God: Restoring Your Soul by Restoring Sabbath.* Nashville: Thomas Nelson, 2007.

Burke, John. *No Perfect People Allowed: Creating a Come-As-You-Are Culture in the Church.* Grand Rapids: Zondervan, 2007.

Butler, Joshua Ryan. *The Pursuing God: A Reckless, Irrational, Obsessed Love That's Dying to Bring Us Home.* Nashville: Thomas Nelson, 2016.

Cain, Susan. *Quiet: The Power of Introverts in a World That Can't Stop Talking.* Kindle ed. New York: Broadway Books, 2013.

Card, Michael. *The Parable of Joy: Reflections on the Wisdom of the Book of John.* Nashville: Thomas Nelson, 1995.

Carson, D. A. *The Gospel According to John.* Pillar New Testament Commentary. Grand Rapids: Eerdmans, 1991.

———. *How Long, O Lord? Reflections on Suffering and Evil.* 2nd ed. Grand Rapids: Baker Academic, 2006.

Crabb, Larry. *Shattered Dreams: God's Unexpected Pathway to Joy.* Colorado Springs: WaterBrook Press, 2001.

Craddock, Fred B. *John.* Knox Preaching Guides. Atlanta: John Knox Press, 1982.

Crouch, Andy. *Playing God: Redeeming the Gift of Power.* Downers Grove, IL: InterVarsity Press, 2013.

Cullmann, Oscar. *Christ and Time: The Primitive Christian Conception of Time and History.* Philadelphia: Westminster Press, 1964.

Culpepper, R. Alan. *Anatomy of the Fourth Gospel: A Study in Literary Design.* Foundations and Facets. Minneapolis: Fortress Press, 1983.

Davis, John Jefferson. *Meditation and Communion with God: Contemplating Scripture in an Age of Distraction.* Downers Grove, IL: IVP Academic, 2012.

Dawn, Marva J., and Eugene H. Peterson. *The Unnecessary Pastor: Rediscovering the Call*. Grand Rapids: Eerdmans, 1999.

Dillard, Annie. *Pilgrim at Tinker Creek*. New York: Harper's Magazine Press, 1974.

Duke, Paul D. *Irony in the Fourth Gospel*. Atlanta: John Knox Press, 1985.

Dylan, Bob. "When You Gonna Wake Up." In *Slow Training Coming*. Special Rider Music. Originally released 1979. http://bobdylan.com/songs/when-you-gonna-wake/.

Edwards, James R. *The Gospel According to Luke*. Pillar New Testament Commentary. Grand Rapids: Eerdmans, 2015.

Gaiser, Frederick J. *Healing in the Bible: Theological Insight for Christian Ministry*. Grand Rapids: Baker Academic, 2010.

Galli, Mark. *Jesus Mean and Wild: The Unexpected Love of an Untamable God*. Grand Rapids: Baker Books, 2006.

Gawande, Atul. *Being Mortal: Medicine and What Matters in the End*. Kindle ed. New York: Metropolitan Books, 2014.

Hays, Richard B. *The Moral Vision of the New Testament: A Contemporary Introduction to New Testament Ethics*. New York: HarperCollins, 1996.

Hengstenberg, E. W. *Commentary on the Gospel of St. John*. Vol 1. Limited Classical Reprint Library. Minneapolis: Klock & Klock Christian Publishers, 1980. Originally published in 1865 by T&T Clark.

Hillenbrand, Laura. *Unbroken: A World War II Story of Survival, Resilience, and Redemption*. Kindle ed. New York: Random House, 2010.

Horton, Michael. *The Christian Faith: A Systematic Theology for Pilgrims on the Way*. Grand Rapids: Zondervan, 2011.

Hoskyns, Edwyn Clement. *The Fourth Gospel*. Edited by Francis Noel Davey. 2nd ed. London: Faber and Faber, 1947.

Hughes, Langston. "Harlem (2)." In *The Collected Poems of Langston Hughes*. Edited by Arnold Rampersad. New York: Random House, 1995.

Isaacson, Walter. *Steve Jobs*, Kindle ed. New York: Simon and Schuster, 2011.

Jeffers, James S. *The Greco-Roman World of the New Testament Era: Exploring the Background of Early Christianity*. Downers Grove, IL: InterVarsity Press, 1999.

Jobes, Karen. *1 Peter*. Baker Exegetical Commentary on the New Testament. Grand Rapids: Baker Academic, 2005.

Johnston, Robert K. *God's Wider Presence: Reconsidering General Revelation*. Grand Rapids: Baker Academic, 2014.

King, Martin Luther, Jr. "Social Justice." Lecture delivered at Western Michigan University, Kalamazoo, MI, December 18, 1963. http://www.wmich.edu/sites/default/files/attachments/u34/2013/MLK.pdf.

Klink, Edward W., III. "Could I Have a Word? Dialogues and Theology in the Gospel of John." A session from the 65th Annual Meeting of the Evangelical Theological Society, "Evangelicalism, Inerrancy, and ETS," Baltimore, MD, November 19–21, 2013. http://www.wordmp3.com/details.aspx?id=16010.

Koessler, John. "Jesus Disappoints Everyone." *Christianity Today*, April 5, 2012, 44. http://www.christianitytoday.com/ct/2012/april/jesus-disappoints-everyone.html.

Koester, Craig R. *The Word of Life: A Theology of John's Gospel*. Grand Rapids: Eerdmans, 2008.

Köstenberger, Andreas J. *Excellence: The Character of God and the Pursuit of Scholarly Virtue*. Wheaton, IL: Crossway, 2011.

———. *John*. Baker Exegetical Commentary on the New Testament. Grand Rapids: Baker Academic, 2004.

———. *A Theology of John's Gospel and Letters*. Grand Rapids: Zondervan, 2009.

Lane, William L. *The Gospel of Mark: The English Text with Introduction, Exposition, and Notes*. New International Commentary on the New Testament. Grand Rapids: Eerdmans, 1974.

Levison, Jack. *Inspired: The Holy Spirit and the Mind of Faith*. Grand Rapids: Eerdmans, 2013.

Lewis, C. S. *The Lion, the Witch and the Wardrobe*. New York: HarperCollins, 2008.

———. *Miracles: A Preliminary Study*. New York: Macmillan, 1947.

Lindsey, D. Michael. *Faith in the Halls of Power: How Evangelicals Joined the American Elite*. New York: Oxford University Press, 2007.

Lukianoff, Greg, and Jonathan Haidt. "The Coddling of the American Mind." *The Atlantic*, September 2015. http://www.theatlantic.com/magazine/archive/2015/09/the-coddling-of-the-american-mind/399356/.

MacDonald, Gordon. *Rebuilding Your Broken World*. Nashville: Oliver-Nelson Books, 1988.

———. *Resilient Life: You Can Move Ahead No Matter What*. Nashville: Thomas Nelson, 2006.

McKeown, Greg. *Essentialism: The Disciplined Pursuit of Less*. Kindle ed. New York: Crown Business, 2014.

McKnight, Scot. *Jesus Creed: Loving God, Loving Others.* Brewster, MA: Paraclete Press, 2004.

———. *Kingdom Conspiracy: Returning to the Radical Mission of the Local Church.* Grand Rapids: Brazos Press, 2014.

Millard, Candice. *The River of Doubt: Theodore Roosevelt's Darkest Journey.* New York: Doubleday, 2005.

Morris, Leon. *The Gospel According to John.* Rev. ed. New International Commentary on the New Testament. Grand Rapids: Eerdmans, 1995.

Munger, Robert Boyd. *My Heart—Christ's Home.* Rev. ed. Downers Grove, IL: InterVarsity Press, 1986.

Munro, Alice. *Lives of Girls and Women: A Novel.* New York: Vintage, 2001.

Neilson, Susie. "How to Survive Solitary Confinement." *Nautilus,* January 28, 2016. http://nautil.us/issue/32/space/how-to-survive-solitary-confinement.

Newbigin, Lesslie. *The Light Has Come: An Exposition of the Fourth Gospel.* Grand Rapids: Eerdmans, 1982.

Nof, Doron. "'Walking on Water' and the Geoscientists' Fear of Social Controversy." *Earth and Science News* 87, no. 39 (2006): 404–409.

Noll, Stephen F. *Angels of Light, Powers of Darkness: Thinking Biblically About Angels, Satan and Principalities.* Downers Grove, IL: InterVarsity Press, 1998.

Oden, Thomas C. *Life in the Spirit.* San Francisco: HarperSanFrancisco, 1992.

———. *Word of Life.* San Francisco: Harper and Row, 1989.

"On the Cocaine Trail." *The Economist,* June 27, 2015. http://www.economist.com/news/books-and-arts/21656126-angry-account-suffering-inflicted-worlds-appetite-illegal-drugs.

Ortberg, John C., Jr. "Slaying Spiritual Skepticism." *Christianity Today,* Fall 1994, 25–30. http://www.christianitytoday.com/le/1994/fall/4l4025.html.

Packer, J. I. *Knowing God.* Downers Grove, IL: InterVarsity Press, 1979.

Parker, James. "The Passion of Flannery O'Connor." *The Atlantic,* November 2013. http://www.theatlantic.com/magazine/archive/2013/11/the-passion-of-flannery-oconnor/309532.

Peterson, Eugene H. *Christ Plays in Ten Thousand Places: A Conversation in Spiritual Theology.* Grand Rapids: Eerdmans, 2005.

———. *The Contemplative Pastor.* Grand Rapids: Eerdmans, 1993.

———. *Eat This Book: A Conversation in the Art of Spiritual Reading.* Grand Rapids: Eerdmans, 2006.

———. *The Jesus Way: A Conversation on the Ways That Jesus Is the Way.* Grand Rapids: Eerdmans, 2007.

———. *A Long Obedience in the Same Direction: Discipleship in an Instant Society.* Downers Grove, IL: InterVarsity Press, 2000.

———. *The Pastor: A Memoir.* San Francisco: HarperOne, 2011.

———. *Practice Resurrection: A Conversation on Growing Up in Christ.* Grand Rapids: Eerdmans, 2010.

———. *Reversed Thunder: The Revelation of John and the Praying Imagination.* San Francisco: HarperOne, 1988.

———. *Subversive Spirituality.* Grand Rapids: Eerdmans, 1997.

———. *Tell It Slant: A Conversation on the Language of Jesus in His Stories and Prayers.* Grand Rapids: Eerdmans, 2008.

Peterson, Roger Tory. *Peterson Field Guide to Birds of North America.* New York: Houghton Mifflin Harcourt, 2008.

Philo, *On the Embassy to Gaius; General Indexes.* Vol. 10. Translated by F. H. Colson. Index by Rev. J. W. Earp. Loeb Classical Library 379. Cambridge, MA: Harvard University Press, 1962.

Plantinga, Cornelius, Jr. *Not the Way It's Supposed to Be: A Breviary of Sin.* Grand Rapids: Eerdmans, 1995.

———. *Reading for Preaching: The Preacher in Conversation with Storytellers, Biographers, Poets, and Journalists.* Grand Rapids: Eerdmans, 2013.

Purves, Andrew. *The Crucifixion of Ministry: Surrendering Our Ambitions to the Service of Christ.* Downers Grove, IL: InterVarsity Press, 2007.

———. *Pastoral Theology in the Classical Tradition.* Louisville: Westminster John Knox Press, 2001.

Rainbow, Paul A. *Johannine Theology: The Gospel, the Epistles and the Apocalypse.* Downers Grove, IL: InterVarsity Press, 2014.

Rasmussen, Carl G. *Zondervan Atlas of the Bible.* Rev. ed. Grand Rapids: Zondervan, 2010.

"Rebranding." *Relevant,* July/August 2015. http://www.relevantmagazine.com/culture/rebranding.

Rolheiser, Ronald. *Sacred Fire: A Vision for a Deeper Human and Christian Maturity.* Kindle ed. New York: Image, 2014.

———. *The Shattered Lantern: Rediscovering a Felt Presence of God.* Rev. ed. New York: Crossroad, 2004.

Rowland, Christopher. *The Open Heaven: A Study of Apocalyptic in Judaism and Early Christianity.* Eugene, OR: Wipf and Stock, 2002.

Saldarini, Anthony J. *Pharisees, Scribes and Sadducees in Palestinian Society: A Sociological Approach.* Grand Rapids: Eerdmans, 2001.

Sittser, Gerald L. *Love One Another: Becoming the Church Jesus Longs For.* Downers Grove, IL: InterVarsity Press, 2008.

Smalley, Stephen S. *John: Evangelist and Interpreter.* Nashville: Thomas Nelson, 1984.

Smedes, Lewis B. *My God and I: A Spiritual Memoir.* Grand Rapids: Eerdmans, 2003.

Strachan, R. H. *The Fourth Gospel, Its Significance and Environment.* London: Student Christian Movement, 1941. Originally published in 1917.

Suk, John D. *Not Sure: A Pastor's Journey from Faith to Doubt.* Grand Rapids: Eerdmans, 2011.

Taylor, Barbara Brown. *An Altar in the World: A Geography of Faith.* Kindle ed. San Francisco: HarperOne, 2009.

———. *Leaving Church: A Memoir of Faith.* San Francisco: HarperSanFrancisco, 2006.

———. *When God Is Silent.* 2nd ed. Lyman Beecher Lectures on Preaching, 1997. New York: Cowley Publications, 1998.

Thomas, Evan. *Being Nixon: A Man Divided.* Kindle ed. New York: Random House, 2015.

Thompson, Curt. "How Neuroscience—and the Bible—Explain Shame." *Christianity Today*, June 23, 2016. http://www.christianitytoday.com/ct/2016/julaug/how-neuroscience-and-bible-explain-shame.html.

Tichy, Noel M., with Eli Cohen. *The Leadership Engine: How Winning Companies Build Leaders at Every Level.* New York: HarperCollins, 1997.

Vanderbloemen, William, and Warren Bird. *Next: Pastoral Succession That Works.* Kindle ed. Grand Rapids: Baker Books, 2014.

Webber, Alan M. "Why Can't We Get Anything Done?" *Fast Company*, May 31, 2000. http://www.fastcompany.com/39841/why-cant-we-get-anything-done.

Weese, Carolyn, and J. Russell Crabtree. *The Elephant in the Boardroom: Speaking the Unspoken About Pastoral Transitions.* Kindle ed. San Francisco: Jossey-Bass, 2004.

Westcott, B. F. *The Gospel According to St. John: The Greek Text with Introduction and Notes.* Edited by A. Westcott. Vol. 2. Eugene, OR: Wipf and Stock, 2004. Originally published in 1896 by John Murray.

Willard, Dallas. *Renovation of the Heart: Putting on the Character of Christ.* Colorado Springs: NavPress, 2002.

Willimon, William H. *Why Jesus?* Kindle ed. Nashville: Abingdon Press, 2010.

Witherington, Ben, III. *John's Wisdom: A Commentary on the Fourth Gospel.* Louisville: Westminster John Knox Press, 1995.

Woodley, Matt. *The Gospel of Matthew: God with Us.* Resonate Series. Downers Grove, IL: InterVarsity Press, 2011.

Wright, N. T. *How God Became King: The Forgotten Story of the Gospels.* Kindle ed. San Francisco: HarperOne, 2012.

———. *John for Everyone, Part I: Chapters 1–10.* The New Testament for Everyone. 2nd ed. Louisville: Westminster John Knox Press, 2004.

———. *Simply Good News: Why the Gospel Is News and What Makes It Good.* Kindle ed. San Francisco: HarperOne, 2015.

———. *Simply Jesus: A New Vision of Who He Was, What He Did, and Why He Matters.* Kindle ed. San Francisco: HarperOne, 2015.

———. *Surprised by Hope: Rethinking Heaven, the Resurrection, and the Mission of the Church.* San Francisco: HarperOne, 2008.

Yancey, Philip. *Disappointment with God: Three Questions No One Asks Aloud.* Grand Rapids: Zondervan, 1988.

———. *The Jesus I Never Knew.* Grand Rapids: Zondervan, 1995.

Zahl, Rachel. *Converting to Judaism: How to Become a Jew.* Charleston, SC: CreateSpace, 2014.

ABOUT THE AUTHOR

JOHN E. JOHNSON GREW UP IN SAN DIEGO, COMPLETING A DEGREE in international relations at San Diego State University. Sensing a call to ministry, he pursued and completed both MDiv and ThM degrees at Western Seminary. It was here God brought significant men into his life who challenged him to give himself to pastoral ministry. He eventually went on to Dallas Seminary, where he earned a PhD in systematic theology.

For over thirty years he has lived in two worlds: pastor and professor—a perfect fit, for one informs the other. After serving three churches (in southeast Portland, Oregon; Wassenaar, the Netherlands; and Beaverton, Oregon), he has recently transitioned from the lead pastor role to devote his time to writing and teaching. He is currently a professor of pastoral theology and leadership at Western Seminary, teaching the next generation of global leaders both at home and abroad.

John is married to Heather, has two children, Kate and Nate, and is an avid tennis player, kayaker, and gardener. Part of his year is spent with his wife in the wilderness of northeast Washington, where he hikes, reads, kayaks, and writes.